Jim Haynes is a first generation Aussie whose mother migrated from the UK as a child during the Depression. His father arrived on a British warship at the end of WWII, met his mother and stayed. 'My parents always insisted we were Australian, not British,' says Jim.

Educated at Sydney Boys High and Sydney Teachers College, he taught for six years at Menindee, on the Darling River, and later at high schools in Northern NSW and in London. He has also worked in radio and as a nurse, cleaner and sapphire salesman and has two degrees in literature from the University of New England and an M.A. from the University of Wales in the UK.

Jim formed the Bandy Bill & Co Bush Band in Inverell in 1978. He also worked in commercial radio and on the popular ABC *Australia All Over* program. In 1988 he signed as a solo recording artist with Festival Records, began touring and had a minor hit with 'Mow Ya Lawn'. Other record deals followed, along with hits like 'Since Cheryl Went Feral' and 'Don't Call Wagga Wagga Wagga'.

Having written and compiled twenty-four books, released many albums of songs, verse and humour and broadcast his weekly Australiana segment on Radio 2UE for fifteen years, Jim was awarded the Order of Australia Medal in 2016 'for service to the performing arts as an entertainer, author, broadcaster and historian'. He lives in Moore Park in Sydney with his wife, Robyn.

ALSO BY JIM HAYNES

The Big Book of Verse for Aussie Kids
Best Australian Racing Stories
The Great Australian Book of Limericks (2nd ed)
The Best Australian Trucking Stories
The Best Australian Sea Stories
The Best Australian Bush Stories
The Best Australian Yarns
Australia's Best Unknown Stories
The Best Gallipoli Yarns and Forgotten Stories
The Big Book of Australian Racing Stories

AUSTRALIA'S MOST UNBELIEVABLE TRUE STORIES

JIM HAYNES

ALLEN&UNWIN
SYDNEY·MELBOURNE·AUCKLAND·LONDON

For Jillian

First published in 2016

Copyright © Jim Haynes 2016

Allen & Unwin
83 Alexander Street
Crows Nest NSW 2065
Australia
Phone: (61 2) 8425 0100
Email: info@allenandunwin.com
Web: www.allenandunwin.com

Cataloguing-in-Publication details are available
from the National Library of Australia
www.trove.nla.gov.au

ISBN 978 1 76011 058 1

Set in 12/15 pt Minion Pro by Midland Typesetters, Australia
Printed and bound in Australia by Griffin Press

10 9 8 7 6 5 4 3 2 1

MIX
Paper from
responsible sources
FSC® C009448

The paper in this book is FSC® certified.
FSC® promotes environmentally responsible,
socially beneficial and economically viable
management of the world's forests.

CONTENTS

PART THREE   LEST WE FORGET

PART FOUR   THOSE MAGNIFICENT WOMEN AND MEN

INTRODUCTION

I have wanted for some time to make a collection of all the odd stories I've stumbled across in almost 30 years of documenting 'Australiana' on radio, or while researching other, more specific, collections on topics as diverse as railways, horseracing, trucking, drinking, Aussie yarns, maritime history, etc.

I always seemed to find a few stories that were too weird to be true, and they didn't always fit into the collection that I was compiling at the time. Over the years I put many of these stories aside for a possible collection of 'unbelievable' stories.

This is that collection.

Rather than make the whole collection a miscellany of 'believe it or not' anecdotes, and for the sake of having some order, I divided the stories into four sections. Looking through the stories I had earmarked for the collection, I found that three obvious sections presented themselves: royal visits, war and aviation. The rest of the stories are in section one.

Australia's obsession with British royalty is odd enough in itself, but the first four visits to Australia by members of the royal family were full of such unusual events that accounts of those visits seem to me decidedly slapstick and verge towards the odd and even hilarious at times.

I suppose we expect wartime to produce tales of unbelievable courage, cruelty and coincidence, but the Battle of the Coral Sea was truly farcical. Were it not for the loss of life involved, it might even be considered comical. My favourite story in the war section, however, is the strange tale of Private John Leak.

The early days of aviation were full of amazing swashbuckling true adventures, but the story of the Flying Van Tassel sisters' Australian tour is hard to beat.

Although three of the sections do have a common theme, the style of the stories varies considerably.

Some of the events narrated in the collection are weird in the sense of 'spooky'. The case of the totally inexplicable phenomenon known as the Guyra Ghost is my favourite of those.

Some of the stories document the lives of characters whose turbulent, multifaceted biographies defy human logic and limitations; characters whose adventures, tragedies and amazing feats rival those of the fictional Baron Munchausen. I cannot decide between Tom Wills and Jorgen Jorgensen as my favourites in that category.

Then there are the ridiculously coincidental historic events that, when told, make people exclaim, 'That's unbelievable!'.

Let me give you an example.

In 1875 and 1876 the Victorian government held a royal commission into the colony's defences and invited Lieutenant General Sir William Jervois, Director of Works and Fortifications in London, to come to Victoria and advise the government on how best to defend Melbourne.

Sir William is best remembered for later being Governor of South Australia and Governor-General of New Zealand. He also had the most impressive, and largest, set of 'mutton chop' whiskers I have ever seen, and believe me, I have looked at thousands of photos and paintings of colonial sideburns!

Sir William and his offsider, Colonel Scratchley, advised that the best plan was to fortify the entrance to Port Phillip Bay and, consequently, fortifications and barracks were built on Point Nepean in 1873. Gun batteries were installed in 1886 and the fort, Fort Nepean, housed a company of the Royal Victoria Volunteer Artillery Regiment.

Skip forward to 5 August 1914.

The German merchant ship SS *Pfalz* was attempting to leave Port Melbourne when Victorian Defence Chief, Lieutenant Colonel

Sandford, gave an order to the Fire Commander at Fort Nepean, one Lieutenant Morris. The order was 'stop her or sink her'.

The *Pfalz* ignored signals to halt and the B1 gun of the Fort Nepean battery (barrel number 1489) fired across her bow. The *Pfalz* then returned to port and the crew was arrested.

Skip forward again to 1.30 a.m. on 4 September 1939. A vessel leaving Melbourne failed to identify itself and the A1 gun of the battery (barrel number 1317) fired across her bow. The ship then identified herself as the local freighter SS *Woniora*.

In 80 years of being manned and ready, these were the only two times that any of the Port Phillip guns were fired in 'action' of any kind.

Why does this matter?

Well, those two shots were the first shots fired in World War I and World War II respectively.

The first was fired within minutes of war being declared in 1914 and is indisputably the first shot of WWI. The second shot, fired within hours of the announcement that Australia was at war in 1939, has strong claims as the first official shot of WWII, though this has been disputed, but it was certainly the first shot fired after the declaration of war was made by Britain and Australia.

All coastal installations were gradually removed after WWII and Fort Nepean became part of Point Nepean National Park in 1988.

In the early 1960s someone suddenly realised the guns that fired the first shots of both world wars were gone. Luckily they were tracked down, one in a scrap yard at Brooklyn in Victoria and the other at an artillery range at Port Wakefield in South Australia.

Today the gun barrels are back at Point Nepean. You can picnic beside barrel 1489, which fired the first shot of WWI, or barrel 1317, which did the honours in WWII.

If you, like me, find it fascinating, weirdly coincidental and slightly bizarre that a virtually useless colonial port battery at the bottom of the world on the south coast of Australia fired the first shots in *both* world wars (both of which originated 12,000 miles away in Europe) then maybe this is the book for you.

Jim Haynes, August 2016

Part One
STRANGER THAN FICTION

This first section of the collection contains stories that range from the truly weird and inexplicable to some that I would label 'typically, farcically Australian'.

When the 19th century novelist Joseph Furphy was asked, in light of the fact that all Australians were 'British subjects' at the time (and remained so until 1947), how he thought about himself and his writing, he replied that he was 'offensively Australian'. I think that phrase is an apt one for several of the stories in this section of the book. The story of the Charters Towers 'riot' is a case in point.

The failure of European settlers to understand the continent they had 'invaded' is the source of quite a few stories covering events with consequences that leave me shaking my head in disbelief.

Here's an example. In spite of being advised by the Indigenous population that the Flinders Ranges were not always as green and fertile as early pioneers found them, white settlers established wheat farms in a period of good seasons, which soon became abandoned ghost settlements when the normal seasons returned. Abandoned and ruined farmhouses are now a picturesque feature of the area.

Early white settlers at Gundagai were advised by the local Aborigines not to build on the south side of the Murrumbidgee River. The advice was ignored and, when a flood wiped out the settlement in 1856 and drowned 89 people, a third of the white population, the Aborigines used their canoes to rescue the survivors—who finally took the advice and shifted the town to the other side of the river.

Most Australians are aware of the infestation of prickly pear that wiped out millions of acres of grazing land in New South Wales and Queensland, but how many Aussies know who brought the pest to Australia?

It was the man credited with founding the British settlement, good old Captain Arthur Phillip himself.

Phillip loaded up with the noxious cactus in South America as the First Fleet headed southward with its cargo of human flotsam.

Why?

Well, the cochineal beetle lives on the prickly pear; you can see it in white fungus-like colonies on the cactus pads. When squashed, the tiny beetles turn bright red and provide brilliant scarlet cochineal dye—which was used to make the famous British military 'redcoats' red. Phillip thought a handy supply of red dye would be a great thing, and he needed the cactus to feed the beetles.

The prickly pear story has quite a few amazing twists and turns. Scientists persevered with importing various cactus-eating bugs until the hilariously named *Cactoblastis* moth was imported, survived and flourished and wiped out the entire infestation. This tiny moth made millionaires out of many speculative farmers and graziers who bought the cactus-infested land for virtually nothing.

After billions of little *Cactoblastis* caterpillars ate the millions of acres of cactus, those lucky land speculators were left with prime grazing land, most of which is still farmed by their descendants to this day. In the tiny town of Boonarga, near Dalby, the beneficiaries of the destruction of the prickly pear at least had the good grace to pay tribute to their tiny saviours. While the vast majority of memorial halls in rural Australia are dedicated to those who served in two world wars, the memorial hall in Boonarga is dedicated to the memory of the little grub that ate the cactus; the hall is called the Cactoblastis Memorial Hall.

As the little *Cactoblastis* ate nothing but prickly pear, it didn't prove to be a pest afterwards either, unlike the notorious cane toad, which didn't actually eat the sugar cane pests it was imported to eat. *Cactoblastis* did its job and then died away with the cactus. The cane toad, we soon discovered, ate everything *but* the pests it was imported to control!

One unfortunate victim of the prickly pear invasion was the poor old emu.

In spite of the fact that there was a lot of evidence to prove that the prickly pear was pretty good at spreading itself rather quickly, the emu copped the blame for spreading the seeds of the cactus by eating them, running a distance and pooping them out. So a bounty was placed on emus and the poor old gangly birds were shot in their thousands. You rarely see an emu in that part of Australia now.

Another place where our national bird emblem should be scarce these days is in the Campion District of Western Australia.

The story behind that is a ripper.

There have only been two times in our history when the army was called out to wage war on home soil—here on the Australian continent.

Once was when the militia were roused to arms in Broken Hill to counter an act of war against our nation that was perpetrated by an ice-cream vendor and a butcher—that story appears in another section of this collection.

The other time was in 1932, in the Campion District of Western Australia, about 300 kilometres northeast of Perth.

The invading army was estimated to be around 20,000 strong. What made it worse was that the area threatened was an area of soldier-settlements, farmed by veterans of World War I.

The Western Australian government asked for protection from the Commonwealth and Defence Minister Sir George Pearce decided to order a full-scale military operation. Soldiers from the 7th Heavy Battery Royal Australian Artillery were armed with Lewis machine guns and 10,000 rounds of ammunition, and they set out for the battlefield.

The enemy?

Emus!

That's right, emus.

It seems huge flocks of emus were devastating the farmland and some soldier-settlers had already quit and left their little bit of the district to the birds.

The first great battle of the Emu War lasted nine days, and guess what? The emus won.

In those nine days the army blasted away at 20,000 emus and managed to kill . . . a few dozen.

The military mastermind who led the campaign, one Major Meredith, reported that the emus were almost impossible to defeat. Not only did they ignore the normal conventions of warfare and terms of engagement by zig-zagging erratically at high speed, they were also almost impossible to kill! Bullets didn't stop them, even if they were hit.

'If we had a military division with the bullet-carrying capacity of these birds,' said a frustrated Major Meredith, 'it would face any army in the world.'

The major was fulsome in his praise of the enemy. 'They can face machine guns with the invulnerability of tanks,' he reported.

One of his soldiers, a hardened veteran of the nine-day Emu War, gave the *Argus* newspaper the benefit of his battlefield experiences:

> There's only one way to kill an emu—shoot him through the back
> of the head when his mouth is closed, or through the front of his
> mouth when his mouth is open. That's how hard it is.

The army decided to retreat, much to the dismay of the settlers.

On 10 November 1932 the *Argus* reported that settlers were 'alarmed at the Defence Department's decision to recall the machine gun party which . . . after overcoming preliminary difficulties . . . had begun to make an impression on the ravaging hordes'.

The army persevered for another month and eventually Major Meredith claimed his men killed 986 emus with 9860 rounds of ammunition.

Twenty years later the emus were still winning, so the Western Australian government decided to build an emu-proof fence.

It was more than 200 kilometres long, 1.3 metres high, cost £52,000 and joined on to the famous rabbit-proof fence.

Did it work? Well, as late as 1994 the Western Australian government was still carrying out emu eradication programs.

A FEW GHOSTS AND SOME COLONIAL CORRUPTION

It comes as no surprise to me that the largest number of good old-fashioned ghost stories in Australia, particularly those from the colonial era, seem to emanate from Tasmania when you consider the fact that the European history of the island was so gruesome, horrific and embarrassing that the name Van Diemen's Land was scrapped in 1856 and the new name, Tasmania, has been used ever since. It was hoped that doing away with the old name would help people forget that during the first half-century of European settlement the island was best known as a place of unbridled savagery, cannibalism, lawless bands of brutal bushrangers who did as they pleased, and the official planned extermination of the original Indigenous inhabitants.

I recall being pleasantly surprised, during my first visit to the island, to find that every hotel I stayed at had at least one resident ghost, usually a convict in the cellar.

Sydney, although it has a much larger population and a slightly older colonial history, has comparatively few resident ghosts and haunted buildings. There is, however, a girl in a white dress who appears near Middle Creek Bridge on the Wakehurst Parkway. If you are alone and stop to give her a lift, the results could be fatal. If a motorist even just sees her and acknowledges her presence, she has been known to take control of their car and take them on a very scary ride indeed. I've never encountered her personally but, when I mentioned the legend on radio, several listeners called in to assure me that they knew someone who knew someone who had once talked to someone who had encountered the spectral girl.

Fisher's Ghost

Sydney's most famous ghost story begins with a bloke arriving at a pub in desperate need of a drink.

It was four months after the mysterious disappearance of a local farmer, Fred Fisher, in 1826 that John Farley, a respected and honest local farmer, arrived at a pub on the rural outskirts of Sydney, in the area that is now the bustling outer suburb of Campbelltown, in a state of shock.

In one version of the story Farley claimed he had seen the ghost of Fred Fisher sitting on the railing of a bridge over a creek. The ghost pointed to a paddock down the creek, then faded away. The body of Fred Fisher was later discovered in the paddock where the ghost had pointed.

The other version says Farley reported seeing a 'ghostly figure' sitting on the bridge railing. Investigations showed blood on the bridge at the spot where Farley saw the spectre and an Aboriginal tracker was brought in and said he smelled 'white man fat' under the bridge. Fisher's body was found in a deep hole in the creek near the bridge.

Frederick George James Fisher was born in London in 1792. He was a shopkeeper and, either innocently or deliberately, obtained forged banknotes through his business. In 1815, Fisher was sentenced to fourteen years transportation to Australia. In 1822, he applied for a ticket-of-leave and secured a property at Campbelltown.

In 1825, Fisher had an argument with a local carpenter and received a light prison sentence. Worried about his farm, he gave his neighbour, George Worrall, power of attorney during his sentence but, after his release in June 1826, Fisher disappeared and George Worrall announced that he'd sailed for England. Three weeks later, Worrall sold Fisher's horse and belongings.

In September 1826, George Worrall was arrested on suspicion of Fisher's murder. During the trial, Worrall confessed—even though the tale of the ghostly sighting could not be told in court, as stories of the supernatural were not permitted in a court of law. Worrall was hanged at The Rocks.

The good citizens of Campbelltown are quite proud of their famous ghost and, like all towns and districts, Campbelltown needs some excuse to celebrate and attract tourists and visitors. For ten days every November, the Festival of Fisher's Ghost is held. There is a street parade, the Fisher's Ghost Art Award, the Fisher's Ghost Fun Run, a street fair, craft exhibition and, of course, fireworks. Which all proves two things: Aussies don't need much of an excuse to have a festival, and no festival is really complete without 'crackers'.

Sydney Town Hall

If there is one place in Sydney that ought to be haunted, it is Sydney Town Hall in George Street, which was built in 1869 on top of, and right in the middle of, the city's first cemetery.

The official 'City of Sydney' was established by the *Corporation Act* on 20 July 1842 and comprised an area of almost 12 square kilometres that included the present-day CBD along with Woolloomooloo, Pyrmont, Surry Hills and Chippendale.

By this time the old cemetery had not been used for more than twenty years. A new cemetery had been established in an area along Devonshire Street, which later became the site of Central Railway Station. There was a complete lack of interest in maintaining the old George Street cemetery. It seems that very few people at the time could remember where anyone was buried, or even who was buried there. Apparently no plans or registers of the cemetery were ever kept, and few headstones remained. The majority of those buried there never had a headstone anyway.

This cemetery, which was known officially at the time as the 'George Street Burial Ground', was established in 1792, the fifth year of the settlement of Sydney, by Governor Phillip and Richard Johnson, the First Fleet's official clergyman. In 1812, Governor Macquarie authorised the building of a new church, St Andrew's, next to the burial ground and an extension of the cemetery, which eventually covered just over two acres of land. After the first timber St Andrew's was built, the cemetery was sometimes known as 'Cathedral Close Cemetery'.

Although the old burial ground had been used for almost 30 years, its management was completely haphazard. The area was never formally gazetted as a burial ground, no trustees were appointed and there is no evidence that the area was ever officially consecrated.

Church of England clergy officiated at funerals, but Reverend William Cowper, who was Sydney's only permanent clergyman from 1810 to 1820, noted that 'the dead of all communions were interred indiscriminately'. There was no register of graves, no official map or plan of the layout, and records of the burials were not kept, although some social distinctions were in evidence and the military chose various parts of the cemetery.

Non-commissioned officers of the New South Wales Corps were buried in an area near the George Street end, near Druitt Street. Some non-commissioned officers of the 46th and 48th Regiments were buried in the corner near Kent Street, and over in the southwest corner soldiers of the 73rd Regiment were buried.

Some vaults were established for the wealthier citizens and officers but all records of those were lost over time. During that period of the city's history, officials and officers were also buried privately, or in the grounds of Government House or on Garden Island.

After it was officially closed in 1820, the cemetery was neglected. By the 1830s, the headstones had been vandalised and most had disappeared. People living nearby allowed their cows, goats and horses to graze there and stray pigs took up residence and dug up some of the graves.

The area was, by the late 1840s, prime real estate, right in the centre of the expanding settlement and it is not surprising that the City of Sydney councillors wanted the site for their new town hall. The 'poor fellows' had no permanent home and, for more than 30 years, the proud City of Sydney Council was forced to hold its meetings in various pubs and official buildings around Sydney.

The cunning councillors started a campaign designed to show that the old burial ground was a disgrace and a health hazard. They commissioned a report, which pointed out that the area had developed an unpleasant aroma that became 'unbearable in hot weather'. This was partly caused by unofficial clandestine burials and grave robbers opening graves to steal lead and other material from coffins. It was also recorded in the report that men 'utilised the old burial ground to answer the call of nature', which no doubt added to the aroma. To top it all off, the place had become 'a resort for bad characters at night'.

The City of Sydney Council asked to be given the land several times, but there was still some public opposition to disturbing graves and the colonial government offered other sites, including Hyde Park, the George Street Markets and the old original Government House site on the corner of Phillip and Bridge Streets, which is now the site of the Museum of Sydney.

The councillors persevered, however, and in 1865 once again applied for a grant of a portion of the old burial ground. This time the government agreed and formally transferred part of the cemetery to the Council in 1869 and construction of the Sydney Town Hall began.

Sydney undertaker Robert Stewart, who was also involved in local politics, was given the difficult task of exhuming the remains and removing them for a decent reburial in the Church of England Necropolis at the new cemetery at Haslem's Creek—now known as the Rookwood Cemetery. The removal and reburial process took place between April and September 1869. Not a lot is known about the actual exhumation process, although quite a lot about what Mr Stewart *didn't* do came to light more than a century later.

In the area Mr Stewart was paid to clear, there was apparently only one legible headstone, that of a certain Captain Hamilton. His relatives took charge of that and it was also taken to the new Rookwood Necropolis.

A stonemason, Francis Murphy, was commissioned to create a large classical monument to identify the relocated graves at Rookwood. Although the inscription records the name of the mayor, it does not list any names of those who were reburied there from the old cemetery.

Evidence of the old burial ground has come to light regularly as the city of Sydney developed. Coffins were found during the construction of parts of St Andrew's Cathedral in 1871–72 and, as the city's infrastructure developed, skulls, coffins and tombs were unearthed during excavations for water mains in the 1890s and when electricity cables were being laid in 1904 and 1924. Tombstones and timber coffins were found in 1929 when Town Hall Railway Station was being built.

Quite substantial vaults and tombstones were then uncovered during the excavation work for the establishment of Sydney Square, between the Town Hall and St Andrew's Cathedral, in 1974.

In more recent times it has become obvious that Mr Stewart's contract was carried out with little attention to detail, indeed there is evidence to indicate that he did not 'carry out' the job at all.

In consultation with the city engineer it had been agreed, apparently, that the area under the footprint of the planned building would be completely cleared of all remains by Stewart, but drainage repair work under the Town Hall in 1991 unearthed seven graves, some with skeletons, along with a headstone to a poor lost soul called Elizabeth Steel. More graves were discovered during building work on the forecourt area in 2003.

All that, however, was merely the tip of a scandalous iceberg of evidence of colonial corruption.

In September 2007, a $60 million restoration project began on the building and the University of Sydney's Archaeological Department took the opportunity to conduct an extensive 'dig', which involved lifting up the timber floor of the Town Hall's huge basement. A layer of concrete was removed and the soil underneath examined in the usual meticulous way of such procedures, and evidence of more than 50 graves was found, a number of which were marked by stone memorials and contained timber coffins.

Archaeologist Mary Casey and her team found positive proof that Mr Stewart rorted the council when he took the money (but not the bodies) and ran. It came as no surprise to Professor Casey, who said, 'We have known from work we've done in the building in 1991 and 2003 that there are definitely remains . . . still surviving in the ground both inside and outside the building.'

As far as I can ascertain, however, there have been no substantial reports of hauntings or other ghostly activity in the Sydney Town Hall. It would be nice to imagine that some long-dead bandsman from a colonial regiment might rise up and play thunderous ghostly music on the Town Hall's Grand Organ, installed in 1890 and claimed to be the largest in the world. It would be wonderful if it occurred during the council's annual Seniors Week concerts but, to date, it hasn't happened.

Darlinghurst Gaol

One building in Sydney that I do believe to be haunted is the National Art School, which was the old Darlinghurst Gaol. Now it is true that creative types, such as the artists, painters, potters and the like who inhabit the building these days are perhaps more inclined to flights of fancy and vivid imaginations than the rest of the population, and I have had first-hand accounts of ghostly goings-on from quite a few of them. But they aren't the only witnesses to unexplained events in the building.

Francis Greenway designed Darlinghurst Gaol in 1820. His plans were used for the walls. But because he was an ex-convict, he was taken off the job and his entire design was not used. Instead, the jail was built using the plans of a jail in Philadelphia, like the spokes of a wheel, with wings radiating from a central point leaving narrow segments of space between them.

Before it closed in 1914, more than 70 people were hanged at the jail. Henry Lawson did time there, for drunkenness and non-payment of alimony. In 1921 it was adapted to become East Sydney Technical College, then the National Art School.

There are three known haunted rooms in the old Darlinghurst Gaol buildings; one of them is now a classroom, but previously this was where prisoners were kept prior to hanging. A security guard employed by the art school told me:

It used to be really bad in here. What would happen was lights would come on and the doors would close. There was a smell too. It was so bad that you couldn't stay in the room. Maybe you could say it smelt like dirty socks or rats. We got the place cleaned and the lights checked but the problem was not fixed. I would race through here at night; I really did not like the feeling. I still don't like it at night. It was especially bad near the stairs, and it happened when there were not many people around.

Apparently, near the staircase outside there are about five spirits, which can also sometimes be heard in the classroom knocking on the blackboard.

Teachers at the National Art School have also been the witnesses of ghostly encounters. One teacher saw a ghost in the men's toilet in Building R: there was just a head and a face, which was blue-grey and old. The teacher fell to the floor with a sickly feeling and felt drained till he left the room. In another report, a spirit followed that same teacher as he was going home, all the way to Glebe Island Bridge. Evidently ghosts don't like to cross water, and the malicious presence dissipated near the fish markets.

WHEN THE END OF THE WORLD WAS NIGH . . . PERHAPS

The 1970s were a wonderful time to be living in Adelaide.

In retrospect, the 1970s seem to be a curious age of bad hairstyles and funny fashions. There were cork high-heeled sandals and miniskirts for women, and platform shoes, flares, long socks and shorts for blokes—and there were kaftans for everyone.

South Australia, however, had Don Dunstan, the member for Norwood, as its premier—and that was enough to make life rather wonderful, or at least interesting, depending on your politics and your sense of humour.

Premier Don Dunstan famously and hilariously caused a furore by wearing pink denim shorts and long socks to work in 1972. He was later 'chucked out' of parliament (or at least asked to leave the chamber by opposition members) for wearing a t-shirt bearing the slogan '100 Years of Redleg Football'.

That year, 1978, the Norwood Football Club celebrated its centenary, and pulled off the most unbelievable premiership victory in Australian football history. Having looked like missing the finals early in the season, they not only made the finals but also defeated the undefeated minor premiers Sturt—who had lost only one game all season—by a point. Norwood trailed by 30 points at three-quarter time, hit the lead at the 29-minute mark and led for just three minutes of the game! Dunstan was rightly pleased.

In a more simple age, before the internet and Facebook, practical jokes like the one perpetrated by Adelaide's *This Day Tonight* news program, on 1 April 1975, actually seemed clever and amusing.

The program announced that South Australia was converting to metric time with 100 seconds to the minute, 100 minutes to the hour, and 20-hour days. Furthermore, seconds would become millidays, minutes would become centidays, and hours would become decidays. The report included an interview with Deputy Premier Des Corcoran, who had agreed to give credence to the hoax. He praised the new time system and said South Australia was leading the way with so-called 'deci-time'.

One viewer wanted to know how he could convert his newly purchased digital clock to metric time.

But the most amazing and amusing event to capture the spirit of the times was the one that never happened—the apocalyptic tidal wave that was to wipe out the City of Churches and end forever the unique Adelaideian lifestyle!

Self-proclaimed clairvoyant John Nash declared he'd had a vision that Adelaide would be destroyed, by a massive earthquake and tidal wave, between 10.30 and noon on 19 January 1976.

This prophet of doom was actually a house painter from Melbourne who had moved to Adelaide and become rather distressed at the progressive politics and philosophies that seemed to be taking hold in the historically conservative city.

Adelaide, and therefore the state of South Australia, has always been 'different' to the rest of Australia. For a start, it is the only state devoid of any convict history or heritage. South Australians had a reputation for appreciating the finer things—wine, gourmet food, what Barry Humphries called 'the yartz'. Adelaide was famous for its churches and a more 'cultural', less 'ocker' attitude to life than other Aussie cities. Whether this was an accurate assessment of the way the city's population thought in the 1970s hardly matters; these things had always been Adelaide's trademarks and evidently they appealed to the conservative, Old Testament beliefs held by John Nash.

South Australia, led by Dunstan's Labor Party government, was leading the way with social reform, debating Aboriginal rights, challenging the White Australia Policy and, shock horror, legislating to decriminalise homosexuality.

To Mr Nash, this was the beginning of the end of civilisation as he knew it. Adelaide was about to become the new Sodom, or Gommorah—or both!

Evidently, a quick glance at the Old Testament was enough to convince Mr Nash that his house painting days in Adelaide were numbered; soon there would be no houses left to paint. His recurring vision of a massive vengeful earthquake and tsunami sweeping across Spencer's Gulf to Glenelg and then engulfing the city was so vivid that he felt compelled to warn the people of Adelaide of their fate, sell his house and move to the relative safety of a small town in New South Wales that, rumour later had it, was soon after hit by a severe flood, in which his house was inundated—but no one seems to have documented evidence of that happening.

And so it was that, in the second and third weeks of January 1976, word spread in the media of Mr Nash's premonition and Adelaide's 800,000 citizens were informed that the wrath of the almighty was about to manifest itself and their city was to be obliterated by an earthquake and tidal wave.

Of course, the media had a field day. After all, the second and third weeks of January are part of what the media call 'the silly season', when news is scarce, Australia is on holiday and many regular news services staff are on annual leave. The prophecies of Mr Nash were truly a 'godsend'—media gold dust!

There were basically three styles of reaction to the dire warnings.

Some media outlets reported that many 'new Australians' (as recently arrived migrants whose first language was not English were called backed then) believed the warnings, panicked and fled to higher ground. Some were reported to have sold their houses and moved permanently. This was due, some reports said, to the superstitious nature of people from countries such as Italy, Greece and parts of Eastern Europe. More kindly reports declared that immigrants with poor English skills reacted in panic merely because they had misinterpreted the news items as being factual, scientific reports based on some legitimate geological and meteorological evidence, rather than the baseless ravings of a religious nutcase.

There were rumours and unsubstantiated media reports of people selling beachfront properties at bargain prices, and beachfront hotels suffered cancellations and a 50 per cent drop in bookings. Some people, it appears, did drive up into the Adelaide Hills with their valuables; and inland caravan parks, as far away as the Riverland centres of Barmera, Renmark and Berri, reported being full the night before the predicted apocalypse, but were almost empty by the end of the following day.

On the other hand, some Adelaide families who had made plans to be away on a school holiday trip that day revealed that they decided to stay at home so the neighbours wouldn't think they had believed the prophecy and skipped town! One woman said, years later, that she had been quite ill on the day but went to work only to prevent colleagues from thinking she believed the prophecy.

As it was the silly season and news was scarce, there was much interstate, and even international, media interest in the prediction. The BBC sent a television crew from London and a Sydney radio station sent their morning program staff to do an outside broadcast. One television channel ended their news bulletin the night before the predicted disaster by showing the city clock striking twelve noon with the camera shaking to imitate an earthquake, accompanied by ominous rumbling noises.

When the fateful day arrived, it proved to be a very typical, pleasant, hot summer's day in Adelaide and thousands headed to the beach. At Glenelg there was a very funny mock 'protest march' with banners proclaiming such things as 'The end of the world is nigh—Repent your sins', 'Don't shake at the quake', 'Surf's Up' and, my personal favourite, 'Fortune Cookies Don't Lie!'.

Around the city there was a festive air of hilarity and camaraderie, which gave evidence of a united front and a general acceptance of the progressive thinking and sense of fun, which were trademarks of the 'Dunstan Era'. Many people went to work dressed for the beach and carrying towels. Some of the more painstaking, dedicated office characters turned up wearing wet suits, goggles and flippers. A few even carried surfboards. One office worker recalled that at 11.50 a.m. a workmate said to him, 'I'm going to the toilet, if the tidal wave doesn't come I'll see you in ten minutes. If it does, I'll see you on Mount Lofty.'

Don Dunstan appeared on the balcony of the Glenelg Hotel and declared he would turn back the tidal wave like King Canute—if it arrived. He also declared that Mr Nash would not be welcome back in Adelaide.

A countdown began as the final seconds ticked away to noon and thousands cheered as nothing at all happened. Many stayed at the beaches to enjoy the sunshine and swim, and the pubs and restaurants of Adelaide's seaside western suburbs did a roaring trade all afternoon.

Next morning *The Advertiser* editorial wrote: 'Hopefully, the lesson we should all have learnt from yesterday's pathetic anti-climax is to rely more on our common sense and less on the silly and unscientific speculation of self-appointed soothsayers.'

Words of wisdom, indeed.

THE ACT THAT BROUGHT
THE HOUSE DOWN

In November 1872 the miners living in the settlement of Millchester, a 'suburb' of the goldmining town of Charters Towers in northern Queensland, did something rather extraordinary and very 'offensively Australian'. Let me explain with the help of that august and popular Charters Towers publication, the *Northern Miner*.

It had been a dry year and cattle prices were up. Even so, the bolshie Queensland miners suspected that the few local butchers, enjoying a monopoly of sorts, were taking advantage of the situation. As the *Northern Miner* explained:

> Some time since our butchers, under the plea that owing to the high price of cattle and the extra expense entailed by the dry weather 4d per pound did not pay them, made an attempt to raise the price of meat from 4d to 5d per pound. This change created a great deal of dissatisfaction in the mining portion of the population.

In the true spirit of fair play and the Eureka Stockade, several 'roll-ups' were called and the butchers were warned that 'action would be taken' if the price of beef exceeded 4 pence per pound.

So 4 pence a pound it was, and peace reigned in what the *Northern Miner* called 'the butchering line' and 'the butchers enjoyed peace and pursued the even tenor of their ways in unmolested quietude'.

There was in Millchester, however, a champion of free enterprise in the person of Mr Adolphus Trevethan, the owner of the settlement's largest butchery.

Confronted by this bullying bolshevist attitude and no doubt thinking, as the *Northern Miner* put it, 'probably that he could charge what he liked', he stood like a beacon of *laissez faire* in the midst of socialist people-power. Brave Mr Trevethan:

> ... again brought up the price, this time to 6d per pound, stating his intention of shutting up his shop if he could not obtain that price.

This was, according to the *Northern Miner*, 'more than a portion of our population could stand'.

That 'portion' was, of course, made up of the miners, for whom we assume the *Northern Miner* was the official 'voice'. That voice went on to say that:

> On Tuesday evening the musical sounds of a bullock bell floated gently on the breeze, and the lively town of Millchester resounded with the cry 'Roll up! Roll up!' Soon a crowd assembled and proceeded to the fated building, which was shut up and in total darkness.

The 'fated building' was, as you may have guessed, Mr Trevethan's butchery establishment and home, which was a substantial building made of solid timber. The *Northern Miner* tells us it was 'composed of pine, and presented rather a respectable appearance'.

This was a mere trifle to the six hundred or so representatives of fair play and 'a fair go' for working men. They procured the stoutest rope available from the local produce store, put it around the building and heaved.

Among the 'war cries' used to urge on the mob, and reported in the paper, there were two that I thought had quite a catchy appeal.

I'm not sure if they were chanted like slogans at modern protest meetings, but one of them has that 'feel':

> Trevethan was always the first man to raise the price! *Pull* his shop down.

Then there was the more basic, but no less catchy:

> Pull the [expletive deleted] house down.

Then it appears that the forces of fair play suffered a setback to their plans. A saboteur, to this day unidentified but obviously an enemy of the working classes (and doubtless Mr Trevethan himself), cut the rope at the back of the building.

There was, however, plenty of rope on hand, and once it was replaced around the building at a higher level, the miners simply pulled the building into the street. This had the side effect of completely demolishing the building. To make their point even more emphatically, they also demolished some outbuildings, which no doubt added another element to Mr Trevethan's frustration.

The demolition was just the beginning of the affair (but it's my favourite bit).

Some of the mob celebrated thirstily in the settlement's two pubs while others stayed in the street and then decided to pull down Walker's Store. This plan was abandoned when they remembered that a lot of the settlement's alcohol supplies were stored there and could be lost in the demolition.

The few police present in the crowd could not prevent the demolition of Trevethan's premises, but two 'ringleaders' were arrested for the crime that night. Next day police sought out and also arrested Daniel Scullen, the man who had been ringing the roll-up bell and inciting the crowd.

At the resulting trial, Constable Callaghan testified that, on the night, he 'saw Scullen on the street . . . shouting "Roll up! Roll up! We're going to pull down the price of meat".'

Callaghan went on to testify that next day, when he arrested Scullen and asked him why he rang the bell:

He said that he did not know—the bell was put into his hand by some one he did not know; he said he was very sorry for the affair, and that it was an unfortunate job for him.

Constable Callaghan then added, 'I found the bell on him.'

On the morning after the arrests an angry mob surrounded the lock-up, demanded the release of the prisoners and threatened to pull down the building. Police reinforcements armed with revolvers confronted them and, after some negotiating, the three men were released on bail.

When Mr Trevethan rode his horse into town and attempted to tether it to a verandah of the North Star Hotel, he was jeered and threatened by a group of miners and soon a crowd gathered. Trevethan's horse became frightened and he led it around the back to the yard then he was jeered and jostled by a mob that pursued him onto the pub verandah. At that point he produced a pistol and waved it. The crowd dared him to fire and closed in upon him, a bottle was thrown at him and he fired at a man who rushed towards him. The bullet grazed the man's neck and passed through the neck of a man behind, a miner named Joseph King.

Police arrived to rescue Trevethan from the mob but he was badly bashed and bruised. He was taken to the courthouse and the mob followed. A rumour spread that Joseph King, who was bleeding profusely but very much alive, was dead. The mob demanded Trevethan be handed over and lynched.

At this point sanity arrived upon the scene in the person of Bishop Quinn, Roman Catholic Bishop of Queensland, who had arrived on the goldfields some days previously. He made a moving and ecumenical speech in which he referred to himself as a friend to the miners—probably a sensible thing to do when 600 or more of them, very angry and fuelled by grog, are facing you. He then appealed to the miners' sense of fair play and justice.

As the *Northern Miner* put it:

First of all he would observe that he believed he was known to many there present as a friend to the miners; that from the time when he first came to know them, he had formed the opinion that, as a body, they were the best preservers of law and order, and the most earnest promoters of impartial justice in the colony. He did not believe that there was a body of men in the colony in whose hands the preservation of peace, support of the lawfully constituted authorities, and the promotion of justice were more secure than in those of the miners.

Bishop James Quinn was born in County Kildare and obviously had the Irish gift of the gab and a silver tongue. He was sent 'down under' as Bishop of Brisbane in 1859 and later, in 1875, clashed with Mother Mary MacKillop. His silver tongue failed to stop her taking her order of St Joseph out of Queensland to Sydney. He was, however, more successful in persuading miners to calm down than he was in making Mary MacKillop submit to his authority:

> His Lordship then observed that he did not at all intend to go into the merits of the case which had caused the present commotion; but that he would say this much, that the act of the man who had fired the shot was a rush act. He did not believe that more ought to be said by any one not duly authorised to pass sentence on him. He would also say, he believed there was no body of men who would more clearly distinguish between a rash impulsive act and one of premeditated malice, than those there present. How far the act was rash and impulsive, and how far malicious, should be determined by the lawful authorities, and that he felt warranted in assuring the people that strict justice would be done. He further suggested, first, that the people should allow Trevethan to proceed to the lock-up, and that they should pronounce no opinion on his case until the magistrates had given their decision.

The bishop then walked beside poor Adolphus Trevethan to the lock-up—and the mob parted like the Red Sea before Moses.

The whole affair fizzled out and was soon over. Joseph King recovered, Trevethan was never tried, and Scullen and the other two ringleaders were tried in Townsville and found not guilty. Adolphus Trevethan chose to leave town and pursue his butchering career elsewhere.

Anarchy on the goldfields did not go unnoticed by the authorities, however. There was one small side effect of the affair. Irish-born 42-year-old William Skelton Ewbank Melbourne Charters, the 6-foot 4-inch, 18-stone Gold Commissioner, a veteran of police work and goldfield administration after whom the town of Charters Towers is named, was sacked.

TWO INCREDIBLE 'ALL-ROUNDERS'

Every now and then in history some rare combination of genetic inheritance, circumstance and natural ability, teamed with an abundance of the powers of concentration, produces an individual whose sporting talent and versatility seem inexplicable and superhuman to the rest of us mere mortals.

Australia has been home to a number of these rare human beings.

'Professor Miller'

William Miller was not born in Australia. He arrived here at the age of five when his parents migrated to Melbourne from their hometown of Liscard in Cheshire in 1852. His father, Alexander, a wine and spirits merchant, was also a champion swordsman and William took up the sport at the age of fifteen. Two years later William was a more proficient fencer than his father and had also taken up the sports of gymnastics and boxing.

In 1862, aged sixteen, he started work with the Melbourne and Hobson's Bay Railway Company. In the five brief years he worked there William received a series of rapid promotions, which saw him filling the positions of stationmaster and telegraph instructor at different times. These responsibilities did not, however, prevent him from entertaining his co-workers with feats of strength such as lifting railway sleepers above his head and balancing his entire weight on one hand.

In 1872 William won the Australian broadsword championship by defeating a sergeant of the Light Hussars. He was so proficient in all forms of sword fighting by the age of 25 that there was no opponent in Australia who could defeat him at the sport. By 1874 he was not only the Australian fencing champion but also the undisputed Australian weightlifting champion and wrestling champion. He also held Victorian state titles in boxing and gymnastics.

It was time to move on. William had married Lizzie Trible, the daughter of an American Baptist clergyman, in March 1872 in Melbourne and in 1874 they headed to the USA, where William became a senior physical culture instructor at the famous Olympic Club in San Francisco. This position did not stop him from competing in two of the sports he particularly enjoyed, boxing and wrestling. Between 1874 and 1880 he managed to compete in the sports at a top level on 72 occasions, winning 55 times and suffering only six losses—the other eleven matches being drawn.

In 1879 William decided to try his hand—or rather his legs— at competitive long-distance walking and defeated the champion walker Duncan Ross in a 24-hour event by walking 102 miles (164 kilometres). He also took on the champion weightlifter Richard Pennell, but failed to better him and had to be satisfied with a draw when both men lifted 1550 pounds (703 kilograms) of solid iron.

Somewhere along the way, William had become 'Professor' Miller. Whether he gave himself the title or it came from an event promoter or the American media, we don't really know. One American sportswriter, obviously a keen student of Greek mythology, called William Miller the 'man built in the form of Hercules'.

Although he stood only 175 centimetres and weighed a mere 90 kilograms, his Herculean calf muscles were 44 centimetres in diameter and his chest was a fraction under 120 centimetres.

It wasn't just his body strength that was impressive, however; his stamina and endurance were in the realm of the superhuman, as his poor victim on several occasions, the champion walker Duncan Ross, knew only too well. In one 50-hour walking competition Miller defeated Ross by 48 kilometres and, in the rematch, poor Ross pulled out defeated after just 64 kilometres, at which point Miller invited Ross's trainer to finish the competition. The trainer also broke down while trying to keep up with Miller and was carried off the track after 80 kilometres. Miller continued alone and walked 160 kilometres in 22 hours

On his return to Melbourne in 1880 he set up a wrestling match with his former pupil William Muldoon, which ended in a draw—after eight hours. Miller and the champion Scottish wrestler Donald Dinnie then competed in a series of three wrestling bouts. In the first of these Dinnie broke Miller's left leg in the opening round, but the Professor declared that he was okay to fight on, and the match was eventually declared a draw. The second match was also drawn but the Aussie champ finally achieved victory in the third and final match.

Miller then moved operations to Sydney where he set up a gymnasium in Liverpool Street. In May 1883 he challenged the legendary champion boxer, Larry Foley, the 'father of Australian boxing', who owned a rival gym, to fight for £500, a fortune in those days.

They had been fighting for 40 rounds when Miller knocked Foley down and spectators invaded the ring and stopped the fight, which was officially declared a draw, although Foley, who was famous for his sportsmanship, always conceded that Miller had won the fight.

Returning to Melbourne in 1884 Professor Miller coached at the Olympic Club for five years and then set up his own gymnasium in Elizabeth Street. He taught himself the art of Greco-Roman wrestling and competed in matches against the British Empire and European Champion Mons Victor, and defeated him. He even challenged two Greco-Roman wrestling champions to fight him as a tag team, two against one, and he won that match as well.

Miller finally met his match in the wrestling ring when he was defeated by the American Clarence Whistler in a bout at the Theatre Royal in Melbourne in 1885. Whistler, who was regarded as the world champion wrestler at the time, was so pleased that he toasted his victory with champagne after the bout then ate the champagne glass, and died from internal bleeding several days later.

'The Professor' wrote articles, books and gave regular talks on fitness, lectured on physical culture at the Hibernian Hall and even appeared in a Shakespeare play that featured a wrestling scene. He continued wrestling and boxing until he returned to the USA in 1903, where he was made manager of the San Francisco Athletic Club and was also an athletic instructor for the New York Police Department.

William and Lizzie had no children and lived in retirement in Baltimore from 1917 until he died, aged 92, on 11 March 1939.

Snowy Baker

In 1884, the year that William Miller called himself Greco-Roman wrestling champion, Reginald Leslie Baker was born in Surry Hills, Sydney, son of George Baker, an Irish-born Sydney Municipal Council clerk, and his wife Elizabeth.

Called 'Snowy' from childhood, young Reg was educated at Crown Street Public School and, from the age of twelve, won a series of swimming championships for his school. While still at school he also swam and played water polo for the East Sydney Swimming Club and learned to ride well enough to do trackwork at Randwick Racecourse in the mornings before school.

In 1901 he started work at the Colonial Sugar Refining Company as a draftsman, and continued his sporting activities, finishing second in the state half-mile final. He played halfback for the Eastern Suburbs Rugby Union team and represented New South Wales against Queensland and the touring British Isles side in 1904. He also played for Australia in the first test against the British Isles. A punishing tackler, he was, according to one sportswriter, 'as hard a player for his weight as has been seen in the game'. Snowy, who weighed 73 kilograms for most of his adult life, also rowed for the Mercantile Rowing Club in championship races and was a very good cricketer.

Snowy served as a trooper with the New South Wales Lancers and gained the rank of sergeant. In the army he excelled in a variety of military sports and won many prizes for fencing, wrestling and horse sports, including tent-pegging. He was also a good shot with a rifle.

In 1902, he took up boxing. In 1905 and 1906 he won the New South Wales amateur middleweight boxing title then went on to win that title in Victoria and also became the heavyweight boxing champion of both states.

In December 1906, according to the legend, 1000 people turned up at the dock in Sydney to see him leave for England to compete in the Amateur Boxing Association's championships. Apparently, a group of twenty young women hired a boat and followed the steamer on which he departed all the way out of Sydney Heads.

Unfortunately for Snowy, and no doubt to the great disappointment of the twenty young ladies who chased him out of the Heads, he contracted enteric fever and pneumonia and was unable to complete in the championships. He did, however, compete in the 1908 Olympic Games. The boxing section of the Olympics that year was held in London in October, which was actually three months after the rest of the games.

Competing as a middleweight for the combined 'Australasian' (Australia and New Zealand) team, Snowy won three fights, all fought on the same day, two of them by knockouts. That got him into the final, which he lost narrowly on points in a split decision, thus earning himself the silver, Australia's first-ever boxing medal at an Olympics. He was the only non-British boxer to win a bout in the entire competition.

Snowy then toured Scotland, Ireland and Scandinavia, performing in exhibition matches in boxing and aquatic sports, before returning to a huge welcome in Sydney in December 1908. Unfortunately we have no record of how many of the twenty young ladies were there to greet him that day but if they were it was all in vain, for on 31 March 1909 at St Mark's Anglican Church, Darling Point, Snowy married 37-year-old Ethel Rose Mackay, widow of the noted tennis player Augustus Kearney.

Snowy soon began to capitalise on fame and opened a training establishment in Castlereagh Street. He also ran mail-order courses in fitness, published a book called *General Physical Culture*, and wrote articles for the Sydney *Evening News*.

From 1912 to 1914 he published *Snowy Baker's Magazine*, which cost a penny and achieved sales of more than 3000 a month during the two years that it existed.

Always the clever entrepreneur and promoter, Snowy went into partnership with controversial powerbrokers like Hugh McIntosh in Sydney and John Wren in Melbourne. He purchased the Rush-cutters Bay Stadium for £30,000, and also set up 'Baker's Stadiums' in Melbourne, Adelaide and Brisbane. He usually acted as referee for big fights in Sydney. He was also involved in the career of Les Darcy and later accused of helping arrange the boycotting of Darcy in the US in 1917. Snowy vehemently denied the charges and was cleared of any blame in the Maitland committee of inquiry.

In spite of trying to enlist three times in the Australian Imperial Force, he could not pass the medical due to an old spinal injury so he threw his energies into fundraising for the war effort and organised concerts, shows and film-nights at the stadium.

As soon as the war was over, Snowy made another career change and became a film star in silent movies. He started with a film called *The Enemy Within*, in which he played a secret agent, but he soon moved into outdoor action films, in which he could use his horseriding skills and athleticism. He played a stationhand in *The Lure of the Bush*, a boxing parson in *The Man from Kangaroo* (a film he also co-produced), a bushranger in *The Shadow of Lightning Ridge* and the title role in *The Jackeroo of Coolabong* (1920).

Like all the classic cowboy heroes of the silent era and early talkies, he had as a constant companion a trusty steed, a grey horse called Boomerang.

In 1920 Snowy left for the United States hoping to make it 'big in pictures' and, although he did appear in a number of early Hollywood movies, he was far more successful as a stunt coach and a riding instructor to Hollywood stars and as a polo player and businessman. In 1933 he became a director of the Riviera

Country Club, near Santa Monica, which he was also involved in managing.

He only made three brief visits back to Australia and died of heart disease in Los Angeles in 1953.

Snowy's reputation is based on the amazing variety of his achievements and skills. He excelled not only at rugby, boxing, rowing, horseriding, fencing, polo and aquatic sports, but also as an entrepreneur, film star, showman, publicist and businessman.

Snowy wasn't the only excellent all-round sportsman in his family, either. Believe it or not, his brother, William, also known as Harold, was a swimmer who won three New South Wales championships in 1906, captained the Australian water polo team, played rugby for Australia three times against New Zealand, and won boxing and wrestling championships. As captain of Maroubra Surf Club from 1900 to 1910, Harold was awarded the Albert Medal for bravery for his part in the famous surf rescue of more than 100 people at Cronulla Beach in 1910. He enlisted in 1915 as a lieutenant in the Light Horse but was injured in a shipboard accident on the way to Egypt, spent the next two years in plaster from his neck to his toes, and had to remain immobile for four years. After his recovery he coached Randwick's first-grade rugby team to their first-ever premiership in 1930. The 'Galloping Greens' went on from that victory to become the most successful rugby club in Sydney.

Additionally, two other brothers, Frank and Ernest, were water polo players and another, Frederick, was an amateur welterweight boxing champion of Australia.

THE WOMAN WHO MURDERED HIS WIFE

On 7 October 1920 the headline in the *Sydney Morning Herald* announced:

EUGENIE FALLENI FOUND GUILTY—SENTENCE OF DEATH

This was the news for which all the curious and pruriently-minded citizens of Sydney had been waiting. It was the culmination of one of the most talked-about murder trials in Sydney's history, and one of the strangest legal cases Australia has ever seen.

The article went on to explain:

At the Central Criminal Court yesterday, before the Chief Justice (Sir William Cullen), the trial was concluded of Eugene Falleni, 45, who was charged with having, on September 28, 1917, at Lane Cove, feloniously and maliciously murdered Annie Crawford.

Now, the more observant among you will have already noticed something either odd or erroneous in the newspaper report, for it is 'Eugenie' who is found guilty in the headline, but 'Eugene' who was charged with the crime.

This is how one reporter described the defendant in court:

The accused woman is strangely interesting. She bore an extraordinary resemblance to a man, for facially she is masculine.

She wore a man's clothes. While in the docks she appeared distinctly nervous. She wears a gold band ring on the little finger, and she 'fiddled' with the dock rail. In her right hand, she carried a grey felt hat. Her hair is almost black and clipped short. It was neatly brushed and parted on the left side of her head.

That final piece of information may be lost on younger readers who don't know that, up until the 1960s, it was customary for males to part their hair on the left, and females on the right.

'Eugene Falleni' was indeed 'Eugenie Falleni', although she was probably born Eugenia Falleni. She also may have been Eugenia Martelli, Harry Leo Crawford, Eugenia Innocente, Jean Ford and, according to the *West Australian* newspaper, 'Eugenie Callini'.

Eugenia married three times: once to a man who was already married and twice to women who believed she was a man. One of those women, Annie Birkett, was brutally murdered by Eugenia.

In Western societies today there is understanding of and sympathy for those who are born 'transgendered', and legislation to protect their rights is being formulated and introduced. A century ago, however, there was nothing but ignorance and morbid curiosity about such conditions.

Eugenia Falleni committed acts of deception and a foul murder. She can be seen, however, as a victim of society's almost total ignorance about her true nature. She was also a victim of poverty and lack of education, and suffered badly from her father's lack of understanding and brutal attempts to make her 'normal'. She was also probably the victim of repeated rape as a young woman.

Eugenia, who was illiterate, was also a victim of her own belief that posing as a member of the opposite sex was a criminal offence and, if discovered, she would be jailed. This led to a paranoid fear of detection, which was partly the reason for her brutal crime.

Her Italian Catholic father was hostile and uncomprehending about her 'masculinity' and possibly told his daughter that posing as a man was a criminal offence in order to force her into behaving like a female. He may even have believed it himself, although no such criminal law ever existed.

Eugenia feared being jailed more than anything, for obvious reasons, and in attempting to prevent it from happening, she performed a criminal act that led to it happening.

After four years of married life together, her wife, Annie, had discovered Eugenia's secret.

The *Sydney Morning Herald* summarised the facts of the case this way:

> ... it was stated that the accused, while wearing male attire and passing herself off as Harry Leo Crawford, went through the form of marriage in 1913 with the deceased, Annie Birkett, a widow, who then became known as Mrs. Crawford.
>
> The charred remains of a woman, subsequently identified as Annie Birkett, or Crawford, were found on October 2, 1917, in the bush some distance from Chatswood, on the Lane Cove River.

It was three years before someone contacted the police with 'certain suspicions' and the body was exhumed and identified, but once it was, Harry Crawford was soon arrested—and was discovered to be female. Amazingly, when arrested, Harry had remarried and was living with his second 'wife', Elizabeth Allison, who was a few years older than her 'husband'. They had married in September 1919 and she described him as a model husband.

The case caused a sensation. Transgenderism, as we now know, has been around as long as mankind has walked the planet, but there was blanket ignorance about it in Australia in 1920. The only words in the common vocabulary that could be found to label Eugenia's condition, such as 'homosexualist', 'pervert' and 'hermaphrodite', were all completely inaccurate.

To the newspaper readers of 1920, Eugenia was not only a freak, she was also a murderer, and that coincidental link made her 'condition' seem decidedly 'evil'.

For most people this morbid curiosity about the strangeness of the case focused on one main mystery: how could a woman posing as a man practise the physical 'deception' of what many then still called 'the marriage act'?

The most sensational piece of testimony came when Constable John Henry Walsh presented a record of an interview conducted during the search of Harry Crawford's home, where the accused lived with his second wife, Elizabeth. It was read in court.

As the constable was searching the bedroom, the accused said, 'You will find it, something there that I have been using.' The following conversation, recorded in the police report, then took place.

Detective: 'What is it, something artificial?'

[Falleni] replied: 'Yes, don't let her see it.'

Detective: 'Do you mean to say that she doesn't know anything about this?'

[Falleni] said his first wife had not known about it either, 'Not until the latter part of our marriage.'

At the risk of being disrespectful and frivolous in the midst of a serious narrative, this part of the story always brings to my mind the limerick that we found so hilarious as teenagers, about the poor policeman from Tottenham Junction. According to the limerick, the unfortunate policeman in question 'lost the use of his sexual function' but managed the situation ingeniously in the following manner: 'For the rest of his life he deceived his wife, By dextrous use of his truncheon.'

Eugenia Falleni did almost exactly the same thing as that mythical policeman from Tottenham Junction, although not 'for the rest of his life'. She also had more to hide than a case of male sexual dysfunction.

The 'article', found 'among male clothing in a locked leather suitcase' in Eugenia/Harry's room at the Stanmore house where she/he lived with her/his wife, was later exhibited in court. It was 'made of wood and rubber bound with cloth in the shape of a phallus or dildo'.

What led to the murder, evidently, was that Annie Crawford had discovered her husband's true gender. It was reported that Annie had been told by a 'neighbour' that her husband was a woman; or maybe she had discovered the truth for herself. In

September 1917 she told a relative, when talking about Harry, that she had 'found out something amazing about him', but Annie kept the details to herself and was killed a few days later.

Eugenia eventually admitted that Annie had discovered the truth and they argued about it. It seems that was why she planned a fatal picnic at Lane Cove on the 'Eight-hour Day' long weekend in 1917.

Reports in the *Sydney Morning Herald*, during the trial in 1920, gave the basic evidence from the scene of the crime:

> Evidently the woman had been burnt to death. With the exception of her stockings and shoes all her clothing had been destroyed. The body was intact, but the injuries by burning were most noticeable on the upper portion. None of the features was recognisable. There were signs of fire on the rocks, the ground, and the trees, but nothing could be seen of a made fire for cooking or any other purpose. The lower part of the body was almost untouched. The fire seemed to have extended about 100ft in another direction.
>
> During a search near the charred portions a carryall, a drinking glass, a mug, and a hatpin were found, also the broken parts of a glass bottle. A brooch and a greenstone pendant, which were on the body, have since been identified by the dead woman's son, Harry Birkett, as her property.

Eugenia/Harry was arrested and the evidence was overwhelming in favour of 'guilty'. The *Sydney Morning Herald* reported that:

> Police-sergeant Gorman stated that the day after the dead body was removed in 1917 he found a bottle containing a small quantity of kerosene a few feet from the spot . . .
>
> The accused, in a statement from the dock, said that she was unnerved by three months' detention in Long Bay gaol, and could not speak as she wished in declaring her innocence of the crime with which she was charged. She knew nothing, she said, about what happened after the woman with whom she had lived for four years disappeared. They had had words from time to time, but no serious quarrel.

Annie's son, also named Harry, gave evidence of the events leading up to the murder. He said his mother met the accused when they were both employed by Dr Clarke, of Wahroonga, where his mother worked in domestic service and Harry Crawford worked as a handyman.

Harry Birkett said that the accused 'was so persistent about his mother marrying him that she at last consented'.

Evidently Crawford, claiming to be a 38-year-old widower born in Scotland, was a considerate and generous suitor and took the widow and her son on outings to the circus and on picnics. Annie had a nest egg from her first marriage and the couple decided to quit working in service and use the money to open a corner store in Balmain, which they did prior to their marriage in February 1913 at the Methodist parsonage in that suburb.

Harry Birkett, whose father died when he was three, was nine when his mother remarried and remembered that they lived at Balmain for about six months after the marriage, but the couple 'did not seem very happy in their married life'.

The couple then separated and Annie and her son lived in Kogarah with her sister until the marriage was patched up and they moved to Drummoyne, where Crawford obtained menial work in hotels and factories. Harry Birkett testified that on 'Friday morning not long before Eight-hour Day in 1917, he went to work as usual, and never saw his mother again'.

Witnesses were called who said they saw the accused near the scene of the crime at the time of the murder. Mrs Ethel Carroll said that she saw 'a man sitting on a rock near the hill, with his head buried in his hands', not far from where the body was after-wards found. Ethel testified that he 'appeared to be excited, and startled' when he saw her and later, as she returned from her walk, he had 'jumped over a rock and walked behind [her] for about six minutes, until he came to another track branching off from the one [she] was using'. This was obviously, the jury decided, the action of someone making sure a passing stranger didn't notice something. Ethel identified the 'man' in the dock was the one she saw that day.

Two dentists testified that dental evidence proved it was Annie Birkett's body that was found.

It really was a very obvious case of murder and the accused was rather obviously the murderer, so you may be wondering by now why the crime took three years to solve. There are several reasons.

Firstly, the murder took place during World War I and at a time when the newspapers were full of war news. Things were going badly on the Western Front and almost 40,000 Australians died or were wounded in the four months between June and November 1917. An unidentified body at Lane Cove didn't seem such a big deal.

Secondly, it was not until 1919 that Annie was reported missing by her sister and son. It was known that Annie and her husband quarrelled and his story that she had 'cleared off with a plumber' seemed to satisfy the neighbours, although there was no history of adultery in Annie's life and she was a shy, reserved woman.

Harry Crawford then sold the furniture and moved with his stepson to a boarding house in Woolloomooloo. At first he told his stepson that his mother was visiting friends but later he switched to the 'cleared off with a plumber' story with him also.

It appears that after a while the landlady, a certain Mrs Henrietta Schieblich, was 'onto' Crawford and scared him enough to get him out of her house several months after the murder.

By that time Harry Birkett was living safely with his aunt in Kogarah, and Crawford was drinking heavily and was often in a deranged mental state. During one bout of hysteria he told Mrs Schieblich that his room was haunted and she apparently replied, 'It's your wife that's haunting you, I think you killed her.' She later lied to him, saying that detectives had called looking for him, and he moved out of the house.

Why didn't Mrs Schieblich report her suspicions to the police? Well, as you can tell by her name, she was German and it was wartime. There was massive anti-German sentiment in 1917 and Mrs Schieblich wanted no trouble with the authorities. She just wanted her suspicious boarder to be gone.

There were very good reasons why Harry Birkett had left to live with his aunt. His stepfather's behaviour was extremely weird after his mother 'left' and there were two incidents involving the young lad that shed a very ghastly light on the disturbed mind of Eugenia Falleni.

It seems that Eugenia, deranged, despairing and suffering depression, actually contemplated killing her stepson and herself. There is very good evidence that on at least two occasions she set out to do this, only to have fits of remorse and change her mind.

On one occasion, soon after the murder, Eugenia took Harry to The Gap, the notorious suicide spot near Watsons Bay in Sydney. According to Harry Birkett's account, they climbed over the safety fence so that they could throw rocks into the ocean and his step-father sat near the edge and encouraged him to sit with him. The boy, however, was nervous and refused and so they returned home.

A few days later the two took an even more bizarre journey. Leaving Mrs Schieblich's boarding house, they walked in pouring rain to the tram stop and caught the tram to Double Bay, where they alighted and walked into the bush.

What really scared Harry, apart from being dragged out at night in a thunderstorm to take a tram ride for no apparent reason, was that his stepfather was carrying a brand new shovel. What the boy didn't know until later was there was a bottle of brandy in his step-father's pocket. What Harry never knew was that there was almost certainly also a five-shot revolver in the pocket, with two bullets in the chamber.

These days, bushland is at a premium in Double Bay—and 'secluded clearings in the bush' are non-existent, but in 1917 Eugenia soon found one and started to dig. The bottle of brandy was produced and Eugenia started drinking and told the boy to dig and also offered him brandy. This continued for some time, with the poor kid getting more frightened and the adult getting almost hysterical, until Eugenia suddenly threw the shovel into the bush and took the boy home.

The police found the revolver, still loaded with two bullets, when they found the dildo. Eugenia had stolen it while briefly employed as a payroll guard.

The theory is that Eugenia intended to suicide and take the

boy with her by grabbing him and jumping off The Gap or, in the second attempt, shooting him and then herself.

Let me finally go back and start where I should have—at the beginning of the whole sad story of Eugenia Falleni.

Eugenia Falleni was born on 25 July 1875 in Italy (either in Florence or Livorno—accounts differ). She was the eldest of the Falleni family's 22 children, seventeen of whom survived birth. All but two of the children were, however, born in New Zealand, after the family moved to Wellington in 1877.

Eugenia was, apparently, always 'a man trapped in a woman's body'. She grew up as what might be called a 'tomboy'. There are two versions of her relationship with her father, a fisherman who also owned a horse and cart and sometimes worked as a carrier.

It seems most probable that a sympathetic grandmother and sister helped Eugenia to lead a double life during her teenage years. She would leave home dressed as a girl then change and become, to all intents and purposes, a young man often engaged in manual work in stables, brickyards or on the docks.

There is another version of the story that implies that Eugenia's father, knowing full well that his oldest child behaved as a man, exploited the fact by allowing her to do menial manual work as a man in order to earn income for the family.

What we do know is that Eugenia's father, seemingly in an attempt to force his nineteen-year-old daughter to be a woman, arranged her marriage to Braseli Innocente in September 1894 in Wellington. The poor girl was taken to Auckland by her husband, where she discovered that he was already married. She then fled back to Wellington, avoided her family, decided to live her life as a man and went to sea as a cabin boy.

Eugenia spent three years at sea as 'Eugene' but at some point her true identity was revealed. There is an apocryphal story that the cover was blown in a drunken conversation with an Italian-speaking captain when she was talking about her childhood and used the female form *piccolina*, rather than the male form *piccolino*, in referring to herself as a small child. Whether she was repeatedly raped, as some versions of the story would have it, or consented to sex for self-preservation or other reasons of her own, she was abandoned, destitute and pregnant, in the port of Newcastle in 1898. Later that year in Sydney she gave birth to a daughter, Josephine.

Josephine was left with an Italian couple and raised by a woman she knew as 'Granny De Angeles', who told her that Eugenia was her mother and her father was a sea captain. Josephine appears to have been a troubled and troublesome child and, having met her mother when she was seven, she knew Eugenia's secret.

Not long after 'Harry Crawford' and Annie Birkett were married, Granny De Angeles, whose husband had apparently deserted her and returned to Italy, died and twelve-year-old Josephine came to live with her mother. If this had not happened it is quite probable that Eugenia may well have maintained the deception.

As it was, however, Eugenia/Harry was now living with three people as a family in the same house, but two of them were a wife and stepson, to whom she/he was masquerading as a male (and who both assumed she was Josephine's father), while her daughter knew the truth.

After the disappearance of Annie and the move to the boarding house at Woolloomooloo, it didn't take long for both teenagers to quit living with Eugenia/Harry. Josephine had 'shot through' by the time young Harry had left to live with his aunt in Kogarah.

Josephine was used as a hostile witness in the court case. Her statement read:

I first remember my mother when about seven years of age. She always wore men's clothing, and was known as Harry Crawford. I was brought up at Double Bay by Mrs. de Angeles, whom I used to call 'Granny.'

Granny told me that Harry Crawford was my mother, and that my father was the captain of a boat. My mother was very cruel to me when I was a child, and often forgot me.

Granny told me that my mother tried to smother me when I was a baby. Mrs de Angeles died when I was about 12 years of age, and my mother took me to a little confectionery shop in Balmain, kept by a Mrs. Birkett, who had a son named Harry.

My mother told me Mrs. Birkett had some money, and always thought my mother was a man. I said to my mother, 'She'll find you out one of these days.'

My mother replied, 'Oh, I'll watch it. I would rather do away with myself than let the police find anything about me.'

My mother told me always to call her father, and not let Mrs. Birkett nor anyone else know that she was a woman. I did not know that my mother was married to Mrs. Birkett, but they occupied the same bed-room. They quarrelled a great deal, and mother used to come out and say, 'More rows over you. I cannot get any sleep.'

I replied to my mother, and she said, 'Oh, a lovely daughter I've got.'

I said, 'What can you expect? A lovely mother I've got.'

In 1917 I met my mother, who told me everything was unsettled and upside down, as Mrs. Birkett had discovered she was a woman. My mother seemed very agitated, and was always reticent about herself.

Josephine's statement was given after police tracked her down after they had arrested 'Harry Leo Crawford' at the Empire Hotel, Annandale, on 5 July 1920. On arrival at Long Bay Prison, Crawford shocked the guards by requesting to be admitted to the Women's Section. At first they refused, but a prison doctor was called. The doctor later said, 'I knew within a matter of seconds that she was a woman.'

Henrietta Schieblich, feeling safe now the war was over, testified that Harry Crawford told her his wife had left him and said he added, 'We had a jolly good row, and I gave her a crack on the head, and she cleared.'

Eugenia/Harry later gave an account of the fatal picnic in which she claimed that Annie slipped and fell, hitting her head on a rock and losing consciousness and, despite her best efforts, died within minutes at which point she panicked and resolved to burn Annie's body to make it unidentifiable. The motivation being fear that if Annie's body was identified, Eugenia would be arrested and her true sex would be revealed.

The last part of the statement was the only part anyone believed.

Annie Birkett's remains, which had been exhumed from the grave in which she had been buried as 'unknown', in 1917 at Rookwood Cemetery, were reburied by her family at Woronora Cemetery.

Meanwhile, second wife, Elizabeth Allison, who was quoted in the media as stating that Harry Crawford was 'an ideal husband' and they had 'a very happy married life', was forced to move house when the case started because she was 'so pestered by calls and sensation seekers'.

Harry Birkett, who was working in a tailoring business at the time of the trial, seemed to have survived the horrors of losing both natural parents and almost being murdered by his deranged female stepfather, and was described as a 'bright young man'. I have no idea what happened to the troubled and unruly Josephine, who seems to have been the main cause of all the rows between Annie Birkett and her 'husband'.

Eugenia was sentenced to death, which was commuted to life, and served eleven years in Long Bay Prison, during which time she lived as a woman, having lived the previous 25 years as a man.

Sympathisers petitioned for her release and, in February 1931, following a visit from Mr Lamaro, the Minister for Justice, she walked free. Eugenia was nearly 60 years old and 'not of robust health'. She was taken by car to an unknown destination and disappeared without a trace.

On 9 June 1938 Mrs Jean Ford, the proprietor of a small boarding house in Glenmore Road, Paddington, stepped off the kerb in front of a car in nearby Oxford Street and was run over and badly injured. She had just finalised the sale of the premises and had £100 cash in her purse.

It was uncertain whether the event was a suicide attempt or merely an unfortunate accident, but Mrs Jean Ford died of her injuries the next day in Sydney Hospital. When all efforts to trace her family failed, the hospital authorities, in desperation, passed the matter on to the police, who came and took fingerprints.

The dead woman was Eugenia Falleni.

THE OVERLAND MAIL

If you have ever had cause to complain about the email that didn't arrive or the parcel that went astray for a few days in the post, you should a spare thought for our colonial ancestors, for whom the seemingly simple process of sending a letter was not only frightfully expensive, but also a rather hit-and-miss business.

Sending any correspondence, official or personal, from anywhere in the world to anywhere else in the world was, up until the 19th century, mostly a matter of transferring dispatch bags from ship to ship. This was usually done in port. Copies of official correspondence would be handed to the captains of visiting ships in the hope that they would deliver them, or at least pass them on to other ships they chanced to meet that happened to be heading for the port the mail was intended for.

Colonial powers, such as Britain and France, had extensive diplomatic and naval systems, which provided reasonably secure methods of transferring mail around the globe; there was, however, no secure system for personal mail.

During the early days of the settlement at Sydney Cove, a minor government official, perhaps the governor's secretary or assistant secretary, would board the ships that arrived in port and attempt some orderly supervision of the distribution of the mail. By the time the colony was twenty years old, however, the standard practice of Sydneysiders boarding ships and claiming mail had become unwieldy and prone to theft and corruption. The *Sydney Gazette*, on 23 April 1809, reported that:

. . . complaints have been made . . . that numerous frauds have been committed by individuals repairing on-board ships on their arrival . . . and personating others, by which they obtained possession of mail.

The *Gazette* announced the establishment of an office on the north side of George Street:

. . . at which parcels and letters addressed to the inhabitants of this colony are to be deposited previous to the distribution, which office shall be under the direction of Mr Isaac Nichols, assistant to the naval officer.

Isaac Nichols, a native of rural Wiltshire, was found guilty of stealing a donkey at the Warminster Assizes in 1790. He was sentenced to transportation and arrived in New South Wales on the *Admiral Barrington* in October 1791, as part of the Third Fleet.

Governor Hunter was impressed by his character and sobriety and appointed him chief overseer of the convict labour gangs. Hunter granted him 50 acres (20 hectares) at Concord when his sentence expired in December 1797, and Nichols became a farmer and also opened an inn in George Street.

In 1799 Nichols was charged with having received stolen property—but the trial was set up by John MacArthur and his cronies of the NSW Corps as revenge against Nichols for not bending the rules to allow them extra convict labourers. Three naval officers (one of whom was Matthew Flinders), acting as a minority of magistrates on the bench, disagreed with the verdict handed down and Nichols was exonerated after an enquiry and given a free pardon.

Nichols added further properties to his holdings and built a substantial house and a shipyard near the hospital wharf.

In March 1809 he was appointed superintendent of public works and assistant to the naval officer and, a month later, he was made the colony's first postmaster. He held the position until his death in 1819, when he was succeeded as postmaster by George Panton, who was also coroner.

A post office was set up in Hobart on the same day that Nichols opened the one in Sydney in 1809.

While there was a system for collecting mail that came into port and distributing it directly in an orderly manner, it took a few more years before a system of actually delivering mail was put into place.

Back then, all communication, transport and freight between the various settlements of New South Wales and Van Diemen's Land was carried out by sea, but a regular overland mail run was established in October 1816 between Hobart and Launceston.

A government messenger left Hobart on a Sunday, walked the 193 kilometres to Launceston and left on the return journey on the following Sunday. This provided a regular service for the exchange of correspondence between the two settlements of Van Diemen's Land and that did not depend on the availability of ships and the vagaries of wind and sea.

Twelve years later, in 1828, the *Gazette* reported that the Hobart–Launceston messenger had been provided with a horse for the journey.

Australia can boast a world first in the history of postage and mail services in the creation of the prepaid mail. On 1 November 1838 James Raymond, who was at the time colonial postmaster-general, introduced a system of prepaid letters, which had never been done before anywhere in the world.

Every schoolboy of my generation knows that Roland Hill in Britain devised the first adhesive postage stamp, the famous 'Penny Black', in 1840. Up until that time it was the custom for people receiving the mail to pay the postage, not the sender. People receiving mail from Isaac Nichols in 1809 had to pay one shilling to collect!

James Raymond's system, which pre-dated the postage stamp by two years, consisted of a prepaid letter in the form of a folded sheet of notepaper with an embossed seal. These were sold for one and a half pence each or one shilling and three pence per dozen. Later the price per dozen was discounted down to an amazingly low one shilling.

Raymond was a landowner and magistrate from County Limerick, Ireland, who had to abandon his property when his life was threatened. Ralph Darling, who was governor of New South Wales at the time, was asked to provide Raymond with a suitable colonial appointment and Raymond arrived in Sydney in 1826 with his wife and nine children and was made coroner at Parramatta on a salary of £50, with additional allowances of £184 in place of rations and lodgings until a more suitable appointment could be found.

In September 1827 Governor Darling made him Searcher and Surveyor of Customs and, when George Panton died in April 1829, Raymond was appointed to succeed the postmaster at a salary of £400. In 1835 his title was changed to Postmaster-General, and his salary had increased to £650 by the time of his death.

Raymond was aware of the ideas being put forward in Britain by Roland Hill, who had suggested the idea of prepaid letters before coming up with the notion of the adhesive postage stamp, but the credit for actually designing and producing the first prepaid postage system in the world goes to James Raymond—and therefore Australia! Hip, hip, hooray.

In fact, the idea was still being used for international airmail in the 1980s, in the form of the Aerogram, the lightweight prepaid blue letter sheet that folded and stuck down into an envelope shape. They may still be used today for all I know—but I haven't seen one in many years.

The same year that Raymond introduced the world's first prepaid letters, a long-distance overland mail run was established between the fledgling settlement of Melbourne and the seat of colonial government in Sydney.

This idea was the brainchild of the enterprising pioneer Joseph Hawdon, who had arrived in the colony in 1834, aged just nineteen, and had joined his older brother, John, in a cattle-breeding venture at Batemans Bay. From there, Joseph and two friends overlanded cattle to Port Phillip Bay and Joseph took up land around the Dandenong district.

The only method of transporting mail around the colony at that time was by sea, which meant the service was erratic and irregular. In 1838 Joseph, therefore, secured a contract to deliver the mail fortnightly overland from Port Phillip to Yass, 280 kilometres south of Sydney. From there it could be taken by coach or bullock team to Sydney.

No one else was interested in the contract as there was, at that time, no track at all between Yass and Melbourne and there were rivers to cross and bushrangers and possibly hostile Aboriginal tribes along the 600-kilometre route, not to mention floods and bushfires and various venomous reptiles and insects. The financial reward was, however, a good one—with the contract being valued at £1200 per year, which was a massive sum in 1838.

Young Joseph was daring and enterprising, but he wasn't silly enough to even contemplate doing the job himself.

Several years earlier, during the overlanding expedition from Batemans Bay to Port Phillip Bay, three members of the party were about to drown when a wagon was carried away by raging waters as they forded the Murray River. At that point a young colonial bushman, a stockman named John Bourke, took charge of the situation and calmly rescued the men and recovered the wagon. Joseph Hawdon remembered the incident and thought Bourke was just the man to operate the mail run. He offered him the job and John Bourke accepted.

The famous American Pony Express—about which we have all heard so much, and about which so many romantic tales have been told and so many movies made—lasted for exactly eighteen months and each rider rode for only one day at a time and changed horses every 20 kilometres or so.

Yet, for three years, using the same horses and packhorses and riding for six days at a time, John Bourke took the mail backwards and forwards over unchartered and hostile bushland between Yass and Melbourne. It was not uncommon for the mail, which had taken six days to travel about 600 kilometres from Melbourne to Yass, to be placed on a bullock dray which would then take six weeks to complete the 280 kilometres from Yass to Sydney.

While most of the world's English-speaking people of my generation have heard of Kit Carson and the Pony Express, and most

Australians have heard of the Birdsville Mailman and his famous truck on that outback mail run, no one these days remembers John Bourke, the quiet and unassuming bushman who, calmly and without fuss, single-handedly pioneered the track from Yass to Port Melbourne and established the overland mail.

THE GIRL WITH PECULIAR DARK EYES

The strange phenomenon that became known as the 'Guyra Ghost' occurred 96 years ago in two towns situated on the Great Dividing Range, in the New England region in northern New South Wales. What happened has never been satisfactorily explained.

It all began in the first week of April 1921 when occasional unexplained knockings and shakings occurred in three houses in the potato-growing town of Guyra. The houses were all associated with the extended family of William Bowen, who worked as a ganger for the Guyra Shire Council.

Soon the unexplained activities concentrated themselves on the small brick and weatherboard cottage where Bowen lived with his much older wife, two other adults, and nine children, some of whom were Bowen's children and stepchildren.

One particular child, Bowen's daughter Winnie, aged twelve, became the focal point of the unexplainable activity. Throughout the whole affair many of those involved seemed to think that Minnie was the 'target' of the weird malicious activity. It is far more likely, however, that the strange forces causing the activity were emanating from her.

Police Sergeant Ridge, the local copper, spent night after night at the Bowen home as the intensity of the strange attacks increased. The cottage was rocked by hundreds of mighty thumps, which were 'sufficient to shake the cottage to its foundations and audible to watchers 100 yards from the house'. Stones the size of walnuts smashed windows and rattled against the outside walls of the cottage.

Sergeant Ridge then enlisted the help of local men who formed a cordon around the house each night, and spotlights were used in an attempt to discover who, or what, was responsible. Other men patrolled the fields around the house, which was situated on the outskirts of Guyra.

There is little doubt that if 'larrikins and mischief makers' had perpetrated the activity, as was suggested by many at the time, they would have been quickly discovered. In spite of the increased vigilance and observation, however, the thumping, shaking and showers of stones continued unabated. Those who were on guard outside swore that the thumpings emanated from inside the house, while those inside watching the family were equally adamant that the source of the powerful activity was outside the cottage.

The terrified residents of the small, quiet farming town found themselves at the centre of an unwanted media frenzy. Many took to sleeping with a loaded firearm by the bed and there were examples of firearms being discharged in the direction of strange noises by some of the town's jittery citizens. One girl was accidentally wounded in the head when her small brother discharged a loaded firearm in the house.

The story was a sensation.

A police detective from Sydney, Constable Hardy, was sent to investigate and produced a report on the activities. Reporters and journalists began arriving, and interviewing anyone who would talk to them. The publicity generated in the media soon had spiritualists and 'experts in the supernatural' arriving in the town and offering various explanations.

One of these was Mr Moors, a friend of the famous author and spiritualist Sir Arthur Conan Doyle. He was given full access to the family residence and made a thorough investigation of the walls and ceilings before announcing that there was no trickery involved in the case. He set up a system of traps designed to detect any human activity and created secret spyholes from which the family could be observed and the rooms monitored. It was all to no avail, however, as no human involvement was detected and the strange activities continued.

It was by now becoming apparent to most reasonable people that there was no chance that the phenomena were caused by human activity. Investigators began to search for explanations in the spirit world—perhaps this was a case of traditional haunting where the spirit of the departed soul was making its presence felt in the mortal world?

There were two ghostly possibilities.

On 5 April 1921, an 87-year-old Irishwoman named Mrs Doran, who had lived in the district for many years, simply disappeared off the face of the earth. She was last seen walking across a field just out of town carrying some potatoes. She was never seen again and no trace of her has ever been found.

It appears, however, that the first examples of strange activity around William Bowen's cottage were already occurring before Mrs Doran did her vanishing trick and so the attention of the paranormal investigators was soon drawn to another, far more obvious, possibility.

Minnie Bowen's half-sister May, who was Mrs Bowen's daughter from a previous marriage, had died three months before the activity began. Fifteen months before she died, May, who was unmarried, had given birth to a son. It is also quite probable that May's death was a case of suicide. There was also unconfirmed gossip to the effect that William Bowen was the baby's father.

Ben Davey, an enthusiastic student of theosophy and spiritualism from the nearby town of Uralla, was keen to test the theory that the activity occurring at the cottage was a result of May's spirit attempting to communicate with the living.

On the night of 15 April 1921 the scene inside one well-lit bedroom of the cottage might well have been from a classic Gothic horror movie, or perhaps an episode of *The Addams Family* or *The Munsters*.

Minnie Bowen—described by one journalist as 'tall, thin and dark, with peculiar dark, introspective eyes that never seemed to miss any movement in the room'—sat being watched by two police officers and a number of others.

At nine o'clock two enormous thumps shook the building. Most of those present were quite justifiably terrified and some were described as being 'white with fear'. Minnie Bowen, however, remained impassive and seemingly unconcerned.

Mr Davey, who had retained his composure, suggested to Minnie that she should ask a question. So the girl asked in a clear voice, 'Is that you, May?'

There was no reply but Minnie later told the investigators that she was aware of her half-sister replying with the words: 'Tell mother that I am in heaven, and quite happy. Tell her it was her prayers which got me here, and I will look after her for the rest of my life.'

It seems rather odd to me for the ghost of a dead girl to talk about 'the rest of her life' and I am inclined to believe that the rather predictable and clichéd words that Minnie Bowen claimed to hear in response to the question were, in fact, the troubled child's attempt to tell the investigators exactly what she thought they wanted to hear.

It seems certain to me, in retrospect, that Minnie was probably the only one who did know what was going on. I'm almost equally sure that she didn't understand it, either.

What was happening around the cottage at Guyra was, in fact, nothing new. Similar events, with almost identical sets of circumstances, have occurred throughout human history.

The centre of the activity is invariably a pubescent child or adolescent teenager, nearly always female. The child is always described as introverted, not especially intelligent and suffering from repressed emotional stress of some kind.

Minnie was a classic case. The passive, uncommunicative girl who was not good at school, forced to care for the unwanted child of her dead half-sister who had no doubt suffered from the ignominy and shame of her unmarried pregnancy. May's pregnancy and death would obviously have had a massive effect on the mind and emotions of a quiet and introverted girl struggling with the transition from childhood to womanhood in an atmosphere of poverty and ignorance.

There are quite a number of well-documented cases from various parts of the world where young teenage girls, very similar to Minnie, have been the centres of almost identical paranormal activity. Objects moving, buildings shaking and stones hurled by invisible forces are quite commonly the phenomena manifested in these cases, which are often referred to as 'poltergeist' hauntings.

If proof was needed that May's ghost was not the cause of the activity, it did not take long for that proof to come. Those who believed that once May's ghostly message was delivered, the haunting would have achieved its purpose and the affair would end, were to be disappointed just two evenings later.

The Bowens returned to the house that evening to find all the timber shutters and battens, which had been nailed over the broken windows, had been smashed into tiny pieces and placed in a large pile on the verandah.

A few nights later, while a policeman was standing guard and spotlights illuminated the house, two large rocks crashed into the wall beside him.

Proof was soon also provided that Minnie, not the house, was the cause of the activity. The girl was sent to live with her grandmother in a weatherboard cottage in the larger nearby town of Glen Innes. It seems that whatever was doing the 'haunting' went along with her.

This *Sydney Morning Herald* report from 11 May 1921 takes up the story:

GLEN INNES, Tuesday.
The Guyra ghost has removed his venue from Mr. Bowen's house to that of Minnie's grandmother (Mrs. Shelton), who resides in Church Street, Glen Innes. The occupants of the house comprise Mrs. Shelton, her son (Alf Shelton), Minnie Shelton, and a baby.

Shortly after tea last night noises were heard like stones bumping on walls. The neighbours made inquiries, and the police were sent for. Constable Stewart was sent along to investigate, and while he and several others who had arrived were walking round the house a stone hit the window of Alf Shelton's bedroom, breaking a pane of glass and becoming entangled in the curtain. This stone was of ordinary white metal, and was similar to many others on the footpath in front of the house.

The constable kept a close watch, with Minnie inside the house, and while there heard four or five distinct sounds resembling knocks against iron at a distance, but he was not sure whether they emanated from inside or outside. He came to the conclusion that the girl was responsible, and declined to stay any length of time.

After his departure the inmates of the house and the neighbours outside were emphatic in their statements that they heard many noises up till midnight as of stones hitting the walls or the roof.

One neighbour, named Mr. Marden, says the noises were like the sounds caused by an axe being struck heavily against the wall. The occupants of the nearest house to Sheltons', named McKillop, a few yards distant, distinctly heard the noises and became greatly concerned. They are threatening to leave the premises if the mysterious noises continue.

The girl, Minnie Bowen, was brought up from Guyra to Glen Innes about ten days ago, and last night was the first occasion when any untoward sounds were heard by the occupants of the house.

When Minnie returned to her father's house at Guyra not long after, the strange activity eventually ceased.

The report on the affair by the Sydney detective Constable Hardy was rather odd. The phenomena were explained away as the naughty actions of Minnie, who had, at one stage during an interview, admitted to throwing stones onto the laundry roof during daylight hours to scare her sister. There was even a suggestion that such mischievous and prankish behaviour was not unusual in the town.

Local resident Mr Alex Hay, described as 'a prominent Guyra businessman', was incensed at this attempt to explain away the whole thing. He gave an interview to the *Sydney Morning Herald*, which appeared on 30 April, in which he expressed the opinion 'that the supposed solution of the affair was quite inadequate'. Mr Hay went on to say that 'the local police were not of the same mind as Constable Hardy, who had reported to headquarters that the action of the girl, with the aid of some accomplices, explained the origin of the knocking, and stone throwing'.

He went on to say, quite correctly, that the report did not adequately explain 'quite a number of incidents'.

The *Herald* article on 30 April 1921 continued:

'I am surprised to learn,' said Mr. Hay, 'that Constable Hardy has been able to furnish such a satisfactory explanation and report to the Superintendent of Police, but it is of no material value to those affected by these mysterious happenings, and is most discrediting to the vigilantes and officials of the Guyra police and public, who spent night after night for three weeks in the vicinity of the Bowens' house, trying by every known method of strategy to find the culprit who was responsible.

'Dealing with Hardy's report, as published, we read that he had solved a similar mystery in the Guyra district 15 years ago. I have just read a telegram received here a few days ago from Police Sergeant O'Neill, who was then in charge of the Guyra district, stating that he had never heard that any such mystery occurred in the last 15 years, and that he had been residing in Guyra for a much longer period than this . . .

'Now, as regards to the actions of the little girl (Minnie Bowen), the report states that she was found throwing stones at the house one night. This report is absolutely incorrect. The facts of the case are as follows: Minnie Bowen, whilst outside the house at midday, picked up two or three small stones and threw them on the iron roof where her sister was washing clothes. Her sister knew at once that it must have been Minnie who threw these particular stones . . .

'Strange to say, throughout the whole episode no stone has ever hit the iron roof, but has always been directed with unerring aim at either the windows or the walls. Consequently, this little girl's stupid playful act does not assist in any way in solving the mystery . . .

'I might also quote another case, during which we posted six trusted men, standing with their backs to the outside wall of a

12-foot room, after which we placed the girl in the inside of the room, with a good light burning, and being closely watched by three men, including Constable Taylor. Notwithstanding this well-organised guard, two very loud knocks came on the wall. As usual, the men on the outside insisted that the knocks came from the inside, while the watchers inside believed that they came from outside. I would like to mention that the six men picked for positions on the outside wall were selected from at least 40, and were absolutely above suspicion . . . every member of the Bowen family has been under strict observation whilst the knocking went on.

'The whole business, after the first two nights, lost all semblance of being a joke, and had any man-larrikin or respectable citizen been caught throwing stones whilst the watchers were on duty it requires little imagination on the reader's part to know what sort of a time he would have had at the hands of 50 or 60 determined men.

'The mystery is still unsolved. Two stones hit the house last night with terrible force. Mr. Bowen rushed out with his gun and fired three shots in the darkness in the direction from which the stones appeared to come, but without result . . .

'There has been one child shot as a direct result of these happenings, consequently it is hardly reasonable to believe that any person short of a lunatic would persist in such mad practices.'

Mr Hay's indignation was quite justified. On many occasions during the 'haunting', strong men weighing 'over 200lb' had attempted to replicate the massive wall shaking by pushing and shoving at the house both inside and out, and had failed miserably. To think that Minnie could have managed it, without paranormal powers, is laughable.

The good people of Guyra soon began to resent the inferences that they were pranksters or country hicks who believed in ghosts. The town put up a 'wall of silence', which is still in evidence to this day, according to recent investigators.

All copies of all editions of the local newspaper from the period of the hauntings have 'disappeared' from the archives and all copies of a documentary film made and distributed at the time have also gone missing.

Minnie eventually married and lived in the nearby city of Armidale all her adult life. Like most of the people of Guyra, she never spoke about what happened during those few crazy weeks in the autumn of 1921.

A family member recently confessed, while reminiscing about Minnie, that she could 'make a piano play, or . . . move furniture and lift objects without touching them'.

The 'girl with peculiar dark eyes' died in 1989, aged 80, when she was knocked down by a car while walking along the Grafton Road outside Armidale.

THE TUMULTUOUS, TRIUMPHANT AND TRAGIC LIFE OF TOM WILLS

Snowy Baker and 'Professor Miller' were truly remarkable men, with skills and abilities beyond the range of normal human athleticism, who also lived unusual, even sensational, lives. However, there is another Australian sporting hero whose life was full of such a strange combination of weird and wonderful, unusual and coincidental feats, achievements and tragedies that eclipses them both and seems way too fantastical to be true. His name was Tom Wills.

Thomas Wentworth Wills was born on 19 December 1835 at Molonglo Plains, near Gundagai in New South Wales. He was the eldest son of Horatio Wills, a pioneering pastoralist and politician whose convict father was transported for highway robbery. Horatio was always on the lookout to improve his lot by developing new grazing country and the family moved to western Victoria when Tom was a child and developed a 510 square-kilometre property called Lexington, in the Ararat district. Tom and his parents lived in tents while the property was developed.

Tom's middle name was derived from his father's friend, the famous statesman and politician William Charles Wentworth, who was a mentor to Tom and whose father D'Arcy Wentworth was also, coincidentally, transported for being a highwayman.

Tom had no siblings until he was aged seven and spent his early childhood playing with the local Aboriginal boys. He learned their language and customs and often played a game with them that they called 'marn grook'. The game involved kicking and catching and keeping off the ground a circular 'ball' made from a basket of intertwined twigs and possum skin.

From 1846 young Tom attended William Brickwood's School for three years and played cricket for both the school and the Melbourne Cricket Club (MCC), where William Brickwood was club vice-president.

Back at Lexington things had changed: the family house had been built and Tom had a younger sister and three brothers. But his life was about to change more dramatically than he could imagine.

After just over a year back home, in 1850, when he was fourteen, Tom was sent on a five-month sea voyage to attend the famous Rugby School in Britain, the birthplace of the game of rugby.

There, Tom played the early version of rugby, became the school's best bowler in cricket and was in the school's First XI, aged sixteen, when they played against the MCC at Lords where he took twelve wickets. In 1855 he took over as captain of the First XI, which was the most prestigious position at the school. He was invited to play for an All England XI, but couldn't leave his studies to play.

Odd as it may seem, although Tom Wills was athletic from an early age, he was prone to illness, and once, when he was ill for months as a four-year-old in 1839, his parents 'almost despaired of his recovery'.

In a very amusing young man's letter to his father back home, he wrote, 'I know that if I [study] too hard I will become quite ill. We hardly get any play during school time.' The rest of the letter, written on enormous broadsheet-sized pages, is filled with accounts of cricket games and lists of his scores.

Tom's room at Rugby was decorated with Aboriginal weapons and he seems to have been very homesick at times. His father wrote to tell him that his Aboriginal friends missed him and had 'told me to send you up to them as soon as you came back'.

In June 1855, aged nineteen-and-a-half, Tom finished school and, armed with a regular supply of money from home, wandered around Britain playing cricket. He played against his old school in

June 1856 as a member of a team representing the MCC. The team also included members of the royal family and a future governor of Tasmania.

It had been intended that Tom would go on to Magdalene College, Cambridge, in 1856, but he did not pass the required matriculation exams. With the permission of Oxford University, however, he played cricket in the Cambridge XI in the inter-varsity match of that year.

This gracious, sportsmanlike gesture was due to the fact that Tom had, by then, become the most notable amateur cricketer in England, playing for both Kent and the Marylebone Club and, on one occasion, after spending time playing in Ireland, for a United Ireland XI.

How a kid who grew up speaking the Djab Warrung language and running around the wilds of the Grampians with Aboriginal boys managed the transition to the upper-class English atmosphere of cricket so successfully that he was granted an exemption to be allowed to play in the most prestigious cricket game on the yearly calendar, I simply cannot imagine.

Tom was touted as 'one of the most promising cricketers in the kingdom'. He had deep blue eyes and hair once described as 'impossibly wavy' and it was written of him in the press that 'few athletes can boast of a more muscular and well-developed frame'.

His six years in England had made him a great cricketer and given him many wonderful contacts and experiences, but there was a dark side. Once he left school, Tom fell into a dissolute way of life that was part of the world of cricket in the 1850s, where drinking, spending and playing were all that mattered. He had no interest in anything academic or career-related and his father despaired.

Tom arrived back in Australia two days before Christmas in 1856. Once again it was like entering a new world for the 22-year-old, as everything at home had changed.

Melbourne was booming from the gold rushes, his father was now a member of the Victorian parliament and the family was living on a property near Geelong. Tom took a position with a law firm in Melbourne, but showed no interest in the law, which he never studied and never practised. Cricket was all the rage in town and he played constantly, mostly for the Melbourne Cricket Club.

It is hard to imagine the bitter rivalry that existed between Victoria and the parent colony of New South Wales in those days. After New South Wales won the first inter-colonial match at the Melbourne Cricket Ground (MCG) in 1856, it became an obsession for Victoria to beat them.

The hatred ran so deep that when touring sides came from England later to play what might be called 'test matches', as they did from 1876–77, some cricketers refused to play in the same team as their rivals from other colonies. Fred Spofforth refused to bowl to the Victorian wicket-keeper and didn't play during that tour, and several others from both colonies also declined to be part of the team.

After a trial game at the MCG, Tom Wills was chosen to captain Victoria against New South Wales in 1858. He was to be their 'great white hope'.

Melbourne came to a standstill for the January match between Victoria and New South Wales at the MCG in 1858. Tom Wills took eight wickets, the most ever for Victoria. On the second day he was knocked unconscious by a ball that rose sharply from a crack in the pitch but came round, played on for two hours, and made 49 not out, which won the game.

The jubilant crowd carried him from the field and the celebrations lasted for several days throughout Victoria, where the newspapers proclaimed him to be 'the greatest cricketer in the land'.

In the midst of this public adulation, however, the darker and more chaotic elements of Tom's character were making themselves manifest in his relationship with the Melbourne Cricket Club, of which he had become secretary in 1857.

He was hardly suited to the role. Outside of sport Tom's life was undisciplined, chaotic and disorganised. His 'continued non-attendance' at meetings and poor administrative skills were blamed when the club fell into debt, while his response to the criticism was to dump the club's books into the garbage and quit. To this present day, the only minute book missing from the club's archives is the one from his time as secretary.

Horatio Wills, now a member of the Victorian parliament, was a strident supporter of an Australian republic and campaigner for the rights of the emancipated convicts—in short, a supporter of the ideas of pioneering statesman William Charles Wentworth—and had written and spoken extensively in support of his ideas and beliefs. His son inherited his capacity to propound ideas and wrote almost daily letters to the newspapers, but his diatribes were mostly about ideas concerning cricket, or sport in general.

This brings us to the main reason that Tom Wills is remembered today, as the man who 'invented' Australian rules football.

It all began with a letter published in the quaintly and clumsily titled publication known as *Bell's Life in Victoria and Sporting Chronicle* in July 1858. As usual Tom was obsessively expounding his ideas on cricket and the letter was titled *Winter Practice*. It began:

> Now that cricket has been put aside for some few months to come, and cricketers have assumed somewhat of the chrysalis nature (for a time only 'tis true), but at length will again burst forth in all their varied hues, rather than allow this state of torpor to creep over them, and stifle their new supple limbs, why can they not, I say, form a foot-ball club, and form a committee of three or more to draw up a code of laws?

What happened next is a little clouded in the mists of time. It appears that Tom spoke to various headmasters about the idea and he and his friend, publican and cricketer Jerry Bryant, attempted to organise an informal 'scratch game' in the 'Richmond paddock' adjacent to the MCG. The event was certainly advertised but no one's quite sure whether or not it occurred. Tom did, however, help umpire a game played over three consecutive Saturdays on the same site, between Melbourne Grammar School and the Scotch College. This game began on 7 August 1858, and a game between the two schools has been an annual event ever since.

A 'scratch match' was played at the end of the cricket season the following year and the Melbourne Football Club came into existence on 14 May 1859. Three days later Tom met with school-teacher Thomas Smith, journalist J.B. Thompson and the famous cricketer William Hammersley at Jerry Bryant's Parade Hotel near the MCG to frame a list of rules.

Various versions of football had been played since medieval times, usually between neighbouring villages, but no one had thought of standardising the rules. In the 19th century each school had its own version of football. These various games had evolved according to the customs of the schools, the number of boys wanting to play, and the individual ideas and notions of the masters who supervised them.

The four men examined and discussed the way the game was played in four different English schools, keeping in mind that what they wanted was a game designed to keep cricket players fit and healthy through the winter. Such practices as attacking a player's legs and hacking at the shins were rejected, as was the game Tom had played at school in England. 'Rugby was not a game for us,' Tom said. 'We wanted a winter pastime but men could be harmed if thrown on the ground.'

The four men came up with a simple list of ten rules and, in doing so, made history. 'Australian Rules Football' became the first codified form of football in the world.

It is hardly surprising that Tom Wills soon became the best footballer in the colony. He had the longest kick and, being much in demand as a player, played for various clubs and institutions, as well as the one that he had recently helped to found, the Melbourne Football Club.

In fact, it was Tom who insisted on using an oval ball during a game in which he was captain of the team called Richmond, playing against Melbourne. (This was not the team we know as Richmond today but an earlier band of players who wore jerseys designed by Tom, who was club secretary and captain. The jerseys were white with a red sash—later to be the colours of South Melbourne Club, which subsequently became the Sydney Swans.)

Tom was never short of ideas and continued to write prolifically about both cricket and football. His thoughts and suggestions helped the new code to evolve into the unique game we know today. Here he is suggesting that the game should not be restricted by any notions of 'offside':

> I think the ground should be free to all, so that the captain of each side could dispose of his forces in any position he likes; and when this is done, and the ball is carried on from one end of the ground to the other, by a succession of good, well-directed kicks, to the hands of those that the ball was intended for . . . it has a very pretty effect, and is the result of some skill.

In cricket, Tom led Victoria to victory over New South Wales again in January 1859 in a game played at the Domain in Sydney, in which he dislocated a finger on the first day, top-scored in the first innings and took 5/24 and 6/25.

At the MCG in February 1860, 25,000 people saw him bowl unchanged in both innings (taking 6/23 and 3/16) and top-score with 20 not out as he led Victoria to yet another win over New South Wales.

Even the Sydney media, ever keen to remind readers that he was born in New South Wales, lavished praise upon the freakish athlete:

> Tall, muscular, and slender, Mr. Wills seems moulded by nature to excel in every branch of the noble game, and with the ball at the wicket, and on the field we find him the admiration of the ground, while in the combination of his successes, his noble eleven recognise with pride the still more arduous duties of an unwearied and most discreet captain.

Within the game of cricket, and the Melbourne establishment, however, Tom was not particularly well liked. After he walked out on the Melbourne Cricket Club, he became the driving force and vice-president of the Richmond Cricket Club. Later he switched to Collingwood Cricket Club where he became president.

His willingness to play as a hired hand or guest with any team that invited him caused consternation among the 'sporting gentlemen' of Melbourne, as it often distorted the outcome of matches and greatly affected betting. Tom's lack of loyalty to one club or team was regarded with contempt by the more 'respectable' elements of Melbourne society. His alcoholism didn't enhance his reputation much, either.

At the end of 1860 Tom Wills shocked the sporting world of Australia and precipitated another of the massive lifestyle changes that were to be a trademark of his life. He announced his retirement from sport and his intention to leave Victoria to set up a new family property at Cullin-la-ringo, in the outback of Queensland, on the Nogoa River.

Tom spent six months in country Victoria, visiting properties, studying sheep-farming methods and preparing for his new life as a pioneer grazier. Part of his motivation was the ultimatum given to him by his father. If Tom 'misconducted himself' or quit the enterprise, he was to be removed from Horatio's will!

It appeared that Tom was, at last, about to make an attempt to become the kind of son Horatio always wanted. He would give up the dissolute and disreputable lifestyle that had caused his father so much anguish and show his true mettle as a proud son of a hard-working, pioneering and nation-building family.

What happened at Cullin-la-ringo, however, would not go down in Australian history as an example of nation building. Cullin-la-ringo would be forever remembered for other, very different, reasons.

In January 1861, Tom, Horatio and a party of their family and employees, numbering 25 in total, arrived in Brisbane by steamer. They acquired supplies and trekked through the bush of the new colony of Queensland, which was just eighteen months old, to their pioneering enterprise in the outback.

At times during the journey they had to hunt to stay alive and the first death occurred when a man was drowned near Toowoomba. They collected 10,000 sheep on the Darling Downs and arrived at Cullin-la-ringo, near modern-day Emerald, on Kairi Aboriginal land, in October, after an eight-month, 1300-kilometre trek.

Horatio Wills had always managed to maintain good relationships with Aboriginal people and used them as workers on his other properties. Although wary, he allowed local Aborigines into the camp, which was merely a ring of tents, and gave them sheep to slaughter as a display of friendship.

Two weeks after Wills had set up camp, Aborigines began entering the Cullin-la-ringo locality in small parties until their numbers were estimated at 200 by the morning of 17 October 1861.

At around 2 p.m. that day the Aborigines suddenly attacked, and six children, two women, and five men from the Wills camp were clubbed to death within minutes. Another six men working just outside the camp were also killed.

Horatio, who kept all the party's firearms out of sight in his tent, was the only one to attempt a defence. He fired one shot before he was overwhelmed and killed.

John Moore, the cook, who was resting after lunch in the shade of the bush several hundred metres away, heard the shot, witnessed the massacre and ran 50 kilometres through the bush to Rainworth Station, the nearest white settlement.

Tom Wills and three others, who were making a week-long round trip to Albinia Station to pick up stores, arrived back two days after the massacre. A rescue party from Rainworth had already buried the dead and were attempting to round up the 10,000 sheep. Most of the party's equipment had been taken and the firearms had been thrown into the campfire.

Cullin-la-ringo was the largest massacre of white settlers in Australia's history.

When the news reached the cities, the press produced the usual mass of misinformation. Tom was at first reported dead and Horatio was accused of ignoring warnings about the local Aborigines.

Tom publicly defended his father but admitted privately, 'If we had used common precaution all would have been well.'

Reprisals were swift and tragic, with much of the local Aboriginal population being slaughtered in the aftermath of the attack.

Tom, who never took place in any reprisals, believed the massacre at Cullin-la-ringo was an act of revenge for an attack made on local Aborigines by squatter Jesse Gregson. He told a cousin, 'If the truth is ever known, you will find that it was through Gregson shooting those blacks; that was the cause of the murder.'

For the rest of his life Tom suffered from nightmares and flash-backs. He slept poorly and drank even more than previously. Sadly, there were many more scandals and tragedies yet ahead for Tom Wills.

Tom, who was now head of the family, vowed to stay and fulfil his father's dreams at Cullin-la-ringo. He is said to have slept only three hours a night, with a rifle beside the bed, until his uncle, William Roope, who was a shareholder in the operation, arrived to help run the property in December. But Tom and his uncle soon fell out and Roope departed. Tom struggled on in isolation for twelve months, and even went blind for a short time after contracting 'sandy blight'.

Still, he made the long trip to Sydney to captain Victoria in a cricket match at the Domain in January 1863. The match turned into a riot over the dismissal of a local batsman by a Victorian umpire. Tom was hit in the face by a rock and two of the Victorian players fled from Sydney, but Tom and the eight other Victorians continued the game. New South Wales were victorious and Tom, who took eight wickets and top-scored in both innings, commented later, 'I for one do not think that Victoria will ever send an eleven up here again.'

The Melbourne press blamed Tom for the defeat, saying he never should have played on with nine men and even accusing him of treachery because, starved of cricket and out of practice, he had played several games for New South Wales in the lead-up to the match.

Tom then travelled on to visit his mother in Geelong, where he became engaged to Julie Anderson, a family friend from a respectable farming family. He upset his family, who had a lot of money invested in Cullin-la-ringo, by delaying his return to Queensland in order to play football for Geelong.

On his return to the property in May, having been made a justice of the peace, he wrote letters to the Brisbane press reporting

Aboriginal attacks on white settlers and attacking the soft attitude of city-dwellers towards the plight of the Queensland Aboriginals.

At the start of the next cricket season Tom agreed to captain Queensland against New South Wales and then made a dash to Melbourne to captain a Victorian team against George Parr's visiting All England XI, only arriving (to thunderous applause) on the final day of the match. He then continued on with the English team as they toured Victoria.

The Wills family were becoming fed up with Tom and accused him of squandering the family fortune on travel, women and alcohol and running up huge debts at Cullin-la-ringo. They were outraged when he broke off his engagement to Julie Anderson, although it was common knowledge that Tom was a notorious womaniser and had a long-term affair with Sarah Barbor, a married woman he called his 'housekeeper'.

Tom's answer to the criticism was to leave with George Parr's English team on a one-month tour of New Zealand.

On his return he was dismissed by the trustees of the Cullin-la-ringo enterprise, who included his mother and most of his family, and resumed his affair with Sarah Barbor and his dissolute life as a hard-drinking cricketer and footballer.

In those days football games were played as a series of invitations, rather than in an organised competition, and during the 1865 season Tom often captained Melbourne and Geelong, two of the game's most powerful clubs. This resulted in arguments and eventually he moved to Geelong for the remainder of his career.

Professionalism in sport was a huge issue in those days and Tom, who always maintained his amateur status, was often accused of all manner of ungentlemanly conduct, including being a 'sham amateur'. His bowling action came under scrutiny and he was accused many times of 'chucking'.

Inter-colonial cricket resumed at the MCG on Boxing Day 1865, nearly three years since the Sydney riot. Most of Victoria's professionals had been involved in a pay dispute with the Melbourne Cricket Club and defected to the New South Wales team, which was captained by Englishman Charles Lawrence.

Tom led the weakened Victorian side, took six wickets and scored the first half-century in Australian first-class cricket—and Victoria won.

Tom's transition to 'professional' sportsman involved, remarkably, his management and promotion of the first-ever all-Aboriginal cricket team.

In May 1866, he promoted a cricket match between the Melbourne Cricket Club and an Aboriginal team from the Western Districts of Victoria, coached by Tom Wills. The Aboriginal players were mostly Jardwadjarli men who shared a common language with the neighbouring Djab Wurrung people, which enabled Tom to speak to them using the Aboriginal language he learnt as a child.

Eight thousand spectators attended the Boxing Day match at the MCG and the Aboriginal team, with Tom as captain, lost to Melbourne, who Tom accused of cheating during the game.

Many people were shocked that Tom would associate with Aborigines after Cullin-la-ringo but others saw him as a champion of the Victorian Aborigines. One journalist wrote, in *The Empire* magazine:

> Although you may not be fully aware of the fact, allow me to tell you that you have rendered a greater service to the aboriginal races of this country and to humanity, than any man who has hitherto attempted to uphold the title of the blacks to rank amongst men.

Members of Tom's family, however, were once again shocked by his behaviour when he took the Aboriginal team to the family property to meet his mother, without giving her any advance warning.

As usual, things would end badly for Tom's new venture. The team went to Sydney in February ahead of a planned overseas tour and Charles Lawrence, who could see the financial potential of the venture, accommodated the team at his Manly hotel.

During the first match in Sydney, however, the police stopped play and Tom was arrested and jailed over a breach of contract dispute involving himself and W.E.B. Gurnett, a conman who was trying to take over as manager. The team was left stranded and broke, with all the money saved for the overseas tour gone.

Charles Lawrence set up a benefit match, and worked his way into the team, replacing Tom as captain. The team returned to Victoria in May and Tom resumed playing football for Geelong and ended his association with the Aboriginal team.

It was later claimed that he was a bad influence and encouraged drinking among the Aborigines, four of whom died over the course of the tour; at least one death was officially linked to alcohol.

The surviving members formed part of the famous Aboriginal team which Lawrence later took to England as the first-ever representative Australian cricket team. Tom was deeply upset at being left out and always resented Lawrence for reviving the team without him.

With limited resources and skills apart from sport, Tom joined the Melbourne Cricket Club as a professional in 1867. The club gave him the title 'tutor' so he could maintain some semblance of the prestige of his amateur past, and he captained Victoria to beat New South Wales in 1867.

After his old colleague William Hammersley wrote in his sporting column that Tom, as a paid servant of a cricket club, should not have 'moral ascendancy' over amateur players, the captaincy of Victoria was given to Dick Wardill on the eve of the March 1869 match against New South Wales, the last ever played at the Domain in Sydney.

At first, Tom refused to play, but relented and then took seven wickets to guide the Victorians to a win. Wardill was out for a duck from the first ball of the Victorian innings.

After that, Tom said that he would never play cricket for Victoria again and announced that he would return to Cullin-la-ringo, but his mother ordered him to stay away from the property.

Tom continued as a 'tutor' playing for the Melbourne Cricket Club but also played football for Geelong. When Geelong played Melbourne at football, he was banned from the game, but Geelong was allowed an extra five men to make up for the loss.

In February 1870, Tom was back captaining Victoria in a 265-run win over New South Wales at the MCG. The next crisis in his career occurred when controversy erupted over his bowling style and he was accused by many critics of 'chucking'. William Hammersley went further and said Tom was ruining the game.

Tom's response didn't help matters. He wrote in *The Australasian*: 'If I cannot hit your wicket or make you give a chance soon, I'll hit you and hurt you if I can. I'll frighten you out.'

In the inter-colonial match in Sydney in March 1871 he top-scored with 39 in Victoria's win but was visibly drunk on the field and wouldn't bowl for fear of being called for throwing.

It was the beginning of the end for Tom Wills, but a series of superb club cricket performances saw him play for Victoria in the next inter-colonial match against New South Wales in March 1872 at the MCG.

As a result of the controversy over his bowling action, however, representatives from both sides met and signed an agreement that he would be 'called' for any suspect balls. Thus, when he opened the bowling, Tom became the first cricketer called for 'throwing' in a major Australian match and, after two more balls were ruled as throws in two overs, he did not bowl again.

He was again no-balled when he captained a Victorian side against a combined team from other colonies in 1872.

Tom accused Hammersley, now his bitter enemy, of a plot to promote English-born cricketers and denigrate native-born Australian players.

Hammersley replied in print:

> You are played out now, the cricketing machine is rusty and useless, all respect for it is gone. You will never be captain of a Victorian Eleven again . . . Eschew colonial beer, and take the pledge and in time your failings may be forgotten, and only your talents as a cricketer remembered. Farewell, Tommy Wills.

Tom sank further into alcoholism, and was desperate to play for Victoria against a side led by the legendary W.G. Grace. But

Hammersley was a selector and Tom had no chance of being picked. He toured with Grace's team, however, playing against them in regional matches, which annoyed Grace who later referred to him as the 'old Rugbeian has-been' but neglected to mention that, in the final match of the tour in the remote South Australian mining town of Kadina, Tom bowled him out and ended with 6/28.

Desperation in the light of poor performances caused Tom to be recalled as Victorian captain to lead the team against New South Wales in Sydney in February 1876. He was out for 0 and 4 and failed to get a wicket in spite of bowling the bulk of the overs. Naturally, he was blamed for Victoria's 195-run loss.

Tom's career as a serious cricketer petered out into local matches and disputes about his bowling style, and finally ended in 1878. He continued to play football and was a much-loved favourite at Geelong. After his retirement from football he umpired, was Geelong Football Club's vice-president from 1873 to 1876, and also donated many trophies, as well as money, for football competitions. He was one of Geelong's delegates at the 1877 formation of the Victorian Football League.

However, Tom was broke and in serious debt when he sold his properties in Geelong and moved with Sarah Barbor to South Melbourne in 1878. While there he convinced South Melbourne Cricket Club to start playing football in winter and it was his idea, instituted at both Geelong and South Melbourne, for football clubs to use an oval-shaped playing field, so that the cricket field became the football field in winter.

In 1879, shunned by his family, he and Sarah moved to Heidelberg, then a village outside Melbourne, and Tom sank into alcoholism, although he did coach the local cricket team, for which, on 13 March 1880, he played his last recorded game.

Contrary to a much-believed myth, he was never an inmate of a lunatic asylum but he became, in the words of cricket historian David Frith, 'a complete and dangerous and apparently incurable alcoholic'.

By late April 1880, Tom was suffering from continual *delirium tremens* and paranoid delusions. On 1 May Sarah admitted him to Melbourne Hospital where he was 'kept under restraint' but managed to free himself and return home. The next day he committed suicide by stabbing a pair of scissors into his heart three times.

He was buried the following day in an unmarked grave in Heidelberg Cemetery at a private funeral attended by six people.

Although his sister was one of the six, his death certificate reads 'parents unknown' and his mother is said to have claimed in her later life that he never existed.

The Melbourne Cricket Club erected a monument over his unmarked gravesite on the centenary of his death. The inscription reads, 'Founder of Australian football and champion cricketer of his time'.

Tom Wills was inducted into the Australian Sports Hall of Fame in 1989 and he was inducted into the Australian Football Hall of Fame in 1996. The International Cricket Hall of Fame, in Bowral, New South Wales, contains an exhibition celebrating his life. The Tom Wills Room at the MCG is the venue for important corporate functions.

A statue showing Tom umpiring the famous football match between Melbourne Grammar and Scotch College in 1858 was erected outside the MCG in 2001. Melbourne's busiest freeway junction is known as the Tom Wills Interchange, and Tom Wills Oval, at Olympic Park in Sydney, is the training base for the Greater Western Sydney football club.

In the entire history of Australian sport, there has never been a more remarkable, controversial, triumphant, troubled, tragic and multifaceted character than Tom Wills.

THE LONELY GHOST OF LADY ELLIOT ISLAND

Lady Elliot Island lies 160 kilometres east of Gladstone along the outer edge of the Great Barrier Reef and it has its fair share of ghosts.

These days the island has a wonderful eco-friendly resort, but for years it had very little of anything, not even vegetation. It did, however, have a lighthouse and two ghosts. A lighthouse and two ghosts may not sound much, but that's a good quota of ghosts per hectare. Lady Elliot Island is a very small island.

Captain Thomas Stuart discovered the island in 1816 and named it after his ship the *Lady Elliot*; the ship was, evidently, named after Lady Elliot, whoever she was.

Not long after the island's discovery a few daring entrepreneurs made another discovery, which made them rich quick, well, relatively quickly. The island was covered in phosphate-rich guano, commonly known as seabird poop, most of it provided by thousands upon thousands of mutton birds using the island for thousands and thousands of years.

Chinese coolies (poor indentured labourers) were forced to live on the island to mine the guano, and eat the birds, so the traders could get rich almost for free. But within a few decades, the guano was gone, along with the birds and the island's vegetation.

The area around the island is notorious for shipwrecks and a lighthouse was built in 1873. In those days a lighthouse needed a keeper and, in 1896, that was Mr Phillips, who had a daughter, Phoebe Phillips.

Poor Phoebe did not have a great social life for a 30-year-old single woman, living on a small island 160 kilometres from the mainland with only her family, and then, even more sadly, her unremarkable and isolated existence ended when she died of pneumonia. Her ghost has been spotted on the island, probably searching in vain for a social life. It has been seen around the 'dead centre' of the island, the tiny two-grave cemetery where Phoebe rests, not necessarily in peace, next to her fellow ghost Susannah McKee.

Susannah, the wife of Thomas McKee, the lighthouse keeper ten years after Phoebe's dad, was from Ireland, and she and Thomas had four sons. Susannah didn't like the island, which was still a barren rock in those days, since all the vegetation had gone west with the guano.

The sons were good company for Susannah while they were at home. However, when her youngest son, the last of the four to leave the island, went off to boarding school on the mainland, Susannah found living on a bare rock in the middle of the ocean more than a little tedious.

The living quarters were small and cramped, the nearest doctor, or any medical attention, was weeks or months away. Also, the tropical climate was a little hotter than Ireland, so meat and other perishables did not keep—and the supply ship was often late.

One day in April 1907, according to her husband, poor lonely Susannah, who was 59 years old, put on her Sunday clothes and went for a stroll along the old ruined jetty below the lighthouse, where the guano used to be loaded onto ships, back when there was some to load.

She then simply jumped into the sea.

Naturally there was speculation that her husband had decided he was better off without her moping all the time. There is no proof, however, that Thomas McKee did anything to get rid of Susannah, although, if you do want to get rid of your wife, or anyone else, it's not a bad idea to do it when you are the only two inhabitants of a small island 160 kilometres offshore.

Anyway, Susannah's body washed up on the shore and

Thomas, thinking she might like the company, buried her next to Phoebe Phillips.

Now, as everyone knows, ghosts of those who suicide often have trouble getting free and entering the spirit world and ghosts of people who were trapped in places they disliked in life often have trouble getting away from those places after they die. Susannah was a prime candidate for becoming a trapped spirit, and that's exactly what happened. Her spirit is trapped on Lady Elliot Island, the island she disliked so much when she was alive.

Susannah's ghost behaved itself for a few decades but became fed up with the isolation again in the 1930s and decided to start manifesting itself around the island.

Margaret Brumpton, the young daughter of the lighthouse keeper Arthur Brumpton, began feeling a presence and soon she was regularly hearing ghostly footsteps in the lighthouse.

Then, one day around sunset, Arthur, not having much to do that evening and being at rather a loose end, was amusing himself by looking down from the lighthouse balcony to the cottages below, apparently one of his favourite pastimes. While engaged in this recreational activity, he saw a female figure, dressed in turn-of-the-century clothing, taking an evening stroll between the lighthouse and the three cottages behind it. Later, Margaret also saw the ghost several times.

When Arthur and his daughter were leaving the island in 1940, perhaps so that Arthur could continue his career on a more popu-lated island, or look after a bigger lighthouse somewhere, they mentioned the incident to the captain of the ship transporting them to the mainland. The captain happened to have photos of people who had once lived on Lady Elliot Island and both Arthur and Margaret immediately identified a woman in one photograph as the person they had seen.

The woman in the photograph was Susannah McKee.

In 1985 the lighthouse became automated and, with the island slowly recovering some vegetation, the first holiday resort was established and staff arrived to work on the island.

It wasn't long before the resort manager, Tili Birkman, began experiencing strange feelings and noticing odd activities that mostly centred in and around the three old cottages.

Spooky feelings and a cold atmosphere were reported by several staff members, but what happened to groundskeeper Jeff Raynor and chef Chris Lister was something else altogether.

The very physical and dramatic haunting occurred on the day that the two men moved into one of the long-deserted cottages. They'd been inside the building, moving furniture and generally getting settled in, but were taking a break from work and were sitting just outside their cottage when an empty plastic ice-cream container came flying out the front door of one of the other cottages and landed right at their feet.

The two men were a bit rattled but Jeff laughed it off and later, as he and Chris were describing what had happened to other staff, Jeff several times made the statement that he did not believe in ghosts.

Late that night, as Jeff was sleeping in the cottage, he suddenly woke for no reason and sat up in bed, startled. There was a brief moment of stillness and then something lifted him and hurled him out of bed and onto the floor where he landed with some force and a substantial thump.

From then on Jeff decided it was more pleasant, and cooler, to sleep on the cottage verandah, instead of inside.

Unfortunately for Jeff, that didn't stop Susannah's restless ghost. Just a few nights later he awoke again, this time in his bed on the verandah, and saw, to his horror, the transparent figure of a woman staring at him from the cottage doorway.

Sometime later a team of painters arrived to paint the old cottages and erected scaffolding to do the job. Oddly, however, every time they climbed onto the scaffolding it began to shake violently, but as soon as they clambered down the shaking stopped.

Since then, Susannah's ghost has been spied peering out through the cottage windows and walking across the island's small airstrip at night.

Lady Elliot Island today is a famous heritage-listed site with a magnificent eco-sustainable resort. It even has vegetation.

It's part of the Marine National Park Zone, where fishing is not allowed, so sea life abounds and the scuba diving and glass-bottom boat trips are amazing.

Only a small number of guests are allowed on the island at a time but, if you're lucky enough to visit, you will have a wonderful experience. While you're visiting the island, here's one thing to remember, though: it might be best if you don't mention, out loud, that you don't believe in ghosts.

Part Two
ROYAL VISITORS BEWARE!

The first four visits to Australia by members of the British royal family were all made by 'Princes of the Realm'. Three of these would become heirs to the throne at various times and two would go on to become king, although one of those would not stay king for long.

The four visits actually brought *five* princes to Australia's shores and Australia seems to have been a rather dangerous place for Princes of the Realm—four of whom, it can be argued, had life-threatening experiences due to unplanned events during their time here.

One was shot by a mentally unstable, self-proclaimed Irish rebel, while another was the victim of a train crash in which the royal carriage fell off the railway line. Two other royal princes were lost at sea on their way here and later met with that ghostly harbinger of death, *The Flying Dutchman*, while sailing from Melbourne to Sydney.

Let me explain, for all the royal buffs among my readers, just who these royal personages were.

The very first British royal visitor to our shores was Prince Alfred, Duke of Edinburgh, second son and fourth child of Queen Victoria and Prince Albert. While serving in the Royal Navy and in command of HMS *Galatea*, he left Plymouth in January 1867 for a voyage round the world. He arrived at Glenelg in South Australia in October 1867 and remained in Australia until April 1868. An account of his eventful visit is also in this collection— and it's certainly worth reading on to get to, I assure you.

In 1881 not one but *two* royal princes graced our continent with their presence. They were Prince Albert Victor and Prince George, the two eldest sons of Edward, Prince of Wales, and Princess Alexandra of Denmark and Wales.

These two jolly young royal sailors were second and third in line to the throne as grandsons of Queen Victoria. They were both cadets and later midshipmen aboard HMS *Bacchante.*

Oddly enough, it was the youngest prince who was destined to become king, for the older prince, Prince Albert Victor, Duke of Clarence and second in line to the throne (after his father Edward), died during the influenza pandemic in 1892, aged 28. It was the younger prince who would become King George V on the death of his father King Edward VII in 1910.

Prince George, as the Duke of York and Cornwall, would again visit Australia in 1901 and become the central figure in the massive, iconic Tom Roberts painting of the opening of our first parliament in Melbourne on 9 May that year.

His father, Prince Edward, was supposed to have performed this ritual as Prince of Wales and heir to the throne. The death of Queen Victoria, on 22 January 1901, however, made Edward the monarch and the task fell to George, now the Prince of Wales and heir apparent.

So George made a second royal visit to Australia and became the first member of the British royal family to do so.

You might think this makes the future George V the first royal personage to make two trips to our continent. He was gazumped, however, from that honour by Jorgen Jorgensen, the one-time King of Iceland, who not only died here but also made two very extensive visits to our shores—both at British government expense.

The first visit he made was as a British sailor in 1800, aboard the *Lady Nelson.*

And the other?

Well, Jorgen was transported to Van Diemen's Land as a convicted felon aboard the convict transport *Woodman*, in 1826.

Unbelievable, perhaps, but true—as we shall see.

The central figure in the last of our royal visit stories was perhaps the most controversial royal personage of the 20th century, and his visit to Australia provided the media with more than enough sensational incidents and patriotic hysteria to fill thousands of newspaper pages.

His later life would be even more sensational and his private comments, made during the tour but only revealed many years later, make for very interesting reading, indeed.

THE PRINCE'S BRACES, THE IRISH MADMAN AND THE NURSES

Being the second son of a reigning British monarch in the 19th century did not carry a great deal of responsibility or importance, unless of course your older brother took it upon himself to predecease you without having sons of his own.

Queen Victoria had nine children, including four sons. Alfred, her second son and fourth child, was born in May 1844. He remained second in line to the throne, behind his brother Albert Edward, Prince of Wales, until Albert and his wife, Princess Alexandra of Denmark and Wales, began producing sons of their own in 1864, causing Alfred to slip further and further down the line of succession.

As a royal prince, Alfred was not particularly colourful or remarkable and his mother and father decided when he was quite young that he should eventually inherit the German dukedom of Saxe-Coburg and Gotha from his uncle and, consequently, insisted that he turn down an offer to become king of Greece upon the resignation of King Otto in 1866. He was made Duke of Edinburgh, Earl of Kent and Earl of Ulster in 1866.

This rather unremarkable member of the royal family is, however, well-remembered in Australia.

While most Australians today probably have no idea who he was, his name is used by millions of us every day in speaking about such places and institutions as the Royal Prince Alfred Hospital in Sydney, the Alfred Hospital in Melbourne, Prince Alfred Park in Sydney, Prince Alfred College in Adelaide, Alfred Street at Circular Quay and Prince Alfred Square at Parramatta—and the story of his remarkable adventures 'down under' is truly one of almost unbelievable circumstances and coincidences.

Alfred realised from an early age that he was never likely to be bothered with the title of king and chose to enter the navy, serving as a midshipman on HMS *Euryalus* and as lieutenant on HMS *Racoon*. In 1867, at the age of 23, he was given command of HMS *Galatea* and set out on a trip around the world, which was designed to 'show the flag' to the far-flung corners of the British Empire.

The prince arrived at Glenelg on 31 October 1867 and visited Adelaide, Melbourne, Sydney, Brisbane and Hobart during a stay of six months on our shores.

At that time, of course, Australia was made up of separate British colonies and the popularity of the prince's visit took colonial authorities quite by surprise. Planning and preparations appear to have been woefully inadequate and crowd control at times virtually non-existent. There were reports of several people being seriously injured, even trampled so badly that they died from their injuries.

It was on the prince's second visit to Sydney, having returned from Brisbane, that an event occurred that must go down in our history as the first act of international terrorism ever perpetrated on Australian soil.

This was at a time when sectarian violence was proving to be a problem for the British government. The Fenian movement in Ireland had led to political assassinations, harsh reprisals and even the suspension of *habeas corpus*.

No doubt Prince Alfred felt safely removed from these problems in the far-flung colonies of Australia, but we should remember that more than 30 per cent of the convicts and soldiers who originally populated our colonies were Irish.

There was certainly a warm welcome from the majority of Sydneysiders, who were pro-British to the core, and the prince also received a warm welcome form Sydney's German population,

500 of whom paraded through the streets carrying torches to meet him and listen to the British royal address them with a speech in fluent German, which was, after all, the prince's first language, as it was for all Queen Victoria's family.

There was no doubting the loyalty of Sir William Manning, the man who planned the fateful picnic at Clontarf, which was to be the scene of Australia's first terrorist act.

Sir William was a wealthy pastoralist and politician. He had been attorney-general of the colony of New South Wales and a list of his honorary positions will show readers just how respectable Sir William was.

He was trustee and vice-president of the Australian Club, vice-president of the Civil Service Club, a steward of the Australian Jockey Club, member of the Royal Sydney Yacht Squadron, a founding president of the New South Wales Rifle Association, elected to the Senate of the University of Sydney in 1861, and was vice-president of the Horticultural Society of New South Wales.

You really don't get much more respectable than that!

Sir William was also President of the Sydney Sailors' Home, and planned to enhance his reputation and social status by planning and hosting a picnic for the prince and Sydney's elite at the beachfront suburb of Clontarf, ostensibly to raise funds for the sailors' home.

This was to be no ordinary picnic. It was a gala occasion with marquees on the lawn, the band of the *Galatea* playing on the shore and a group of Aborigines to provide entertainment consisting of native sports and dances. There was a marquee for lunch, another for the ladies and, of course, a special royal marquee for the prince himself, should he feel the need for privacy or be overwhelmed by the excitement of the occasion and feel in need of rest.

What the event lacked, evidently, was adequate security. There were no barricades or barriers to prevent the public from enjoying the scene at a distance or, indeed, quite close up. The only thing keeping the public at a safe distance appears to have been the aura surrounding the prince and the social elite of Sydney. Any well-dressed person acting in a respectable manner was capable of

approaching easily to within striking distance of the royal personage, and Henry James O'Farrell was quite well dressed that day.

Henry O'Farrell was born in Dublin in 1833. His father was
a butcher who migrated with his family to Melbourne in 1841 and
improved his lot by becoming a land agent, which enabled him to
send his boys to a Catholic boarding school.

On leaving school at seventeen, Henry attended St Francis's
seminary and became a deacon. He studied for the priesthood in
Europe but a dispute with Bishop Goold, later to become the first
Archbishop of Melbourne, prevented him from being ordained
and he became a sheep farmer and later a grain merchant in partnership with his cousin, Joseph Kennedy.

In 1864, Henry's brother Peter, a leading Melbourne solicitor, had
his reputation ruined in a libel suit and was forced to leave Melbourne
in disgrace. At the same time their cousin, Henry's business partner
Joseph Kennedy, died of *delirium tremens* and these events, along
with his failure to become a priest, his own alcoholism and increas-
ing debt, led to a serious mental breakdown for Henry in 1867.
During bouts of paranoia Henry was known to wave pistols around
and threaten to kill people who he was convinced were attempting
to poison him. He also suffered epileptic fits and his sisters took him
to Melbourne and attempted to care for him.

In September 1867 he travelled to Sydney where he stayed at
the Currency Lass Hotel until asked to leave because of his strange
and erratic behaviour. His sisters sent him money to enable him to
board at the Clarendon Hotel and on 11 March 1868, having used
the money to purchase two pistols, he practised target shooting
in Waverley.

Next day he was part of the crowd of onlookers at the Clontarf
picnic for Prince Alfred, Duke of Edinburgh.

What happened next was described in such melodramatic
and colourful detail by the *Sydney Mail* newspaper that I cannot
improve upon it and, as Banjo says, quote it *verbatim*:

When the Prince left the luncheon-tent, at the Sailors' Home
Picnic, he escorted the Countess of Belmore to the door of the

Royal tent, and then turned to converse with his Excellency the Governor, the Chief Justice, and Sir William Manning. They remained talking a few seconds, and then his Royal Highness and Sir William Manning sauntered across the green towards the clump of trees bordering the beach, and under which the Galatea Band was stationed.

The subject of conversation was the Sailors' Home, and his Royal Highness, to mark his appreciation of the institution, handed Sir William a cheque as a donation to the institution. Sir William made his acknowledgments for the donation, and then asked his Royal Highness whether he would go round to Cabbage Tree Beach to see the aboriginals, as they were then ready for some sports.

Before his Royal Highness could reply a treacherous assailant, who had just left the crowd of persons congregated under the shade of the trees, stole up behind him, and when he had approached to within five or six feet pulled out a revolver, took deliberate aim, and fired. The shot took effect about the middle of the back of his Royal Highness, an inch or two to the right of the spine. He fell forward on his hands and knees, exclaiming, 'Good God, my back is broken.'

Sir William Manning, hearing the discharge, and seeing his Royal Highness fall, turned and sprang at the would-be assassin, who then jumped back and aimed the murderous weapon at Sir William. Seeing the pistol directed towards him, Sir William stooped to evade the shot, and, losing his balance, fell.

Fortunately the charge did not explode; but as Sir William Manning was in the act of rising, the ruffian took aim a third time; just at the moment Mr Vial, of Castlereagh Street, who happened to be behind, sprang upon the dastardly assailant, pinioned his arms to his side, and thus the aim of the pistol was diverted from the body of Sir William Manning to the ground.

The weapon was discharged, however, and the shot entered the foot of Mr George Thorne, senior, who fainted, and was taken away by Mr Hassall, and other friends.

In the meantime a number of people, attracted by the discharge of firearms, and seeing his Royal Highness fall, ran to the spot, and

three or four of them, among whom was Mr T. Hales and a young
gentleman named McMahon, lifted his Royal Highness to carry
him into his tent. It was evident from the demeanour of his Royal
Highness that he was suffering great pain, and he asked his bearers
to carry him gently. This wish was complied with as far as possible,
and thus he was borne into his tent. Here he was taken in charge by
Dr Watson, of H.M.S. Challenger, who together with Dr Wright of
Sydney, Dr Powell of the Galatea, and Assistant-surgeon Waugh
of the Challenger, were immediately in attendance.

The dress of his Royal Highness was removed, and upon
an examination of the wound it was found that the bullet had
penetrated the back, near the middle, and about two inches from
the right side of the lower part of the spine, traversing the course
of the ribs, round by the right to the abdomen, where it lodged,
immediately below the surface. No vital organ, fortunately,
appeared to be injured, the course of the bullet being to all
appearance, quite superficial.

It was, later, ascertained that the bullet had probably been
diverted from its deadly course by striking the metal clasp and
a rubberised portion of Prince Alfred's braces. This had, perhaps,
saved his life and prevented the first royal visit to Australia from
ending in the first case of royal murder on this continent.

Prince Alfred was now safe in the royal tent and, although in
a great deal of pain, he was receiving the best available medical
attention and it appeared he would survive the incident.

Things were not looking quite so good for Henry O'Farrell,
however. Let us return to the colourful account in the *Sydney Mail:*

While this painful examination was in progress another scene,
which almost defies description, was going on in another part
of the ground. No sooner had Mr Vial grasped the arms of the
man who had fired the shots, than M. Benjamin Mortimer (an
American gentleman), Mr Whiting (of the firm of Dryman and
Whiting), A.L. Jackson, and other gentlemen seized him; and, had
it not been for the closing in around them of the police and other

persons, they would speedily have placed him beyond the reach of the Law Courts.

The people shouted 'lynch him,' 'hang him,' 'string him up,' and so on, and there was a general rush to get at him. The police, headed by Superintendent Orridge, got hold of the assassin, and they had the greatest difficulty in preventing the infuriated people from tearing him limb from limb. In this the police were ably assisted by the Chief Justice, Lord Newry, and the men of the Galatea Band. Both Lord Newry and Sir Alfred Stephen exerted themselves to get the prisoner on board the steamer lying at the wharf, while Mr Orridge, with herculean strength, kept back the crowd as much as possible.

The task of putting the prisoner on board the ship was not an easy one, and it was fully ten minutes before they could get him on to the wharf. By that time all the clothing from the upper part of his body was torn off, his eyes, face, and body were much bruised, and blood was flowing from various wounds; and when he was dragged on to the deck of the Paterson he appeared to be utterly unconscious.

No sooner was he on board than a number of sailors had a rope ready to string him up, and it was only by the interference of Lord Newry that his life was spared. Some of the police were very roughly used, Detective Powell getting about the worst of it. In the scuffle he fell over some stones, and had a chance of being trampled to death.

The whole of the police on the ground were under the command of Mr Fosbery. The people, out of whose hands the prisoner had been rescued, immediately gave vent to their disappointment, and at an indignation meeting, summarily convened, determined to bring him back from the steamer, and dispatch him at the scene of his crime.

A rush was then made for the steamer, which had just hauled off a few feet from the wharf, and they shouted to the captain to haul in. For a moment this officer appeared to waver, but the Hon. John Hay, who was on the bridge, doubtless divining the intentions of the crowd, peremptorily ordered the captain to haul off. This he did, and the vessel accordingly proceeded on her way to Sydney.

To say that the loyal British citizens of Sydney attending the picnic were outraged, embarrassed, and on the verge of hysteria would be, perhaps, an understatement. This was the biggest thing to happen in the 80-year British history of Australia and the *Sydney Mail* reporter was at great pains to graphically illustrate the 'effect of this dastardly attempt to assassinate the prince, among the immense number of persons congregated at Clontarf':

> A large number of ladies fainted, others were seized with hysterics, and the whole multitude was convulsed.
>
> Suddenly a joyous throng had been converted into a mass of excited people, in whose breasts sympathy for the Royal sufferer, and indignation for his murderous assailant, alternately prevailed; while pallid faces and tearful eyes told of the deep anxiety that was felt in reference to the extent of the injuries the prince had sustained.
>
> People crowded by hundreds around the tent in which the sufferer lay, until they were informed that they must keep back, in order to allow free ventilation; they at once fell back thirty or forty yards, and formed a complete cordon around the tent, and anxiously awaited the result of the examination.

Meanwhile, inside the royal tent, the prince—who had, according to the *Sydney Mail*, 'never lost consciousness, although feeling faint and weak from the shock to his nervous system, and from loss of blood'—was telling his carers about the sensation of being shot at close quarters. It felt, he said, 'as though [he] was being lifted off the ground'.

When he was told of the near panic, grief and hysteria among the hundreds waiting outside, he gave instructions, as one would expect from a member of such a noble, stoic and Teutonic bloodline, that someone should go out and, 'Tell the people I am not much hurt, I shall be better presently'.

At about five o'clock His Royal Highness was placed on a mattress, which was placed on a litter. He was then carried by officers of the *Galatea* to the wharf and conveyed by boat to the wharf at Government House, where he convalesced in the care of a group of British nurses led by Sister Osburn.

We shall come to Sister Osburn's role in the story presently, but for now let me assure the troubled reader that the prince, although he could not lie down at all that evening, was cared for by Miss Osburn and another of her group of trained nurses, who stayed on duty all night and, thankfully, there was 'no appearance of haemorrhage'.

The condition of Henry O'Farrell, now ensconced in Darling-hurst Gaol, was not too flash, either.

O'Farrell was described by the *Sydney Mail* as 'a man of good education, and in manner not unpleasing, fair-complexioned, about five feet eleven inches in height, and apparently about five and thirty years of age' with a 'slight beard and moustache, and a military air', who was 'perfectly self-possessed'.

His condition, having been rescued from the lynch mob, might be described as rather battle-scarred:

> His clothes were torn to ribbons by the excited crowd, and he received many severe bruises, his eyes being blackened, his nose swelled very much, and his lips puffed out like those of a negro.

The *Sydney Mail* had found out quite a lot about Mr O'Farrell in a relatively short length of time and informed its readers that:

> According to his own statements—although he says very little and maintains much reticence with respect to himself and his dastardly deed—he is a native of Dublin, but left Ireland at a very early age. He has been in many countries, has spent a considerable time on the European continent, and in America, and about three months ago came from Victoria to New South Wales.

The *Sydney Mail* then goes on to inform readers of sundry facts that today would be expected to be left to the judge and jury:

He has expressed a hope that the Prince would not die, and says that he did not mean to kill, but merely to 'frighten him'—a statement which is absurd on the face of it. Two revolvers were found on him, one of which had not been discharged, and every chamber of which was loaded. The other, the weapon with which the attempt at assassination was committed, was picked up by one of the Galatea's bandsmen after the prisoner's capture. The latter is a small Colt's revolver, such as could easily be carried in the pocket.

The article ends by telling readers that 'immense crowds' gathered at both Government House and the offices of the *Sydney Mail* awaiting news of the prince's condition and assures us that the prince's youth and strong constitution will help him survive.

Sister Lucy Osburn and the British Nurses

Just who were these trained nurses who were on hand to care for the prince and give him the up-to-date modern medical attention that enabled him to recover so quickly?

Believe it or not, the first properly trained nurses had arrived from England just one week before the prince was shot, on the clipper ship *Dunbar Castle*. Had the prince been shot during his first stay in Sydney, several weeks earlier, there would have been no nurses to care for him.

So, how did they get to be in Sydney at all?

Well, in 1867, the New South Wales Colonial Secretary, Henry Parkes, despairing of the dilapidated state of the Sydney Hospital, had written to Florence Nightingale and asked for her advice and help. The hospital was decrepit, dirty, equipped with decades-old technology and run by men who had no concept of the recent advances in medicine. Parkes pushed through an Act requiring the inspection of hospitals and suggested that the government bring to Sydney nursing sisters trained by Florence Nightingale, who could modernise the hospital, run the infirmary and dispensary, and train other nurses.

Florence sent six trained nurses, led by her protégé Sister Lucy Osburn, to work at the Sydney Hospital. They arrived in the colony on the *Dunbar Castle* on 5 March 1868, exactly one week before the assassination attempt. Lucy Osburn and her nurses cared for Prince Alfred and restored him back to health.

A fascinating character from our colonial past, Lucy Osburn was born in 1836 at Leeds, her father was the famous Egyptologist, William Osburn. Lucy was well educated and spoke several languages. Her hobby was breaking in Arab horses but she was passionate about the new female career of nursing and worked in hospitals in Holland, Germany and Vienna. She studied midwifery at King's College Hospital and attended Florence Nightingale's Training School at St Thomas's Hospital—all against her family's wishes.

When, in response to Henry Parkes's efforts to solicit help from Florence Nightingale, Lucy was appointed lady superintendent of the Sydney Infirmary and Dispensary at a salary of £150 in 1867, her father disowned her.

Sister Osburn was appointed for three months and stayed sixteen years, fighting constantly all that time against bureaucracy, misogyny, prejudice, professional jealousy and rivalry. She is one of the unsung heroines of our colonial history.

On her arrival in Sydney, Osburn discovered that the accommodation to be built for the nurses had not even begun. The older 'rum hospital' (so called because it was built in exchange for Governor Macquarie giving the contractors the monopoly on imports of rum into the colony) was rat-infested and the kitchen was filthy. Even so, by the end of the year, she had managed to train sixteen new local nurses.

Her attempts to modernise the hospital were constantly frustrated and obstructed by Alfred Roberts, the visiting surgeon whose cronies attacked her in the Legislative Assembly.

She got rid of the prostitutes, vagrants and derelicts who had previously been used to tend the inmates, and cleared the hospital of rubbish, including destroying many of the germ-laden books that were scattered around the wards, which led to her enemies accusing her of bible burning.

She even fell out with her mentor Florence Nightingale who, having no real concept of the conditions under which Lucy worked in Australia, accused her of 'having views of her own beyond the Nightingale system'.

A Royal Commission in 1873 completely exonerated Osburn who had accused the all-male management committee of the hospital of 'other neglect and interfering between the head of nursing and her nurses'.

In 1874 Osburn's salary was raised to £250 and, in 1881, the *Sydney Hospital Act* abolished the infirmary's old name and set up new conditions of management. This huge step forward in our medical history was largely due to the efforts of Sister Osburn.

She battled on until 1884 when she finally resigned and returned to London. She was suffering from diabetes and had contracted several diseases while working in the poor conditions at the hospital, including dysentery. She intended to return to Australia to live, as she had made many friends here and felt that Sydney was her home. Her poor health, however, made it easier for her to remain in London, where she worked as a district nurse and then became superintendent to the Southwark, Newington and Walworth District Nursing Association. She died of diabetes in 1891.

The Royal Prince Alfred Hospital

While Sister Osburn was nursing the prince back to health, the outraged people of Sydney were leaving no stone unturned in their efforts to show their undying support and loyalty to Britain and the royal family.

This was a period of great political and religious conflict between Irish Catholics and the non-Catholic establishment in both Britain and the colonies of Australia. 'Fenian terrorism' was reported regularly in newspapers and there had been a shooting incident between Orange Lodge and Catholic factions during the prince's visit to Melbourne, which had apparently begun as a sectarian disagreement.

The assassination attempt generated an outpouring of prejudice and racism against Catholics and the Irish. Many public meetings were held around the country, with nearly 20,000 people attending a meeting in Sydney the day after the shooting. By the following week, there were daily 'indignation meetings' everywhere.

Anti-Irish hysteria was evident even in parliament and the New South Wales government passed the *Treason Felony Act* on 18 March, making it an offence to refuse to drink to the queen's health. Newspapers and politicians tried unsuccessfully to paint O'Farrell's act as part of a conspiracy, although it was patently obvious that the man was seriously mentally ill. Some even found fanciful and sinister evidence of a plot to disgrace and destabilise New South Wales by the rival colony of Victoria, seen by many in New South Wales as a hotbed of Irish Catholic sentiment and independent thinking. After all, O'Farrell had travelled from Victoria to perpetrate the dastardly deed.

Clemency for O'Farrell was refused, despite the prince's own proposal that he refer the sentence to the queen. In spite of O'Farrell being obviously mentally ill, he was hastily tried and found guilty then hanged at Darlinghurst Gaol on 21 April 1868.

Queen Victoria herself was the target of seven assassination attempts during her reign and was clever enough to make sure that she created no martyrs to provide fuel for enemies of the crown. Not one of her would-be assassins was hanged. Two were 'put under care suited to their mental condition', two were imprisoned 'at Her Majesty's pleasure', one was banished, another transported for seven years, and the other, hilariously, was sent to Dartmoor Prison and 'ultimately released on his promise to go to Australia, where he was working as a house-painter as lately as 1882'.

Insanity and religious fanaticism were obviously inherent in the O'Farrell family as Henry's brother Peter attempted, at Brighton Beach in Melbourne in 1881, to assassinate Bishop Goold, the man who had blocked Henry's ordination many years earlier. He, too, failed to achieve his aim.

Meanwhile, the devoted citizens of New South Wales opened a public subscription fund to build a memorial to Alfred's safe recovery. Eventually some element of common sense prevailed and it was suggested that the 'perfect memorial' would be a hospital—and so the idea of the Royal Prince Alfred Hospital was born.

The monies collected were placed in a fund and, in 1873, the *Prince Alfred Hospital Act* was passed, establishing a board of directors responsible for planning and building the hospital on land belonging to Sydney University in Missenden Road.

The Royal Prince Alfred (RPA) was planned as a clinical school for the university's new medical faculty and, appropriately, as a training school for nurses, and from the start included the latest medical and diagnostic techniques and technologies.

Florence Nightingale supplied advice on the design via her group of nurses now at the old hospital in Sydney and by sending copies of her publications, *Notes on Hospitals* and *Notes on Nursing: What it is and what it is not.*

The project offered the opportunity for Sydney to build a well-designed hospital with trained staff and modern technology. It was everything the old 'rum hospital' in Macquarie Street was not!

It opened as a 146-bed hospital and received its first patients in 1882 at the Missenden Road site. During that year 1069 patients were admitted. The hospital has since established a national and international reputation for excellence as a training and referral institution.

The prince authorised his coat of arms to be used as the new hospital's crest and King Edward VII granted the hospital its 'Royal' prefix in 1902.

Prince Alfred, the Duke of Edinburgh, remained in the navy and was stationed at Malta for many years as commander-in-chief of the Mediterranean fleet and he later became admiral of the fleet. In 1874 he married Maria Alexandrovna, the only surviving daughter of Emperor Alexander the Second of Russia, who gave his daughter a dowry of £100,000 plus an annual allowance of £28,000, just in case the British royal family didn't provide for her basic needs.

The marriage was, by all accounts, not a happy one. Maria was, apparently, a self-centred snob who complained bitterly that her position at court was below that of the Princess of Wales and all of Queen Victoria's daughters. She insisted on taking precedence before the Princess of Wales (the future Queen Alexandra) because she and her father considered the Princess of Wales' family (the Danish royal family) as inferior to their own.

Queen Victoria refused most of her demands, but did eventually give her precedence second only to the Princess of Wales.

Alfred and Maria did manage to produce five children. They had one son Alfred, known as Young Alfie, who became the hereditary prince of Saxe-Coburg and Gotha when his father succeeded to that title in 1893. They also had four daughters, all of whom married into various European royal families (one became the Queen of Romania).

Maria Alexandrovna is best known for the wonderful achievement of having a biscuit named after her. To commemorate the wedding of Alfred and Maria, a small English bakery named Peek Freans produced a biscuit with the royal bride's name and a coronet on it. Known as the 'Marie' biscuit, it became incredibly popular throughout Europe, and indeed the world, and turned Peek Freans into a large international company.

Decades later, the Marie biscuit, in one of those strange quirks of history, became the symbol of Spain's economic recovery after the civil war, when bakeries produced the rather bland, plain biscuit in mass quantities to take care of a surplus of wheat.

So, that's the story of how Sydney got a wonderful new hospital, thanks to the combined efforts of Lucy Osburn, Henry Parkes, Florence Nightingale and Prince Alfred, Duke of Edinburgh and later Duke of Saxe-Coburg and Gotha.

Oh, and not forgetting the efforts of a mad alcoholic Irishman, Henry James O'Farrell.

THE CONVICT KING OF ICELAND

ADAPTED IN PART FROM *THE ADVENTURES OF CAPTAIN JORGENSEN* BY MARCUS CLARKE

Certain characters from our colonial past were larger than life in that they had lives that we can barely comprehend: lives full of strange twists and turns of fate, achievements that seem barely humanly possible, and seemingly impossible coincidences.

The pickpocket and jewel thief George Barrington, the darling of the British press and a man who was so famous ladies boasted that he stole their jewellery, ends up a constable in Parramatta! Then there was James Hardy Vaux, the only man as far as we know to be transported three times to New South Wales, who wrote a dictionary of slang terms.

How about the convict Mary Bryant? She stole the governor's boat and escaped and made it back alive to her native Cornwall. Or 'Chinese' Morrison, who started a major war between Japan and Russia, walked from Peking to Calcutta and, as the first European to penetrate the New Guinea jungle, was speared through the head and survived.

Then there's Tom Wills, the alcoholic champion cricketer who invented Australian rules football and whose family was massacred by Aborigines—his unbelievable story appears in this volume.

Of all the amazing colonial tales featuring those protagonists, however, none can compare to the truly mind-boggling story of the Danish-born adventurer, Jorgen Jorgensen. The story of his life reads more like the fictional and fantastical adventures of Baron Munchausen than a factual account.

Jorgensen was a seaman, explorer, captain of a warship, adventurer, gambler, spy, man of letters, political prisoner, expedition leader, entrepreneur, dispensing chemist, bushranger hunter, policeman, convict transported for stealing bedroom furniture from a landlady, and—wait for it—the King of Iceland!

There is no character in Australia's colonial history whose life is as strange and as bizarrely multifaceted, complex and confusing as that of Jorgen Jorgensen, alias John Johnson, alias Jorgen Jorgenson (with an 'o'—he changed it officially from 'e' while living in England).

What is really strange is that his connection to Australia, and especially to Tasmania, occurred in two quite separate long-term episodes, which happened a quarter of a century apart.

Jorgensen was, at various times in between his two Australian 'lives', a Danish naval war hero in a war against Britain, merchant, British sailor and privateer, author, English spy, inmate of Newgate, Tothill Fields and Fleet Street prisons (as well as several prison hulks), and the ruler of Iceland referred to in Icelandic history as 'The Dog Days King'.

He also left us many writings, plays, political pamphlets, religious works and proposals, along with an 'autobiography' which, Marcus Clarke so accurately stated, 'is written in a vain and egotistical strain, with much affectation of classical knowledge.'

If you find it hard to believe that the King of Iceland was a convict in Tasmania, then you will be enthralled to read the amazing, unbelievable history of Jorgen Jorgensen.

He was born in Copenhagen in the year 1780, and was the son of a mathematical-instrument maker. He received a good education but, though his parents appeared to have been in easy circumstances and would have started him in business, the boy decided to 'go to sea'.

'When I saw a Dutch Indiaman set sail,' said Jorgensen, 'with its officers on deck, dressed out in their fine uniforms, my heart burned with envy to be like them.'

His father, however, did not approve of his son's notions, and bound him as apprentice to an English collier, and kept him on board her for four years, in an attempt to make him disillusioned with the seafaring life. At eighteen Jorgen quit the collier, and shipped on board the *Fanny*, a South Sea whaler, bound with stores to the Cape of Good Hope.

At the cape he joined the *Harbinger*, bound for Algoa Bay on Africa's east coast with a cargo of convicts. In 1798, the *Harbinger* had a narrow escape from being taken by a French ship of 44 guns, but beat off her enemy and accomplished her voyage without mishap.

Young Jorgensen returned to the Cape of Good Hope and, in 1880, now calling himself John Johnson, joined the crew of the British ship *Lady Nelson*, a brig of 65 tons commanded by Lieutenant Grant, which was sent originally as a tender to the *Investigator*, commanded by Captain Flinders on his surveying voyage around the Australian coast.

They sailed to Sydney then to King Island via Bass Strait and then returned and completed the survey of Port Phillip, Western Port, Port Dalrymple (Launceston) and the Derwent.

While in Sydney Jorgensen met Matthew Flinders and also the French explorer Nicolas Baudin, who was a guest of Governor King although their nations were on the brink of war in a time of an uneasy truce.

Jorgensen actually explored the unknown limits of the colony with Baudin and recalled:

On the occasion of his making an exploring tour into the interior of New South Wales, I was induced to accompany him, and all his ambition was to advance further than any Englishman had ever been before. We had travelled about 100 miles from Sydney, and had ascended the Hawkesbury a considerable way, some marked tree or remains of a temporary hut giving constant indications that a European had been there at some former period.

I had become so impatient at his incessant reasons, thus continually discovered, for penetrating further, with so futile an object as that of returning to Paris and boasting that he had been where no traveller had been before him, that, espying a large white rock projecting from a little eminence, I ran forward, and, standing upon it, called out to him with a show of exultation that that was the point beyond which no white had been. Baudin then marched about 20 paces further, and returned quite satisfied.

This episode would return to his mind many years later in London, as we shall see.

In 1803 the *Lady Nelson* set sail from Sydney to form a settlement at the Derwent. They set up the camp at Risdon but soon after it was moved to site of Hobart Town.

Returning to Sydney and tired of His Majesty's service, Jorgensen took charge of a small vessel going on a sealing voyage to New Zealand. He then returned to Sydney and shipped as chief officer of a whaler, the *Alexander*, which sailed for the Derwent. Jorgensen wrote later, 'I can boast of having stuck the first whale in that river.' He also claimed to be the first European to climb Mount Wellington.

The *Alexander* then spent a year whaling and sealing around Australia and New Zealand, and returned to London, via Tahiti, Cape Horn and St Helena, and docked at Gravesend in London in June 1806.

Jorgensen had convinced two Maori men and two Tahitians to sail with them. His vague plan was that they should learn European ways and return home as ambassadors for civilisation and Christianity. He introduced them to Sir Joseph Banks, who took charge of them, paid their expenses and then placed them under the care of the Reverend Joseph Hardcastle, 'in order that by initiating them in the truths of the Christian religion they might be able to confer a similar boon on their own countrymen.'

All four of the Pacific Islanders died in England within a year.

Jorgensen, however, was off on other adventures by then. He went back to Copenhagen, which he found had been bombarded by his recent friends, the English.

During the Napoleonic Wars, Denmark and Norway had a policy of 'armed neutrality'. In 1801, and again in 1807, the British attacked the Danish capital to ensure that the Danish–Norwegian fleet did not fall into the hands of the French. These wars were also known as the 'Gunboat Wars' due to the Danes' tactic of sending small heavily armed ships against the larger English vessels.

Having returned home a hero, with inflated stories of his many adventures, Jorgensen now decided to become a truly national hero and turn on his British friends.

He convinced his father and seven other merchants of Copenhagen, all 'touched with a spirit of reprisal against the English', to purchase a small vessel, equipped with 28 guns, which was armed, commissioned and manned by the government, with Jorgen Jorgensen (no longer 'John Johnson') as captain.

With a crew of 83 men, the vessel, named *Admiral Juul*, broke through the winter ice 'a month before it was expected that any vessel could get out' and captured three English merchant ships.

Encouraged by this success, and relying on his knowledge of the English coast, Jorgensen sailed to the Yorkshire coast off Flamborough Head where he came upon two sloops of war, the HMS *Sappho* and the HMS *Clio*. Finding that flight was impossible, Jorgensen, now the bold Danish privateer, determined to give battle. Notwithstanding that the *Sappho* was a much larger warship with a crew of 120 men, Jorgensen kept her at bay for three-quarters of an hour by firing seventeen broadsides. At last, with his powder spent, and his masts, rigging and sails shot to pieces, he was compelled to surrender, and was taken to Yarmouth.

Our hero was now a prisoner of the British, but all was not as it appeared. Due to his strong British connections, he had, according to his side of the story, 'chanced to obtain an interview' previously in Copenhagen with a 'public officer connected with the British Ministry'.

This mysterious individual now sent for him to travel to London, where Jorgensen suggests that he was made an offer of secret-service employment. Never one to miss an opportunity, Jorgensen was introduced to 'several of the high official characters of that eventful period' and, never short of ideas and plans for adventures, he suggested a scheme for the relief of Iceland.

Iceland, a territory of Denmark, was a victim of the Danish and English war. The inhabitants derived their means of support from the export of wool and fish. This trade was now prohibited, and with British supplies cut off by the Danish ships, the island was in a state of famine. The fate of the islanders had attracted the attention of English merchants, who were looking for some daring fellow willing to run the blockade.

Jorgensen called upon his old acquaintance, Sir Joseph Banks, and represented himself as the man for the job. Permission was obtained from the British government to freight a ship with provisions, and Jorgensen, taking the command, sailed from Liverpool on 29 December 1807. Many predictions were made as to the failure of the expedition, the danger being increased by inclement weather and the winter season.

Though the vessel was only 350 tons, the insurance cost the speculators 1000 guineas, for, according to Jorgensen, 'the enterprise was considered almost desperate' and it was 'madness to attempt such a voyage, which from the high latitude of the country, must necessarily be made at that season of the year almost in the dark'.

The ship made it through to Reykjavik and left its cargo with the 'supercargo', an agent who specialised in managing cargo sales and distribution.

Finding that matters turned out well, Jorgensen hastened back to Liverpool, in order to bring out another cargo. He speedily loaded two vessels, one with flour and another with provisions, and started again for the north.

During his absence, however, the governor of Iceland, Count von Tramp, had issued a proclamation prohibiting all communication with the English. When the two vessels anchored in the port of Reykjavik with their flour and provisions aboard, they were ordered to go away again, full as they came.

Jorgensen made out that he would retreat as demanded and pretended to prepare to sail. He 'knew his duty to his employers', however, and vowed he would land his cargo.

The next day being Sunday, and with the 'people at church', he landed with twelve of his men and, making straight to the governor's residence, stationed six men at the front and six at the back, with orders to fire on anyone who should interrupt him.

Then, with a brace of pistols in his belt, he walked into the Count's chamber, and informed him that he could consider himself deposed.

Count von Tramp, 'who was reposing on a sofa', made an attempt to resist but, as there was no one in the house but the cook, a few servants and 'a Danish lady', he was speedily over-powered, carried down to the beach, and placed under hatches in Jorgensen's ship. Jorgensen then helped himself to the contents of 'the iron chest' containing the island's tax collection.

When the good people of Reykjavik came out of church, they found that a revolution had taken place.

The ever-modest Jorgensen later noted: 'I am not aware, unless some more deep-read historian than myself can cite an instance, that any revolution in the annals of nations was ever more adroitly, more harmlessly, or more decisively effected than this. The whole government of the island was changed in a moment. I was well aware of the sentiments of the people before I planned my scheme, and I knew I was safe.'

The next day he issued a proclamation stating that the people, tired of Danish oppression, had called him to be the head of the government. This proclamation seemed to satisfy everybody.

The few English on the island imagined that Jorgensen had concerted the plot with the Icelanders, and the Danes believed he was supported by the English government. Having secured his position, our hero issued some new laws.

He cut local taxes by 50 per cent, released all people from debts due to the Crown of Denmark, compelled tax defaulters to make up deficiencies from their private estates, advanced money for the benefit of public schools and fisheries, and placed a duty on the 'British goods' which he had himself imported.

He established trial by jury and free representative government, and increased the salaries of the clergy, who then 'not wanting in their gratitude . . . preached resignation and contentment under the new order of things'.

He erected a fort with six guns, raised a troop of cavalry, and hoisted the ancient and independent flag of Iceland, a pale blue flag with three salted cod in the top left corner. The inhabitants appeared to enjoy the new state of things, and when the king made a tour of his dominions, they mostly received him with acclamation.

Indeed, it was prudent that they should do so, for when one magistrate or head-man of one of the northern villages, some 150 miles from Reykjavik, refused to do homage and 'surrender the iron chest', the new monarch piled brushwood around his front door and lit it, 'upon which he immediately submitted'.

Earlier, at Liverpool, Jorgensen had written to New York requesting that a ship might be sent to Iceland with tobacco, and soon after his return to the capital from his royal tour, he had the satisfaction of seeing a vessel enter the harbour 'with a valuable cargo from New York' which he exchanged for part of his (heavily taxed) British goods.

This commercial enterprise was so successful that Jorgensen decided to visit London and 'enter into an amicable treaty with Great Britain in order to permit vessels with British licenses to import grain'. He set sail with two ships, the vessel that had brought him from London and a Danish ship belonging to the deposed Count von Tramp. Unluckily, the Danish ship caught fire and, though every effort was made to save her, she burnt to the water's edge with all her cargo.

This accident compelled them to return to Iceland for provisions, where they found a British warship, HMS *Talbot,* in the harbour, but not yet at the dock. Jorgensen transferred passengers on the British warship and sailed in haste for Liverpool, which he reached in eight days.

The warship had obviously been sent to find out what on earth was going on in Iceland and Jorgensen, fearful that what the English captain of the *Talbot* would find in Iceland might do him injury, hurried up to London and sought support from Sir Joseph Banks. Banks, justly incensed at the extraordinary breach of trust of which his privateer captain had been guilty, refused to have anything to do with him.

The captain of the *Talbot*, in his report of the 'Iceland affair' to the British government, said that 'King Jorgensen' had 'established a republican government in Iceland, for the purpose of making that island a nest for all the disaffected persons in Europe', and added 'that he was highly unqualified to hold the command of a kingdom, because he had merely been an apprentice on board an English collier, and had served as midshipman in an English ship of war'.

Hearing of this, and fearing the consequences, the king went into hiding for a week or so, but one day, while dining at the Spread Eagle Inn, in Gracechurch Street, London, he was arrested and taken before the lord mayor. Jorgensen was charged with being 'an alien to an enemy, at large without the king's license, and with having broken his parole'.

In vain Jorgensen pleaded that he was really acting in the interest of England; the lord mayor had no taste for romance, however, and the poor king was put into Tothill Fields prison, there to console himself by the recollections of other monarchs who had been placed in similar positions.

During five weeks in Tothill Fields, Jorgensen recalled he 'met with persons the effect of whose intimacy steeped his future life in misery'. This mostly referred to the political prisoner Count Dillon, of whom more, anon!

Then he was moved to the prison hulk set aside for Danish prisoners, and kept there for nearly twelve months, at the end of which time he was permitted to reside at Reading on his parole.

Jorgensen now cultivated literary tastes, and wrote a little book, entitled *The Copenhagen Expedition Traced to other Causes than the Treaty of Tilsit*. He would continue to write pamphlets, plays and colourful autobiography for many years from that point.

After a ten month residence at Reading, he received permission to return to London, where he was reacquainted with some of the gentry he had met when they were political prisoners in Tothill Fields and was 'thoroughly initiated into all the horrors and enticements of the gaming-table'. He appears to have lived a bohemian lifestyle, writing, gambling, being now rich, now poor, strolling in the parks and living in an attic.

During this time Jorgensen and fifteen others apparently won the state lottery valued at £20,000, but he soon gambled away his share of the winnings. In order to escape his debts he fled to Lisbon and Madrid where he fell into more gambling and was robbed and left with only his jacket and trousers. He then joined the crew of a British gunboat that was taking mail back to England. His plan was to jump ship as soon as they docked in England.

Unfortunately for Jorgensen the gunboat off-loaded the mail to a coastal ship and never reached the shore. It was then sent to cruise off Cape St Vincent where Jorgensen assisted in the capture of several privateers, and gained a promotion. On arriving at Gibraltar, however, he either became genuinely ill or 'malingered' and was placed in the hospital, and finally invalided back to Portsmouth in 1813. He was placed on board the invalid-hulk *Gladiator*, a hospital ship. The berthing of the invalids would not appear to be conducive to their recovery according to Jorgensen, who wrote that, 'Between 700 and 800 persons were collected in this horribly pent-up place, which could not have afforded moderate accommodation for half of them, even had they been in good health'.

He was in a difficult situation in trying to get off the *Gladiator*. If he said he was not ill, he would be accused of malingering and be punished, or at best sent back to sea. He wrote letters to his superiors and eventually was dismissed and resumed his aimless life in London.

Being one day at a coffee house in the Strand, he met Count Dillon, a member of the French-sympathising Irish-rebel family, whose acquaintance he had made in Tothill Fields prison, where the count was a political prisoner. Dillon, thinking Jorgensen was still an 'enemy of England', talked freely about rebel schemes and Jorgensen, always ready to turn an honest penny, saw a chance to sell information to the government.

Dillon told him of a supposed plot between the Americans and the French, 'to send out an armed expedition' to take possession of the Australian colonies. This idea originated from the reports given by the zoologist Francois Peron, who was supposedly spying for Napoleon while part of the Baudin expedition with the *Geographe* and the *Naturaliste*, visiting Sydney in 1801.

Jorgensen had met Baudin in Sydney, and had no suspicions of any underhanded intentions to spy. Indeed it appears that Baudin may not have known Peron was a spy and the two men apparently did not get on. Peron undermined Baudin's authority and attempted to write him out of the history of the expedition after he died in Mauritius on the way home.

The expedition, according to Dillon, was to consist of two armed French and American vessels which, meeting at a certain rendezvous, were to sail together into the South Seas, and 'participate in the plunder of the colonies'.

Jorgensen hurried to the Colonial Office, and laid his intelligence before 'a gentleman high in office', who remarked that it was a 'wild scheme' and even if it was successful, England would lose little or nothing as those colonies were 'not worth keeping for they already cost the Government £100,000 a year!'.

This rumoured expedition did, however, sail in 1813, when Britain and the United States were once again at war. The two French ships, commanded by Count Dillon, were wrecked off Cadiz but the Americans proceeded, and captured and burned seventeen whalers, creating a deficiency in the supply of sperm whale oil, which resulted in an enormous price rise in London.

Jorgensen bemoaned the British neglect of the Pacific colonies:

It is indeed much to be regretted that the navigation, fisheries, and trade of these seas has so long been looked over by the authorities at home. The immense archipelago of the Pacific is studded with islands, and inhabited by millions of friendly-disposed people, ready and anxious to exchange their commodities for British manufactures. The benign influence of the Christian religion, which is rapidly extending itself by the aid of our gospel missionaries, is doing much to raise these people in the scale of civilised society; and although the Americans are hourly taking advantage of our comparative supineness, the approach of an English flag is always, and we trust ever will be, hailed with superior satisfaction. The pearl fishery is said to be more profitable and less hazardous than that of the sperm whale, and the sandalwood and beche-de-mer, which are produced so abundantly on the northern coasts of our New Holland, are known to yield the Dutch, through the medium of the Malays, an immense revenue. Nothing surprised Captain Flinders more, in the course of his navigation of these countries, than the immense fleets of Malay boats extensively engaged in this traffic which he met with in the Gulf of Carpentaria.

Having once again run into debt from gambling, Jorgensen was arrested and sent to the notorious Fleet Debtor's Prison for two years.

When evidence of the destruction of the British whaling ships proved part of his story to be true, however, he was quick to remind His Majesty's ministers of the service he had rendered.

He was subsequently supplied with money to pay his debts, but instead of discharging his liabilities, he went to a gaming-table and lost every penny and was sent back to debtor's prison, where he 'amused himself' by writing histories, pamphlets and stories and made enough money to live on.

One day he was sent for by the Foreign Office, and 'had the pleasure to be engaged on a foreign mission to the seat of war'. In other words, he became a spy.

Amply supplied with money for expenses, and provided with an order to 'draw on London' for any funds he might require while travelling, it would appear that Jorgensen at last had fallen on good days. He could have at once left London for Paris with money and credit.

Instead of going to Dover, however, he went to a gambling house and lost not only his money, but the clothes he had been provided for his journey.

Totally destitute, Jorgensen resolved to seize his chance of advancement and exchanged his only suit for a sailor's jacket and trousers, walked to Gravesend, and embarked as crew on board a transport bound for Ostend.

At Ostend he met an officer who knew him, and testified to his identity, and an 'order' on the Foreign Office was cashed without difficulty.

His brief for spying on the Continent seems rather a vague business. He wrote later that he was 'sent to ascertain what effect the subjugation of Napoleon was likely to have on British Commerce'. He was in Brussels when the celebrated Battle of Waterloo was fought nearby and spent three days wandering over the field of Waterloo after the battle.

Jorgensen lived the high life in the aftermath of the British victory until he was ordered on a special mission to Warsaw and went out for a last night in Paris and gambled until he had nothing to sell but his shirt, which he sold for seven francs to a sergeant. Jorgensen then buttoned up his coat and, leaving Paris by the east gate, set out along the north road on foot. It was December, and bitterly cold. Arriving at Joncherie, 120 miles from the capital, he walked boldly into the best hotel, and ordered the best dinner they could give him. He then bluffed the local authorities into giving him money and shelter.

In the aftermath of Bonaparte's defeat he managed to 'con' his way around northern France, sometimes purporting to be sympathetic to the fallen emperor and other times using his passport to extract money from those in charge under the new regime.

When he got back to London he was paid for his services, and decided to emigrate to South America, the natural home of adventurers like himself. But he soon lost every penny gambling and the next three years of his life were a 'continual whirl of misery and disappointment at the gaming-table'.

In 1820, having sunk lower and lower, he was arrested for pawning certain articles of bedroom furniture belonging to his landlady in Tottenham Court Road and was sentenced to seven years transportation.

Pending the start of his sentence, Jorgensen was sent to Newgate Prison, and became assistant to the surgeon, Mr Box. His behaviour was exemplary and he became the prison 'dispenser', had his sentence commuted and retained his post as dispenser for nearly two years.

When it was found that the stolen articles for which he had been sentenced were pawned in the name of one of his fellow lodgers, Jorgensen received his pardon, on condition that he should quit the kingdom within a month from the day of his liberation.

Unfortunately, however, having money in his pockets, the savings of his 'prison gratuities', he again sought the gaming-table, and overstayed his leave. Several weeks over his allotted time to leave England, he attempted to ship on board a man-of-war, and was on his way to take the tender in the river when he met an old prison acquaintance, who asked him to dinner and, hearing that he had 'outstayed his time', called the police.

Jorgensen was tried and sentenced to transportation for life, but spent three years in his former situation in the prison hospital, during which time he wrote an account of his 'Continental tour' and a religious work, *The Religion of Christ the Religion of Nature*.

He was sent to Van Diemen's Land in the *Woodman*, which sailed from Sheerness with 150 convicts and a detachment of military with their wives and children, in November 1825.

Some of his writings in Newgate make interesting reading. He noted that it was not a good idea to waste the court's time with arguments of innocence:

> I well remember one day when five men were arraigned at the bar, the four most guilty of whom, being asked their plea by the court, answered promptly, 'Guilty, my Lord,' and were sentenced to a few months' imprisonment, while the fifth, sensible of his comparative innocence, pleaded 'Not guilty,' occupied the time of the court with his defence for three-quarters of an hour, and was sentenced to seven years' transportation.

The *Woodman* arrived safely at Hobart Town on 5 May 1826, and Jorgensen remembered sadly, as he saw the city, that 'twenty-three years before he had assisted in forming Risdon, the first settlement in the island'.

Next day the usual muster of prisoners took place. The convicts in their prison clothes were landed and marched up to the prisoners' barracks, where they were inspected by the governor, Colonel Arthur, and in due course 'assigned' or sentenced to such further imprisonment as their conduct during the voyage had rendered desirable.

Jorgensen had 'letters of recommendation' from two of the directors of the Van Diemen's Land Company to their principal agent and had made application to be placed in his office on government service. This application was granted, and Jorgensen found that he had committed a great error; the government pay being small and the work arduous.

'A prisoner clerk,' he reported, 'received only 6 pence a day and 1 penny for rations; the former paid quarterly, and the latter every month.' He had hoped that the government would have extended some mercy towards him, but he was disappointed.

Meanwhile, strange rumours concerning him were afloat. Some said he was a political pamphleteer, imprisoned for having written against the government—others, that he had been a political spy, employed against the British Crown.

At last there was found for him an employment more suited to his ambition than copying letters in a government office. A party had been formed to explore the company's land, and to trace a road from the River Shannon to Circular Head, and Jorgensen was placed in command. It was the early part of September, and the rivers were swollen with recent heavy rains.

Each man had with him six weeks provisions, slung swag-wise on his back (no small weight to carry), and the journey was most laborious. The settlers, however, received them with much kindness and, until their arrival at the Big Lake, northwest of the ford of the Shannon, they got on well enough. At the River Ouse, which runs parallel with the Big Lake, however, their difficulties commenced. No ford was to be found, and for more than 30 miles Jorgensen followed the course of the stream, searching in vain for a crossing place.

Being now nearly 50 years of age, Jorgensen was becoming knocked up, and considered a retreat. Reaching a 'cataract pouring down between perpendicular and impracticable rocks', the party discovered a ford by accident when their dogs pursued a kangaroo.

They retreated to Dr Ross's farm for supplies and having rested a few weeks, retraced their steps and penetrated to the source of the Derwent, and ascending the mountains, then foot-deep with snow, tried to reach Circular Head. But provisions ran out and the weather forced Jorgensen to lead his companions to a stock hut, where the stockmen, observing their tattered clothes, long beards and firearms, took them for bushrangers. The stockmen refused to give them shelter until Jorgensen produced his maps, compass, journal and letters.

It was lucky that they did not succeed in making Circular Head by that unexplored route, for the provisions which were to have been buried there had not been delivered and, had they reached the Bluff, they would all have died of starvation.

In the early part of January 1827, Jorgensen led a party along the western coast of the island from Circular Head to the Shannon with three others, including Mr Lorymer, one of the company's surveyors.

The coast was barren and flinty and they found many wrecks of beached vessels and 'a mountain of sand which, after ascending with great difficulty, measured on the top seven miles in length'.

After finding themselves in scrub so dense that they could not cut their way through it quicker than '200 yards a day', they were nearly swallowed by the quicksands on the seashore. Then Lorymer was drowned in an attempt to cross the Duck River on a raft. Wet, exhausted and fainting from lack of food, the three survivors at last reached Circular Head. Jorgensen lay between life and death for four days, but slowly recovered. That was our hero's last expedition on behalf of the Van Diemen's Land Company.

Back in Hobart he received his ticket-of-leave, and became editor of a colonial newspaper, but soon fell out with the owner and decided on a new venture.

At that time, Van Diemen's Land was infested with desperadoes who, having escaped from the various prison gangs on the island, had taken to the wilds as bushrangers. The government had determined to put an end to this and the custom was to punish with death all captured runaways.

However, this was found to be counterproductive for, when a man had no chance of escape from the gallows whatever he confessed, he held his tongue and confessed nothing; but when hope of mercy was held out, many betrayed their associates.

So the Crown employed a few daring and trusted agents as go-betweens for the government with the convicts and bush-rangers. Jorgensen was chosen as one of these agents, and installed as constable of the field police and assistant-constable to the police-magistrate for Oatlands.

The circumference of the Oatlands district was more than 150 miles, and Jorgensen was obliged to visit all the farms and stock huts in the districts of Oatlands, Clyde, Campbell Town, the Swan ports and the Richmond district, and protect settlers from bushrangers and hostile Aborigines. For two years he camped out alone in the bush at places like Murderer's Plains, Deadman's Point, Killman's Point, Hell's Corner and Four-square Gallows.

After two years of this life, during which he several times narrowly escaped death from bullets or starvation, Jorgensen took part in the 'war of extermination' against the Tasmanian Aborigines and was part of the infamous 'black line' that attempted to herd the Indigenous inhabitants into a large corral over that narrow strip of sand known as East Bay Neck, connecting Forestier's Peninsula with the mainland, and then drive them across the second isthmus, to what would become the penal settlement of Port Arthur.

By a government order issued from the Colonial Secretary's Office on 9 September 1830, the whole population of the island was called to arms. 'The Lieutenant-Governor calls upon every settler, whether residing on his farm or in a town, who is not prevented by some overruling necessity, cheerfully to render his assistance, and place himself under the direction of the police-magistrate of that district in which his farm is situated, or any other district he may prefer.'

The whole field police, all ticket-of-leave men and a multitude of convicts, either in assigned service or otherwise at the disposal of government, were ordered to join the line; and this immense force, consisting of more than 2000 armed men, moved slowly across the island. It all achieved very little but it paved the way for the remaining Aborigines to be resettled on Flinders Island and hostilities had ceased by the end of 1831.

Jorgensen's adventures were drawing to a close. One afternoon in 1830, turning over the leaves of the gazette just brought by the mail-boy, he observed his own name. He had obtained a conditional pardon!

He was free, but now had to feed himself as the roving bands of police, one of which he led, were disbanded in the spring of 1831 and he was left without employment. He received a grant of 100 acres of land, but with a touch of his old extravagance, he 'sold it almost immediately' and probably gambled away the proceeds.

As a convict, Jorgensen was fearless and desperate; as a free man he could appreciate the value of life: 'Prior to my receiving a pardon I had fearlessly plunged into rapid rivers, up to the armpits, with a knapsack on my back, containing a weight of 60 lbs. to 70 lbs.'

He wrote that one day after his pardon, at George Espie's farm where he had often crossed the river during floods, 'I would not venture to cross. Mr Espie expressed some surprise at my backwardness, as he had formerly seen me cross without any apprehension. I replied, "Yes, Mr Espie, I was then a prisoner, and life of little matter; but now that I am free, I must take more care of myself."'

In January 1831 Jorgensen, then 50, married a 30-year-old illiterate Irish convict, Norah Corbett. Both he and his wife were granted full pardons in 1835.

The month after he got his pardon, he took up his abode in Hobart Town; however, he was 'sadly put to it to make both ends meet'. He and his wife took charge of a dairy farm but, as Jorgensen knew nothing about farming, and confounded seedtime with harvest, the pair were speedily discharged.

He then wrote 'a tolerably large pamphlet on the Funding System', which brought him in more than 100 guineas, which was soon spent and he was again destitute. Then a letter from the Danish envoy in London to Lord Glenelg was passed on to

Colonel Arthur, informing him that the 'mother of J. Jorgensen, a prisoner of the Crown' was dead, and that he had come into a comfortable little fortune.

Norah died in July 1840, and Jorgensen on 20 January 1841 in the Colonial Hospital of 'inflammation of the lungs'.

Two men who knew Jorgensen well were William Hooker, who said his 'talents were of the *highest order*: but for his character, moral and religious, it was always of the lowest order', and Thomas Anstey, police-magistrate of the Oatlands district, who said Jorgensen was his own worst enemy but added: 'He acted successively as my assistant-clerk, constable of the field-police, leader of several roving bands in quest of the aborigines, and one of the directors of the Oatland volunteers, in the levy en masse against the aborigines. In all those capacities he discharged honestly and fearlessly the arduous duties which were entrusted to him.'

Writing of the Icelandic revolution Jorgensen revealed himself in a rare moment of truth: 'I . . . fully determined to seize the first opportunity to strike some blow to be spoken of . . . It was not love of liberty . . . which influenced me on this occasion . . . I have in the course of my life been under the malignant influence of other passions.'

Apart from his writings Jorgensen's explorations in 1826–27 have been considered as the most permanent contributions of his Australian years.

Jorgensen never called himself 'King of Iceland', though he certainly thought of himself as the island's ruler and head of government.

Icelanders use the term 'Dog Days King' when referring to Jorgensen in their history, as his nine-week reign coincided with the period when Sirius, the Dog Star, is visible in the heavens over Iceland.

Yes, it's true, a man who gambled away a few small fortunes, sold his landlady's bedroom furniture and was transported to Van Diemen's Land where he explored the uncharted wilderness, rounded up bushrangers and couldn't manage a dairy farm, was once the 'King of Iceland'.

THE PRINCES WHO SAW A GHOST

In 1881 not one but *two* royal princes graced our continent with their presence. They were the two grandsons of Queen Victoria, Prince Albert Victor and Prince George, who were the two eldest sons of Edward, Prince of Wales.

Prince Albert Victor was born in January 1864 and his brother, George, on June 3 1865, giving us the date for the 'King's Birthday' (or 'Queen's Birthday') official holiday, which is celebrated to the present day.

The two boys joined the navy in 1877 at the ages of thirteen and eleven and, in 1879, the royal family assented to a government idea that a special squadron be formed to cruise the world and visit the far-flung ports of the British Empire—to showcase both the princes and the new-style ships of the navy.

It was a massive public relations flag-waving expedition, led by the fastest warship of the day, HMS *Inconstant*, a fully rigged ironclad steamship of almost 6000 tons.

The princes were assigned to HMS *Bacchante* as cadets and later qualified as midshipmen. They were given a special cabin and took along a tutor, John Dalton, who was assigned as a chaplain to the navy for the three-year duration of the voyage. Reverend Dalton also edited and amended the journals kept by the princes and made their two journals into one narrative, which was published in 1886 as *The Cruise of Her Majesty's Ship Bacchante*.

It is probable that most of the journal was written by the younger prince, who appears to have been more intellectually gifted and dedicated to work than his older brother. Dalton may also have heavily edited and improved the writings.

Albert Victor was born prematurely and was prone to seizures. Dalton wrote that his mind was 'abnormally dormant' and he needed his younger brother's 'company to induce him to work at all'.

The man given the task of preparing Albert Victor for university, the poet James Stephen, commented, 'I do not think he can possibly derive much benefit from attending lectures at Cambridge . . . He hardly knows the meaning of the words *to read*.' The prince's elderly relatives appear to have agreed. The Duke of Cambridge called him 'an inveterate and incurable dawdler' and Princess Augusta of Cambridge referred to him as '*si peu de chose*' (a little nothing).

Albert Victor eventually joined the Hussars after spending a brief time at both Trinity College Cambridge and Heidelberg University in Germany. He was excused from exams and Cambridge gave him an honorary degree in 1888.

In his brief adult life Albert Victor was rumoured to be bisexual and sexually obsessive and was at one time apparently treated for gonorrhea. One of the more absurd theories about him was that he was Jack The Ripper.

It is fanciful, of course, to suggest that three years spent living on a vessel named after the licentious female followers of Bacchus, god of sexual abandon and drinking, perhaps influenced the prince psychologically, although there is no evidence that he was in any way alcoholic.

He never married, although he unsuccessfully courted several princesses and offered to renounce his right to the throne to marry Princess Helene of Orleans, who was Catholic and with whom he was infatuated. Her father refused to let her convert to the Church of England and the affair ended. He was involved with two chorus girls, Lydia Miller who committed suicide by drinking acid, and Maude Richardson who was apparently 'bought off' by the royal family for £200. He was eventually engaged to the German Princess Mary of Teck, but he died before the wedding and she married his brother George instead and became Queen Mary.

But all that was years ahead when the idea of the three-year cruise was proposed in 1879. At first Queen Victoria was not keen on sending her two grandsons to sea and was fearful that the *Bacchante* might not be a safe enough vessel to convey them around the world for three years. So the admiralty sent *Bacchante* to sea during a gale to prove she was sturdy enough to weather storms.

As an extra precaution a squadron of naval vessels accompanied the *Bacchante* and *Inconstant*. These ships changed over the course of the three years but included HMS *Topaz, Diamond, Tourmaline, Carysfort* and *Cleopatra*.

Bacchante was an ironclad, fully square-rigged, screw-propelled corvette of 4070 tons. She was armed with fourteen 7-inch muzzle-loading rifle guns, machine guns and two 64-pound torpedo carriages.

The crew of the *Bacchante* is listed fully in the princes' journal and consisted of:

Officers 39
Petty Officers 55
Seamen, Stokers, Carpenters, Servants 208
Boys 36
Marines 49
Complement 387
Supernumeraries allowed 63
Total 450

All these were accommodated for three years in a vessel whose 'extreme length over all was 307 feet (between perpendiculars 280 feet), her extreme breadth 45 feet, depth of hold 15 feet 7 inches'.

One assumes that the supernumeraries were mostly there to look after the princes' needs.

Having said that, the two boys were spared nothing as far as work on board and their midshipman education was concerned. They also had to learn every detail of the ship and each port of call and record it all in a journal they wrote up every evening.

The *Bacchante* even had its own concert group, which performed to raise money for a sailors' charity while the ship was in port:

> The 'Snowdrop Minstrels' (the Bacchante's negro troupe) gave an entertainment at the courthouse this evening, on behalf of the Seamen and Marines' Orphans' Home at Portsmouth, at which they got £18.

Whether the 'Snowdrop Minstrels' were black crew members or a 'blackface' group of white sailors, I have no idea!

After visiting South Africa, the squadron set sail for Australia and were within sight of land on 12 May 1881 when a heavy storm developed and the squadron was scattered and *Bacchante* was lost from sight. The squadron searched for three days before *Bacchante* was sighted. She had broken her rudder and become helpless in the storm.

One of the princes (we can never tell which one was writing which part of the edited journal) wrote:

> At 10.30 P.M. the fore topmast staysail split, and ten minutes afterwards the ship broached to.
>
> ... It was now one of the most magnificent sights we ever gazed on, though we never wish to be in similar circumstances or to see quite the like again.
>
> The moon above was breaking in full glory every few minutes through the densest and blackest storm clouds, which were here and there riven by the blast; the sea beneath was literally one mass of white foam boiling and hissing beneath the gale. For a few seconds, when the Bacchante first broached to, it was doubtful what would happen, but no one had time to think of the peril we were in, for at once the old ship came to the wind and lay-to of her own accord. Having gone into the cabin under the poop just before she broached to, experienced a curious sensation of grinding beneath the screw-well and counter and by the rudder chains. It might be compared to the somewhat similar sensation felt when a boat's bottom touches rock or sand and grinds over them, and

bumps for a few seconds. We knew, of course, it could not be thus with us, but suspected it was caused by the wrench the rudder then suffered. Owing to the strain there had been on the upper deck wheel (which had during the day several times nearly taken charge, in spite of the dozen men that manned it), the main deck steering gear had also been connected that evening, and was being used at the time of the accident, in addition to the upper deck gear.

As the ship refused to pay off, there was nothing for it but to let her remain, as she was, lying-to. It was then conjectured that something had happened to the rudder, as with the helm put hard a starboard no appreciable difference was observed. (It was not, however, till the next morning that we realised our position of being practically rudderless on the open sea, all the other ships of the squadron having gone right away out of sight since yesterday evening.)

The gale continued, and there was of course still a very heavy sea, but she proved herself a good sea boat, and shipped, comparatively, but little water. The lower deck was, however, all afloat through the sea washing up through the scuppers, and they had one or two heavy sprays down the hatches into the ward-room, but nothing more to speak of.

. . . At 7 A.M., as the current was drifting us helplessly further south and further away from Australia, we furled sails and again tried to get her off the wind, but with no effect whatever. By this time, it being daylight, it was discovered, by looking over the stern, as the ship pitched, that the rudder was amidships, whilst the tiller in the captain's cabin was hard a starboard. This showed us that the rudder head had been twisted about 22°.

The journal goes on to explain how they managed to improvise a clumsy steering method and stay afloat through the gale until finally coming safely to port at Albany on 16 May. No doubt their formidable grandma, Queen Victoria, would not have been 'amused' had the *Bacchante* not survived the gale and the damage—especially after her misgivings about the voyage and the ship's seaworthiness when the venture was proposed.

The two young princes stayed in Albany for three weeks and then travelled to Adelaide on the steamer *Cathay* and, after several weeks in Adelaide, travelled overland along the Coorong and Murray River by coach, horse and train via Ballarat to Melbourne, where they again caught up with the 'detached squadron'. The two teenagers hunted kangaroos, saw a football game, were given cockatoos as pets, inspected Ned Kelly's armour and had quite a jolly time in the Australian colonies.

It was on the voyage from Melbourne to Sydney that the princes encountered the ghostly spectre of the *Flying Dutchman*. The princes were now travelling on the squadron's flagship, HMS *Inconstant,* commanded by Admiral Sir Richard Meade, 4th Earl of Clanwilliam.

The legend of the *Flying Dutchman* came into nautical folklore quite late, and it is not mentioned until the 18th century. The story goes that a blaspheming Dutch captain sailed into the teeth of a monstrous gale attempting to round the Cape of Good Hope and refused to listen to pleas from crew and passengers to turn back, swearing he would round the cape if it took all eternity.

When the crew threatened to mutiny, he swore an oath defying them and the Almighty to stop him, then he shot the leader of the mutineers and a ghostly figure appeared and announced that he would henceforth sail the seas and never return to port.

The ship is sometimes seen as a ghostly spectre, other times as a fireship and occasionally as a very real vessel. There are reports of the ship trying to pass mail to other ships and appearing to ram vessels in bad weather and then suddenly disappearing.

Detailed accounts of encounters with the ghost ship have been given by many ships, including a British naval vessel in 1835 and, more recently, a German U-Boat crew in World War II. In 1939, dozens of swimmers at Glencairn Beach, South Africa, saw the ship pass close to shore and all, independently, later described what was obviously an 18th century Dutch East Indiaman, although none of the witnesses knew what they were describing. In 1942 four separate independent witnesses described the same vessel entering Table Bay, Cape Town. In both of these cases, it suddenly disappeared.

One of the best accounts of the legend is found in the 1795 publication, *A Voyage To Botany Bay*, the supposed journals of George Barrington, the famous jewel thief and society dandy who was transported to Sydney Cove as a convict in 1791. These publications were most likely written by greedy journalists in London using other legitimate accounts of the new colony and whatever else they could think up—and using Barrington's name and notoriety to sell books. But the explanation is interesting. Here it is:

> I had often heard of the superstition of sailors respecting apparitions and doom, but had never given much credit to the report; it seems that some years since a Dutch man-o-war was lost off the Cape of Good Hope and every soul on board perished; her consort weathered the gale, and arrived soon after at the Cape. Having refitted, and returning to Europe, they were assailed by a violent tempest nearly in the same latitude. In the night watch some of the people saw, or imagined they saw, a vessel standing for them under a press of sail, as though she would run them down: one in particular affirmed it was the ship that had foundered in the former gale, and that it must certainly be her, or the apparition of her; but on its clearing up, the object, a dark thick cloud, disappeared. Nothing could do away the idea of this phenomenon on the minds of the sailors; and, on their relating the circumstances when they arrived in port, the story spread like wild-fire, and the supposed phantom was called the Flying Dutchman. From the Dutch the English seamen got the infatuation, and there are very few Indiamen, but what has some one on board, who pretends to have seen the apparition.

All we can say is that, in 1881, the legend was believed by many people, especially sailors. Certainly the thirteen witnesses on the *Bacchante*—and others on *Tourmaline* and *Cleopatra*—who saw the *Flying Dutchman* around 4 a.m. on 11 July 1881, had no doubt about what they saw. Here is the account direct from the princes' journal:

July 11th. At 4 A.M. the Flying Dutchman crossed our bows. A strange red light as of a phantom ship all aglow, in the midst of which light the masts, spars, and sails of a brig 200 yards distant stood out in strong relief as she came up on the port bow. The look-out man on the forecastle reported her as close on the port bow, where also the officer of the watch from the bridge clearly saw her, as did also the quarterdeck midshipman, who was sent forward at once to the forecastle; but on arriving there no vestige nor any sign whatever of any material ship was to be seen either near or right away to the horizon, the night being clear and the sea calm. Thirteen persons altogether saw her, but whether it was Van Diemen or the Flying Dutchman or who else must remain unknown.

The princes' journal then quotes in German a stanza of verse about the legend. The family of Queen Victoria all spoke fluent German, in fact it was the language always used by the queen and her family in private. The account continues:

The Tourmaline and Cleopatra, who were sailing on our starboard bow, flashed to ask whether we had seen the strange red light. At 6.15 A.M. observed land to the north-east. At 10.45 A.M. the ordinary seaman who had this morning reported the Flying Dutchman fell from the fore topmast crosstrees onto the topgallant forecastle and was smashed to atoms. At 4.15 P.M. after quarters we hove to with the headyards aback, and he was buried in the sea. He was a smart royal yardman, and one of the most promising young hands in the ship, and every one feels quite sad at his loss.

There is no doubt the future king believed the legend and believed that he and others saw the *Flying Dutchman* that night. Admiral Meade then became ill in Sydney and the princes' journal adds that this, also, was part of the curse of seeing the ghost ship:

At the next port we came to the Admiral also was smitten down.

The next sentence in the journal shows us, however, that the young royal sailors had more important things to consider that day:

The midshipmen's half-yearly examination began today with the Algebra paper.

Admiral Meade soon recovered from the curse of the *Flying Dutchman* and lived on to became Admiral of the Fleet in 1896.

Perhaps the curse of the *Flying Dutchman* had some effect on Prince Albert Victor. He led a brief and rather unspectacular life characterised by little achievement and suffered an early demise. However, the meeting with the ghostly harbinger of doom doesn't seem to have harmed his brother, the future King George V, much at all.

THE NAZI 'DIGGER' PRINCE

If the first royal tour, by Prince Alfred in 1867–68, suffered from a lack of planning, the fourth royal visit, by Edward, Prince of Wales, in 1920, appears to have suffered from an obsessively enthusiastic and bureaucratic amount of 'over-planning'.

Edward VIII was born on 23 June 1894. The prince served with the Commonwealth Forces in World War I and his visit was one of the most popular of all royal visits to Australia. Travelling on the battlecruiser HMS *Renown*, which served as the 'royal yacht' for the duration, he visited not only Australia but also Barbados, California, Honolulu, Fiji, New Zealand, Samoa, Acapulco, the West Indies and Bermuda.

Between late May and August 1920, Edward visited 110 cities and towns in all states of Australia. The year before he had made a similar tour to Canada. Edward's father, King George V, who had himself made two visits to Australia as a prince, saw these tours as an opportunity for his heir apparent to meet with and understand his subjects in the various countries of the British Empire.

There is also evidence that the king was keen to remove his son from the temptations of an idle life in England. Edward was a notorious womaniser and had a penchant for married women in particular. He was also rumoured to be bisexual and had a habit of making friends among the more disreputable coteries of fashionable high society.

As we shall see later, Edward was never the most discreet and diplomatic of royal personages in his private life and conversations.

The visits were also regarded a kind of 'royal thank you' for the loyalty and sacrifice given by the member countries of the British Empire in the war. Meeting with ex-servicemen of WWI was certainly a large part of the prince's official duties on tour, and the tours were also designed as jingoistic exercises to maintain loyalty to Britain throughout the empire.

Events called 'democratic levees' were held in a number of cities he visited at which people were allowed to file past the prince, who stood and raised his hat as the procession went by.

The *Sydney Morning Herald* reported on one such event held at the Sydney Town Hall on 18 June 1920:

> It was the meeting between the prince and the great democracy. For hours the people filed past His Royal Highness. Many of them waited for hours in the queue for the opportunity. The queue, in which the people stood about twelve deep, was the longest ever seen in Sydney . . . The Prince stood for an hour on the dais in the Town Hall, while the people passed at an average rate estimated by the Town Hall Clerk (Mr Nesbitt) at 170 per minute . . . It is estimated that about 50 000 walked past the Prince and that about 100 000 people were in the streets outside the Hall.
>
> It was almost impossible for the Prince to notice people individually, and some of the crowd who were not as tall as those in front had difficulty in seeing the Prince at all.
>
> The only definite thing that one can say about the people who passed before His Royal Highness is that they were representative of the whole community—clergy, accountants, journalists and professional men of all descriptions, manual workers, and women and children filed passed.
>
> That the Prince should have gone through the ordeal unaffected was not to be expected. He was raising his hat continually for nearly two and a half hours.

Edward's personal recollections of the tour were certainly not particularly happy or gracious ones. He resented being poked and prodded while on his Canadian tour and had hated the streamers and confetti. Entries in his staff diary, published later in his autobi-ography, *A King's Story: The Memoirs of HRH the Duke of Windsor*, show that he was even less happy with the behaviour of his subjects while in Australia:

> In that Dominion even a motor car was no sure protection against the hearty greetings of my father's subjects. The unofficial diary kept by my staff (the diary not intended for perusal by my father) contains the following entry recorded in Melbourne:
>
> 'Confetti is appearing in great and unpleasant quantities, and the touching mania has started, only owing to the heartening disposition of the Australians the touches are more like blows and HRH arrived half blinded and black and blue.'

While it is easy to sympathise with members of the royal family who have to endure endless public ordeals, and it is true that the prince's tour of 1920 was ridiculously overburdened with official engagements and public appearances—there were 337 in Western Australia alone!—Edward's later reminiscences do appear to give him the air of one who would much rather have avoided his subjects altogether:

> The 'touching mania', one of the most remarkable phenomena connected with my travels, took the form of a mass impulse to prod some part of the Prince of Wales. Whenever I entered a crowd, it closed around me like an octopus. I can still hear the shrill, excited cry, 'I touched him!' If I were out of reach, then a blow to my head with a folded newspaper appeared to satisfy the impulse.

It was during the Western Australian leg of the prince's tour, in July 1920, that an unplanned event took place which at least added an air of excitement, spontaneity and even humour to the whole dreary affair. The prince and his entourage were involved in a train wreck.

On 11 July 1920 the *Sunday Times* Perth Special Correspondent

John Sandes reported, in a delightfully tongue-in-cheek fashion, that:

> The elaborate and detailed 'Official Programme', covering the engagements of our Royal visitor, has so far been almost faithfully adhered to. In this respect the State Reception Committee can be congratulated. The itinerary has been very closely followed, with one notable exception.

The 'notable exception' was the train wreck in which both the royal carriage and the official carriage departed from the rails and fell over on their sides. The *Sunday Times* correspondent, doing his best to extract as much farce and humour from the situation as was probably allowable at the time, reported it as follows:

> On Monday, July 5, from 4.30 to 5.30 p.m., the Royal train, according to schedule, was to 'stop in a quiet locality for one hour's exercise'.
>
> This ramble in the bush was to have eventuated shortly after leaving Bridgetown en route to Bunbury. It did not occur.
>
> Yet a most sensational accident to the Royal train, providentially unattended by any serious consequences, provided a remarkable variation for the wayside detail quoted.
>
> The derailment and capsize of the Royal and Ministerial parties' coaches 'in a quiet locality', about 10 miles south of Bridgetown, between Wilgarrup and Manjimup, accorded to many of those travelling the 'special' exercise of a nature wholly unexpected . . . comprising the rescue from overturned coaches of the Prince of Wales, his personal staff, the Premier of the State and two members of his Ministry, the Minister for Defence and General Sir Talbot Hobbs.

The reporter, who no doubt accompanied the royal party for the entire tour of duty in Western Australia, shows a deal of sympathy for what he sees as the prince's 'ordeal'—not the train wreck, but the actual tour itself!

The 337 items on the programme—many of them calculated to cause the Prince a nightmare—must be rigidly enforced. Just how the strain tells on the young Heir Apparent may be gathered from his delightfully humorous quip, after emerging from the Royal coach.

The quip referred to does indeed show that, while Edward VIII may be remembered by most of us as a loathsome, unctuous and thoroughly unlikeable person, he was not devoid of a sense of humour.

The heir to the throne emerged from the upturned carriage relatively unscathed. He was holding some official papers in one hand and his silver cocktail shaker in the other and he commented to his companion Lord Mountbatten and all others within earshot, 'At last, we have done something that is not in the programme.'

The *Sunday Times* went on to record that the prince:

. . . even seemed to enjoy a degree of satisfaction from the untoward happening . . . He joked with those around him, and walked along the then torn up railway track in a light-hearted manner.

We can only imagine the attitude of Edward and his young cousin Lord Mountbatten toward the situation in which they found themselves. Mountbatten perched himself on top of the overturned carriage, surveyed the wreckage and reportedly commented, 'That's the best thing I've ever been in.'

The *Sunday Times* reported:

After the accident whisky was forthcoming for those who felt nervewracked. The amber fluid was in great demand.

The circumstances of the actual derailment read more like an episode from some clichéd backwoods *Dad and Dave* story than a chapter from a dignified royal tour:

A cow on the line had caused the engine drivers of the two locomotives to bring the train to a standstill only a few minutes previously, and it was only travelling about twelve miles an hour. Barring a few jolts experienced by those in the foremost carriages there had been nothing to indicate that anything very serious had happened.

Commissioner Pope and his officials, when they saw the two cars in the rear lying on their side, were momentarily awed and dazed by the realisation of what had transpired. Orderlies and attendants with others soon climbed up on the overturned coaches, and when it was ascertained that the Prince and his staff, and also those in the Ministerial car, were safe and none seriously injured in either coach there were feelings of intense relief . . .

Strangely enough the only one of the Prince's staff likely to carry any permanent mark on his body as the result of the accident is Surgeon Commander Newport, physician to the Prince, who suffered an ugly gash on one knee, necessitating stitches being inserted when he reached Bunbury.

It was this event, more than any other, which led to Edward being given the nickname 'The Digger Prince' by the press and he was generally thought to be a 'good sport' by his adoring Australian subjects. Hence the tour was considered to be a wonderful success as a public relations exercise for the British royal family and the empire.

The train trip south from Perth to Pemberton and Bunbury seems to have provided opportunities for members of the official party and the media in attendance to have a few good laughs at the locals' expense. It was not only the farcical nature of the train wreck itself that gave rise to amusement.

John Sandes' account of the journey begins like this:

When the train bearing H.R.H. steamed out of Perth station on Sunday night last there was a large gathering of citizens to cheer him off. Rain set in with the departure of the Royal train, and with one or two brief intervals the 44-hours' trip was marked by heavy rain and hailstorms.

Along the route on Sunday night small groups of enthusiastic occupants of the rural areas congregated at the various stations and sidings, adding their quota by cheers as an expression of goodwill to the Prince and loyalty to the British Throne.

At one or two places, where the train pulled up for a minute or two, His Royal Highness either conversed, through the window of the Royal car with the assembled countryfolk or stepped out on to the railway platform and passed a few words with the people. In all these little railside gatherings the voices of children pre-dominated in the cheers that were heard as the train passed on.

The whole trip was undertaken in pouring rain and the royal party had to endure several local welcomes as well as such unforgettable experiences as watching the felling of a giant tree and 'the cutting up of a huge karri log, and the final process of running out the desired lengths and widths of pieces and planking'.

The prince was, naturally, prevailed upon to participate in various activities and made an effort to appear willing:

> A log-chopping contest was witnessed on returning to Pemberton. The Prince had a bet, but did not pick the winner. Being invited to try his hand on a log, H.R.H. essayed to make chips fly, but lost his balance on the wet and slippery timber, and sustained a fall, which made him limp for a few minutes when walking back to the train.

The *Sunday Times* regular columnist 'Norwood' found a number of humorous angles to the train trip. He had it on good authority that his colleague's account of the felling of the giant tree was written from second-hand accounts as:

> Special Correspondent John Sandes took no risks at the tree-felling exhibition. He only felt safe when he was nearly out of sight of the proceedings.

Norwood also found a reason to be thankful that the Premier of Western Australia, Sir James 'Jim' Mitchell, who had been trapped in the fallen train carriage, was rather famously overweight:

> Premier Mitchell's 'portly' frame served him in good stead when being assisted through a corridor window in the Ministerial car. It prevented him falling back again.

The weekly columnist also gives us an insight into some of the private amusements enjoyed by the royal party, perhaps told to him in confidence by his colleague John Sandes. He spilled the beans by letting the world know that the children at Pinjarra could not keep time with the music when singing their patriotic tribute to the prince, and this amused Admiral Halsey, the prince's equerry, so much that he 'sported a super-abundant smile and tried to keep the instrumentalists in time with the young vocalists'.

The singing of 'God Bless the Prince of Wales', according to Norwood, 'was well meant' but was so out of time that it 'resembled a jazz band on the razzle'.

The opinion of the cynical pressmen regarding the damp and dispiriting display put on by the weather and the local people evidently caused one of the travelling reporters to remark, as the train left town, 'Pemberton for the Pembertonians'.

Although Edward kept his disparaging comments about Australia 'in house' at the time, he certainly didn't spare the feelings of his Aussie hosts in later years, when the burden of being king had been lifted from his shoulders. Indeed he paints a picture of himself and his staff as very hard done by, martyrs to the dreadful burden of privilege:

> My staff and I bore stoically our share of knocks and bruises, which we came to regard as part of our daily round. The poor Admiral's feet were continually being trodden on [in the] melee. The end of many a hard day found him limping around his room or soaking his crushed extremities in a hot bath.

On the subject of the planned capital, Canberra, he found some cause for faint praise of the Aussie spirit of optimism, but his superior, sneering attitude soon took over:

The boundless faith of Australians in their own destiny was perhaps most vividly exemplified for me by their enterprise in creating a remote backcountry brand-new federal capital. When I was there nothing was yet to be seen save a few tin shanties, power stations and numerous cornerstones . . . to which I contributed one exactly in the city's centre.

It is interesting to compare the prince's smarmy official pronouncements about Australia in his farewell to Australian children, to his more unreserved comments in later life. Here is his official farewell to the children of Australia in 1920:

Girls and boys

My wonderful first visit to Australia is nearly over and I want to tell you before I sail how sorry I am to be going and to give you all my best wishes . . .

I should like you all to remember my first visit, which I have enjoyed so much myself, and so I have asked that as a special favour to me you may have an extra week's holiday some time this year.

Australia is a magnificent country and I think you very fortunate to have it for your own. Make up your minds to serve Australia well, for the future of every country depends before all things on the spirit of its girls and boys.

Once the need for diplomacy and a hint of common decency and respect for another culture were removed from Edward's life, however, he showed his true colours.

When told that the parliament of Australia would not accept his solution that he might remain king and enter into a 'morganic' type of marriage with Wallis Simpson, that restricted her from ever becoming queen, he commented that there were 'not many people in Australia and their opinion did not matter'.

He dismissed the Indigenous people of Australia and their 60,000-year-old culture by saying:

> They are the most revolting form of living creatures I've ever seen! They are the lowest known form of human beings and are the nearest thing to monkeys.

Still, we should not forget that we are dealing with a man who was so vain he insisted that a tradition dating back to Charles II be broken for his personal satisfaction.

It was the custom on English coins that the head of each new monarch should face the opposite way to his or her predecessor. Edward's head was supposed to face right, but he insisted that this tradition should be disregarded in his case—he wanted his head to face left on the coinage of Britain, in order to show what he considered a better profile and the part in his hair.

Luckily for tradition, no such coins were minted or issued, though the masters were made with his head facing left. The mint decided to honour the custom and, as no coins were ever issued in Edward's reign, they acted as if his head had faced right and placed his brother's head facing left, then later Elizabeth II's facing right.

On a far more serious note, we should also not forget that Edward admired and sent birthday cards to Hitler and told his old friend the Spanish diplomat Don Javier Bermejillo, in June 1940, that he blamed 'the Jews, the Reds and the Foreign Office for the war' and suggested that 'if one bombed England effectively this could bring peace'.

Bermejillo, who believed that 'the Duke of Windsor seemed very much to hope that this would occur', passed a report of the conversation on to General Franco and it was then passed on to the Germans, who began bombing Britain on 10 July 1940.

While many Australians still believe we should respect the symbolic authority of the monarchy and the royal family, perhaps we should be more judicious about which of its members we choose to lionise and respect.

The whole melodramatic, romantic nonsense of the abdication is, perhaps, best summed up in a limerick of the day, which puts all the twaddle and rigmarole into perspective:

There once was a monarch named Ed,
Who took Mrs Simpson to bed.
As they bounced up and down
He said, 'Bugger the crown,
Give the thing to my brother, instead.'

Part Three
LEST WE FORGET

Of all the fields of human endeavour, there is, perhaps, none that produces more truly strange and unbelievable stories than war.

Although rivalry, competition and conflict are obviously part of human nature, there is still something quite puzzling about what men will do to one another when given the opportunity to do it for a reason, be it nationalism, religion, revenge, commercial gain or supposed justice.

There are many unbelievable stories from that period of time in Australian history when Britain invaded and settled this continent and established the colonies that eventually combined to form the nation we know today.

Some of the saddest and most unbelievable of these stories concern the conflict between the European settlers and the Indigenous inhabitants of the continent, but those stories are not told in this collection as I find them mostly too poignant and upsetting to be 'unbelievable' in the sense of 'interesting and entertaining'.

I have, instead, restricted myself to telling and retelling some stories from the major conflicts in which Australia has been involved since European settlement. Some of the stories concern things that Australians 'know' but don't really know much about. I have tried to explain why the Battles of Villers-Bretonneux were such amazing events for our nation, and why the Battle of the Coral Sea was one of the strangest ever fought.

Events like the Battle of Brisbane and the Cowra breakout

shocked and puzzled Australians when they occurred, and it is fascinating to look at them in retrospect and attempt to see what it was about them that seemed so inexplicable. I certainly found it interesting and enlightening to research these events and attempt to explain why they occurred and why they were so puzzling.

One of my favourite characters from our colonial past is the totally unlikeable Colonel Henry Despard, who did his best to lose the Maori Wars and then precipitated the mutiny of the 99th Regiment in Sydney.

Seen with the benefit of hindsight, and in the light of a different era, he comes to us from the pages of history as a kind of archetypal British buffoon, whose place in Australian colonial military history was established by two major errors of judgement.

Despard was born in 1784 and saw active service in several campaigns in India between 1808 and 1818. He then spent twenty years as a staff officer, inspecting regiments until 1842, when he took command of the 99th Regiment of Foot, stationed in Sydney.

On 1 June 1845 Despard and two companies of his regiment arrived in Auckland and he took command of all British troops in New Zealand, in a battle against the Maoris led by Chief Hone Heke.

With a force of 600 men, the largest British force ever seen in New Zealand, Despard laid siege to Ohaeawai, the first Maori stockade, or *pa*, designed to resist artillery fire. Its 100-strong garrison was protected by a complex of bunkers and trenches. Although no breach had been made in the stockade, Despard lined his troops up shoulder to shoulder and marched them at the impenetrable defences. More than 120 men were killed or wounded due to Despard's insistence on using tactics that had been out of date since the Napoleonic wars.

Despard then attempted to negotiate a peaceful settlement but his negotiating skills were on a par with his military tactics. When Maori chief Waaka Nene offered his services to help the British, Despard replied that 'when he required the assistance of savages, he would ask for it'.

In spite of having 1300 British troops, several hundred Maori warriors and substantial artillery support, Despard returned to New South Wales having achieved not one victory.

Not long after his miserable performance in the Maori Wars, Colonel Henry Despard returned to Sydney where he was the catalyst for the infamous mutiny of the 99th Regiment.

The mutiny was a protest against Despard's decision to discontinue the daily allowance of grog normally supplied to troops on foreign service and his attempts to separate the troops from the townspeople. Despard was of the opinion that the troops might have to be used against the unruly part-convict population, and the 'foreign service' grog ration encouraged the troops to be far too similar to the people they were there to control.

Despard also gave an order that prohibited citizens from walking on any part of the grass-covered area in front of the barracks when listening to the band play. This had been the town's chief entertainment for many years, but Despard thought it unmilitary and likely to lead to dangerous fraternising.

The 99th Regiment locked themselves in the George's Square Barracks in protest and 'forgot their obligations to their Queen and country,' by refusing to obey the lawful commands of their Officers, or to perform any further duty'.

In other words, they went on strike, setting a precedent for what would later become a proud Aussie tradition.

A dispatch was sent to Colonel Bloomfield of the 11th Regiment in Hobart directing him to proceed to Sydney without delay, with as many men as could be spared, to disarm the mutineers of the 99th Regiment. The barque *Tasmania* was chartered and 400 men and officers embarked for Sydney. Three days later they were in sight of Sydney Heads but an offshore gale kept the vessel from entering the harbour for seven days.

The 99th Regiment somehow found out that a vessel full of troops was outside of Sydney Heads and offered to return to duty. The 11th Regiment arrived in Sydney on 8 January 1846 and marched four deep, with fixed bayonets, to the barracks' main gate.

They entered the Barrack Square to a most hearty welcome and cheers from the 99th Regiment and their women and children together with as many citizens as could fit into the barrack grounds.

Thus ended the mutiny of the 99th Regiment. The grog ration was restored to the regiment, and Sydney's citizens were again allowed to walk on the grass in front of Barrack Square and listen to the band play on Thursday afternoons.

And Colonel Henry Despard?

Well, he returned to England and was given a knighthood.

A decade later, a far more serious and significant conflict occurred in Ballarat in Victoria, and became the colonies' most famous: the Eureka Stockade.

Between 1851 and 1860, an estimated 300,000 people came to the Australian colonies from England and Wales, another 100,000 from Scotland and 84,000 from Ireland. It was, of course, gold that brought many of them, along with others from Germany, Italy and North America, and about two-thirds of the new arrivals headed to the colony of Victoria.

In an attempt to maintain some level of bureaucratic control over this unruly population, the British administration came up with the idea of miners' licences and in June 1854 the system of twice-weekly licence checks was introduced.

The trigger for the Eureka rebellion was the acquittal of publican James Bentley for his role in the death of a drunken miner. Bentley was a friend of the magistrate, and the diggers of Ballarat, sick of privilege and corruption and wanting to see justice done, burnt down Bentley's hotel.

On 11 November 1854, 10,000 diggers met to demand the release of the three diggers who had been arrested for the burning of the pub. At the same time, they decided to demand the abolition of the licences, as well as the right to vote for all males in the colony. At another meeting on 29 November, the diggers displayed the Eureka Flag and decided to publicly burn their mining licences.

Next day the diggers marched to the Eureka diggings and constructed the famous stockade.

Early on Sunday 3 December, troops attacked the stockade and, within twenty minutes, 22 miners and five soldiers were dead. Thirteen men stood trial, but all were acquitted and, after a 'Gold Fields Commission' was held, all of the diggers' demands were met.

The story of the Eureka Stockade is a truly remarkable episode in our colonial history. It is a story of 'people power' and the triumph of democracy over privilege and bureaucracy. It is also an early example of the success of multiculturalism, unless, of course, you were Chinese.

The 'vote for all males in the colony' was certainly not intended to be extended to include the Chinese, who were seen as temporary, unwanted aliens by the vast majority of Australians at the time. In 1855 the Colony of Victoria passed Australia's first immigration act, to restrict the number of Chinese in the colony. A tax was charged for bringing Chinese into port and ships then off-loaded their human cargo in Adelaide to avoid paying the tax. The Chinese then walked overland to the goldfields.

The worst violence against Chinese miners occurred later in New South Wales. The 'European' diggers' excuse for the racist aggression was that they objected to the 'puddling' methods used by the Chinese when extracting gold—because it wasted water. Six anti-Chinese riots occurred at the Lambing Flat goldfields in 1861 and, on 14 July 1861, around 3000 European diggers attacked about 250 Chinese miners and many were gravely injured, their camp destroyed and all their belongings lost. A small police force attempted to protect the Chinese, who had fled to a nearby property, and a lopsided battle ensued. The official death toll was one miner and two Chinese, but it is likely that 40 Chinese died. After this tragic event the New South Wales Government passed the *Chinese Immigration Restriction and Regulation Act* in 1861, Queensland introduced restrictions in 1877 and Western Australia in 1886. This was the beginning of the infamous 'White Australia Policy'.

Contrary to popular belief, the Australian term of respect and affection 'digger' did not originate on the battlefield. It was a term used to differentiate 'European' miners, who originally dug shafts to mine gold, from the despised Chinese, who 'puddled'—it was always meant to mean 'white man'. Indeed the phrase 'he's a white man' was a term of respect and honour in Aussie parlance until the 20th century and the slogan of the famous and influential *Bulletin* magazine, that most Australian of all publications, was 'Australia for the White Man'.

When it comes to major conflicts involving Australian troops overseas, the first remarkable story that springs to my mind is that of the Battle of Elands River.

It's strange how history changes from generation to generation, as new events become 'famous' and others fade away in the mists of time. Before the landing at Gallipoli on 25 April 1915, the iconic event in military history, well known to all Australians, was the Battle of Elands River. In fact, the famous writer Sir Arthur Conan Doyle, who was a war correspondent during the Boer War, once said: 'When the ballad makers of Australia seek for a subject, let them turn to Elands River.'

Elands River was a staging post and supply depot on a rocky ridge in the Western Transvaal; it contained 1500 horses, oxen and mules, together with 100 wagons and enough supplies to maintain a force of 3000 men for a month.

The Boers, who were fighting a guerilla war, desperately wanted the supplies, which were valued at more than £100,000. On 4 August 1900, Colonel De La Rey's commando force of around 3000 men surrounded and laid siege to the post which was defended by 200 Rhodesian militiamen and 300 Australians from the various colonies, who had never been shot at before.

The Boers had twelve modern artillery pieces, which pounded the post in its exposed position. They also had snipers positioned on three sides of the camp. The defenders had one Maxim gun and one old seven-pound muzzle-loader. Unfortunately, the supplies at Eland River Post did not include ammunition.

More than 2500 shells landed on the post during the first two days of the siege. Most of the 1500 horses, mules and oxen were killed in the horrific bombardment. The one gun the defenders had was old and faulty. Major Tunbridge had to dismantle it for repairs and reassemble it four times during the siege.

On the third day, a force commanded by General Carrington arrived to relieve them but was driven back by the Boers and retreated all the way back to Mafeking. The men defending the post saw them come, and go. Five hundred men were trapped without cover under the blazing sun, with the stench of more than a thousand dead animals in the air. They had no access to water except by night patrol and they had just seen their 'rescuers' retreat.

On 8 August, the Boer commander, De La Rey, sent a messenger under a flag of truce and offered to escort the force to the nearest British post, provided that none of the supplies within the camp were destroyed, 'in recognition of your courage in defence of your camp'. He even offered to let the officers retain their weapons.

Australian officers sent a written reply, which read:

> If De La Rey wants our camp, why does he not come and take it?
> We will be pleased to meet him and his men, and promise them
> a great reception at the end of a toasting fork. Australians will
> never surrender. Australia forever!

Our nation was exactly eight months old at the time. The 'Australians' fighting were actually soldiers from different colonies who had left home before Federation.

When De La Rey sent a second offer of honourable surrender and safe passage, Colonel Hore, in command of the post, replied:

> Even if I wished to surrender to you—and I don't—I am
> commanding Australians who would cut my throat if I accepted
> your terms.

Finally, when a message from De La Rey to Boer Commander De Wet stating that the garrison was still holding out fell into the hands of one of his scouts, Lord Horatio Kitchener himself, who had been leading a huge force of near 20,000 men chasing De Wet, detoured to Elands River and the siege was lifted. Losses were twelve dead and 58 wounded.

Fifteen years later, the Anzacs landed at Gallipoli and the Battle of Elands River faded from the memory of most Australians.

It was on 1 January 1915, four months before the landing at Gallipoli, that the first act of official, international war on Australian soil occurred—at Broken Hill. It was also the first act of international Islamic terrorism to be perpetrated in the nation of Australia.

The enemy, who were two in number, turned out to be a halal butcher and an ice-cream salesman who managed to kill four people and wound seven more, before being killed by a posse of police, army and locals.

The two-man army consisted of Badsha Mohammed Gool, a former camel driver who operated an ice-cream cart, and Mullah Abdullah, the local imam and halal butcher.

Australia was, at that time, officially at war with the nation of Turkey (more correctly the Ottoman Empire), which was one of the Central Powers and, although neither of them was Turkish, the two men fought under a Turkish flag, which they flew proudly from their official military vehicle, Gool's ice-cream cart.

Gool was a member of the Pashtun tribe, from Afghanistan, and Abdullah was from what would today be Pakistan. He had arrived in Broken Hill around 1898 and had also worked as a cameleer before becoming the local mullah whose job included killing and preparing animals according to halal Islamic custom. Several days before the attack, Mullah Abdullah was convicted by the local chief sanitary officer for operating an abattoir without a licence, when he was caught killing sheep at his home.

In the union-controlled town of Broken Hill, the Butchers Trade Union and the local abattoir had a 'union only' employment rule. It was, therefore, impossible for the non-union Abdullah to legally prepare halal meat for the Muslim community.

On New Year's Day each year, the local Manchester Unity Order of Oddfellows held a community picnic at Silverton, 26 kilometres west of Broken Hill.

Due to an odd quirk of history, the rail line which ran from Broken Hill, in New South Wales, to Cockburn, on the South

Australian border, operated on the South Australian narrow 3'6" gauge and was privately owned. All New South Wales railways were standard gauge and had to be owned by the government. To get around this, the company that owned and operated the 58-kilometre line was called the Silverton Tramway Company.

In 1915 the 'picnic train' from Broken Hill to Silverton was crowded with 1200 people in 40 open carriages. Gool and Abdullah hid behind an embankment 3 kilometres from town and ambushed the train with two rifles. Seventeen-year-old Alma Cowie and William Shaw, a sanitary department foreman, were shot dead, and William Shaw's daughter, Lucy, was injured, along with six other people on the train.

The two desperadoes then retreated towards the cameleers' camp where they lived. On the way they killed Alfred Millard who had taken shelter in his hut.

The train pulled into a siding and the police were telephoned and they contacted the local army base. Soon afterwards, the police, local militia and an army unit set out in pursuit.

A 90-minute shoot-out ensued at a place known as Cable Hill. A policeman was wounded before the shooting from the hill became sporadic and misdirected, which led the police to assume, correctly, that Mullah Abdullah was dead and Gool was wounded.

The unfortunate fourth fatality was 69-year-old local man James Craig, who lived 500 metres away and ignored his daughter's warning about chopping wood during a gun battle and was hit by a stray bullet and killed.

At one o'clock the forces of righteous retribution rushed enemy stronghold. One eyewitness stated that Gool stood with his hands raised and a white rag tied to his rifle, but he was shot down and later found to have sixteen bullet wounds. Both bodies were secretly disposed of later that day by the police.

Both men left letters saying that what they did was an act of war for the Ottoman Empire against the British Empire.

Gool had a letter tucked in his belt, which stated that he was a subject of the Ottoman Sultan and ended, 'I must kill you and give my life for my faith, Allāhu Akbar.'

Mullah Abdullah stated in his letter that he was also dying for his faith and in obedience to the sultan's orders, but added a rather poignant and pathetic statement that, 'owing to my grudge against Chief Sanitary Inspector Brosnan it was my intention to kill him first'.

Sadly, however, it seems that Mullah Abdullah shot the wrong sanitary official.

That night a lynch mob tried to march to the 'Afghan camp', but was stopped by the police.

Oddly, after this event there was no further hostility towards the Muslim community in Broken Hill during the war, but the German Club was burnt to the ground by an unruly mob and the firemen who came to fight the blaze had their hoses cut to prevent them putting out the fire. The next day the mining companies in Broken Hill fired all employees who qualified as 'enemy aliens' under the *War Precautions Act* and six Austrians, four Germans and a Turk were ordered out of town by the mob.

War, as we all know, often brings out the best in people. It can also bring out the worst.

PRIVATE LEAK, THE LARRIKIN

On 28 January 1915 a man calling himself John Leak enlisted as a private in the 9th Battalion, 3rd Brigade, 1st Division of the Australian Imperial Force in Rockhampton, Queensland. The 9th Battalion was recruited almost exclusively from Queensland.

His army records, accessible through the National Archives of Australia, show that he was born in Portsmouth, England, in 1892 and came to Australia sometime before the war began. His file shows that his parents were dead and his next of kin was a brother living in Canada. His profession is given as 'Teamster'. In other words, he was a bullock driver. There were still many teams of bullocks carting freight in that part of Queensland in 1915.

Private Leak embarked with the 5th Reinforcements for the 9th Battalion on the transport HMAT *Kyarra A55*, arriving at Gallipoli and joining his unit on 22 June 1915. He served there until the evacuation on 19 December.

After the Gallipoli withdrawal, the battalion returned to Egypt, and was brought back to strength with reinforcements, before sailing for France in March 1916. The battalion disembarked at Marseilles and headed to northern France to engage in the Somme offensive on the Western Front in July.

The Australian divisions, commanded by General Birdwood and flanked by British divisions, moved towards Pozières on 22 July 1916. Pozières, situated on a ridge overlooking the Somme, was a vital objective for the Allies and was taken after four days of savage fighting.

Private Leak survived the fighting at Pozières, but was severely wounded at the Battle of Mouquet Farm one month later on 21 August 1916.

The Battle of Mouquet Farm was fought just one and a half kilometres northwest of Pozières. The purpose of the operation was to extend British control of the strategic ridge that extended from Pozières to the ruined town of Theipval by capturing a relatively small area of farmland.

The Australian divisions that fought in this battle were the 1st, 2nd and 4th—the three that had served at Gallipoli.

During the second week of August, the 4th Division led the attack, gaining a small amount of territory on the fringe of the farm. Because the German artillery maintained constant shelling from their well-entrenched positions within range of the farm, this small gain cost the 4th Division 4649 men.

In the third week of August, the 1st Division took up the attack, replacing the 4th. The 1st Division, depleted by the loss of one-third of its men during the Battle of Pozières a month earlier, made little progress and, in the next week of fighting, lost another 2650 men, killed and wounded. One of the wounded was Private John Leak.

The 2nd Division, led by Major-General Gordon Legge, then took over. In a dawn attack on 26 August, they succeeded in reaching the farm, only to discover well-entrenched shelters, which had been reinforced by troops of the German Guard Reserve Corps.

The Australians were forced to retreat and suffered another 1268 casualties. The 4th Division was then brought back into the fray and captured the farm again on 29 August, but could not hold it against German counterattacks. The Australians captured the farm *again* on 3 September but were again forced to retreat in the face of German artillery fire and counterattacks.

These two operations cost the 4th Division a further 2405 casualties.

The farm remained an island of German resistance after the Australian divisions were withdrawn on 5 September and was not captured until British forces swept past and completely surrounded it some three weeks later.

In the futile attempt to capture Mouquet Farm, 11,000 Australian casualties were sustained. In the first six weeks of the Somme offensive, the three Anzac divisions of the Australian army had suffered casualties of 23,000. Of these, 6741 had been killed. This figure is roughly comparable to the fatalities suffered by these divisions during the eight months of fighting at Gallipoli, when 5833 men were killed in action and a further 1985 died later from wounds.

Leak was hospitalised from the wounds he received in the fighting at Mouquet Farm, repatriated to London for further treatment and recovery, and did not rejoin the 9th Battalion until 15 October 1917.

Leak continued fighting with the 9th Battalion until 7 March 1918, when he was severely gassed in Belgium, and again hospitalised. In the time between his two bouts in hospital, he was constantly found to be in breach of army regulations and was punished on a number of occasions.

John Leak was a larrikin; throughout his army career he appears to have been a repeat offender when it came to such crimes as insolence, disobedience and going absent without leave. A look at his 'charge sheet' record reveals a long list of offences and there is plenty of evidence to mark him out as 'an habitual offender'.

The most common of his crimes was 'absent without leave', but his service record shows a long list of offences under the heading 'CRIME', which is written in bold capitals.

The entries include 'Entering sergeants' mess & demanding drink', 'Neglecting to obey RSM in that he refused to leave Sergeant's Mess when ordered to by the RSM' (for which he served fourteen days detention) and, in 1917 alone, being 'absent without leave on at least six occasions'.

The punishments handed out to Private Leak varied from forfeiting his pay on three occasions, to detention in military prison on three other occasions.

Finally, in November 1917, after Leak was absent without leave from November 1 to November 6, he was called in to face his commanding officer, who told him that he was sick of handing out punishment after punishment and was passing the problem on to a higher authority: Private John Leak was to be court-martialled as a deserter.

Within days Leak went before a Field General Court Martial, charged with being a deserter. He was found guilty and sentenced to 'Penal Servitude for Life'. Had he served in the ranks of the land of his birth, the British Army, he would almost certainly have been shot by firing squad. As it was, he served less than a month of the life sentence. Within days of the verdict being handed down, the sentence was commuted to two years and, soon after that, it was suspended and Leak rejoined his battalion in the trenches.

In his defence, Private Leak gave his side of the story, which was that he and a mate, having been gassed in action, had requested permission from the company commander to seek medical treatment. Not only was this request denied but also, according to Leak's testimony, the two men were accused of malingering.

Leak went on to say that, as he feared that his mate's eyesight had been permanently impaired, they both went to find the medical help that they desperately needed.

It does appear that the court-martial was, perhaps, an attempt to scare the 25-year-old soldier into mending his ways. The most likely explanation is that Leak's commanding officers were fed up with his behaviour and, when their patience ran out, decided to change what would probably have been another 'absent without leave' charge into something more serious. So the charge was upgraded to 'desertion', in order to teach him a lesson.

If that is the case, the plan failed. On 25 April 1918, Leak went absent without leave again, deserting from hospital without permission and turning up again four days later.

(This particular desertion occurred, coincidentally, on the third anniversary of Anzac Day. That day may have marked the low point in the military career of John Leak, but it also happens to be the day that Australian troops recaptured the French village of Villers-Bretonneux and stopped the advance of the German

Army once and for all, an action that was, perhaps, the crowning glory of the Australian AIF in World War I.)

This time, the punishment handed out to Private Leak was the forfeiture of eleven days pay, but it was like water off a duck's back to the bullock-driver from Rockhampton. In June 1918, less than two months later, and within days of returning from hospital where he had been recovering from being gassed at Hollebeke, he was in trouble again, serving seven days field punishment for 'insolence to an NCO'.

In spite of his clashes with army authority, John Leak served until the end of the war and survived the conflict, having been wounded three times, gassed three times and disciplined for breaches of army regulations on more than a dozen occasions. On 9 February 1919 he embarked for Australia on a troop ship and was officially discharged from the AIF in Queensland on 31 May.

Leak then picked up the threads of his life in Australia. He returned briefly to Rockhampton before spending two years on the southern Darling Downs, where he took up a soldier-settler's block near the small village of Berat, north of Warwick.

After two years he abandoned the block he had been given and moved south to New South Wales where he applied, unsuccessfully, to be given another soldier-settler's block. He appears to have drifted from place to place and job to job for two years before moving briefly to South Australia and then on to Esperance in Western Australia where he worked as a mechanic and ran a garage.

On 12 January 1927, using the name William J.E. Leak, he married Ada Victoria Blood Smith. The couple reportedly lived in a tent and had either seven or eight children before moving back to South Australia, where Leak worked drilling for water in rural areas before retiring to Crafers in the Adelaide Hills, where he died, aged 80, in 1972.

This marriage is rather odd and surprising for, on 30 December 1918, less than six weeks before his departure from England by troop ship, John Leak had married Beatrice May Chapman in the Parish Church of St John The Baptist, in Cardiff, Wales. The couple were never divorced, and Beatrice May Chapman was still very much alive, and recorded on the census. An article in the *Cardiff Times* gave a report of the wedding, complete with background details about the happy couple, on 4 January 1919.

Was Beatrice, commonly known as 'May', part of the motivation for Private Leak's frequent absences without leave? He was certainly in a relationship with her as early as 1916, when she was nineteen years of age.

There is a photograph, taken on 30 December 1916 and reproduced in the *Cardiff Times* article, of him holding her hand, surrounded by her family, outside Buckingham Palace and, at some point during the war, he changed his next of kin on his official army record to 'Miss May Chapman of 62 Bridge Street, Cardiff'. When he enlisted he had given his next of kin as his brother George, of Saskatchewan, Canada.

One version of the story, gleaned from comments made by Leak in a previous article published in the *Cardiff Times*, suggests that he first met Beatrice May Chapman when her father was helping him to trace his family during a visit the young soldier made to Wales early in 1916. This article suggests that John Leak was born in Queensland, although his parents were both Welsh. The article also quite specifically states that he believed his father was from Bryn Mawr and his mother was from Mountain Ash, both of which are in south Wales.

This information is, of course, in conflict with that given or implied by Leak on his enlistment—that he was born in Portsmouth, to English parents who migrated to Australia at some unknown time before the war. It is also in conflict with the information given on his second marriage certificate, that he was born at Peak Hill, in Canada.

'John William Leak' was, and still is, a man of mystery.

He gave his age as 23 when he enlisted in 1915. Twelve years later, on his second marriage certificate, his age was given as 28. Perhaps this seven-year discrepancy indicates that, like many other young men, he lied about his age in order to enlist, and was just sixteen at the time.

On the other hand, he may have lied about his age, as well as his first name, on the West Australian marriage certificate in order to disguise the fact that the marriage was bigamous and therefore illegal.

Those who have thoroughly investigated the life of John Leak, using all the military and public records available, have been unable to find any record of him being born anywhere at any time. There is no record of his birth in Wales, Canada, Australia or Portsmouth, and the best estimate of his date of birth that can be gained from circumstantial evidence is 'sometime between 1892 and 1899'.

Tom McVeigh, former National Party Member for Darling Downs in federal parliament, and a member of the Malcolm Fraser ministry, spent many years researching the life of John Leak and writing a book about him.

McVeigh is of the opinion that Leak certainly lied on the day he enlisted and when he claimed to be a 'teamster from Emerald'. Even at the age of 23, according to McVeigh, the Englishman would not have had the experience to lead a team of bullocks.

It could be that the young man lied about his age and profession as well as the name of the town he came from, choosing Emerald simply because it was far enough away from Rockhampton for the information not to be easily checked, yet not so far away as to arouse suspicion about why he was enlisting at Rockhampton.

The young man may, of course, have also lied about his name. On his first marriage certificate he gave his father's name as James Leak. No mother's name was required. He was consistent on the second marriage certificate, again giving his father's name as James Leak, but adding his mother's name as Sarah Wilson.

As yet, however, no evidence has been found of these two people being born, married or living in Britain; nor is there any evidence, in shipping or migration records, of them ever leaving Britain or arriving in Australia or Canada.

Tom McVeigh was born at Allora, close to Berat, where John Leak lived for two years after the war. Tom spent his life farming in the district and had heard stories about Leak from people of his parents' generation, although he himself was not born until almost a decade after the World War I veteran had left the district.

Evidently the returned soldier was made welcome in the district at first and invited to many Sunday dinners. But he soon proved to be shiftless and untrustworthy and, according to Tom, 'after about two years he just shot through, owing money all around the town'.

Tom's research also indicates that John Leak 'pulled a variety of lurks' in the various towns he lived in briefly in New South Wales, after he shot through from Berat.

What Tom found particularly frustrating in his search for the truth was the fact that John Leak gave different accounts of his birth and background in different interviews over the years. It appears that he and his second wife had eight children and seven of those survived their father. Unfortunately, his children's stories about their father's origins were also 'inconsistent and unsupported'.

It is true, of course, that, if you are a bigamist, you have every reason to lie about your past, but it is also possible that the man we know as John Leak did not know where his parents came from. It seems significant to me that the first thing he did when he arrived in Britain in early 1916 was to go to Wales and enlist the help of William Chapman, his first wife's father, to trace his Welsh heritage.

It is also interesting that the article in the *Cardiff Times* specifically mentions that he could not find anyone who knew his parents in either of the two towns in which he thought they had lived. If you know anything about towns in Wales, you will know how ludicrously impossible it is that anyone could live in those towns for any length of time and not be known and remembered.

There is at least some possibility that the man who called himself John Leak didn't actually know who he was.

In an interview the year before he died, the enigmatic war veteran indicated that his only wish on returning to Australia in 1919 was to forget the war and have nothing to do with the army or the memory of the conflict in which he'd served.

He told a story about arriving by train in Rockhampton, seeing a flag-waving welcoming party waiting for him on the station platform, and immediately jumping on a southbound train to escape the fuss. He claimed that he never returned to Rockhampton.

Leak never joined the RSL and he never marched on Anzac Day. In fact, he went so far as to say, 'I don't believe in war.'

The more cynical among us might be tempted to suggest some inconsistency here. For a man who didn't believe in war, he was happy enough to accept a soldier-settler block of land in Queensland and apply for another in New South Wales.

Further evidence that he did not entirely turn his back on his military past is the fact that, in 1951, he wrote to the army seeking payment of certain entitlements that he had not bothered to claim in 1919. The army received the letter but took no action for, although it contained his service number and details of his service, it unfortunately did not contain a return address. It was filed away as 'no address supplied' and the army made no attempt to track him down.

Although there does seem to be ample evidence that John Leak was a shiftless, unreliable, self-serving and dishonest opportunist, the more sympathetic readers of this story may find some excuses, or at least alleviating circumstances, for his behaviour.

He did at least make an 'honest woman' of Beatrice May Chapman before leaving Britain and there is circumstantial evidence to suggest that there was an understanding that he would arrange her passage to Australia. Perhaps there was insufficient time to do this between the date of their marriage and his embarkation for home.

Whatever the reason, the Australian government did not fund her passage and it seems certain that her husband could not afford to at the time, or at any time in the decade after he left her behind. She stayed in Wales and lived with her parents until at least 1935 when she was recorded on the census under her maiden name. After that there is no record of her at all and she's not mentioned in her father's funeral notice in 1955, although the rest of the family are.

The lies and confusion that John Leak perpetrated about his past may not all be related to the fact that he was a bigamist, or often 'moved on' when he owed money. There is at least some evidence that he himself did not know much about his origins and heritage.

It is also true that he had been through the horrors of war, been wounded three times and gassed three times. He certainly suffered in later life from emphysema, continual bouts of bronchitis and, like so many WWI veterans, probably also from untreated post-traumatic stress disorder, or 'shell shock', as it was known then.

There is no doubt that Private John Leak had experienced distress and the horror of war at first hand. Which brings us, finally, to the whole point of this story.

Perhaps the inquisitive reader has wondered by now why we are bothering to talk about this enigmatic layabout at all. Some of you may be wondering why he seemed to get off so lightly so many times when he flouted army rules so blatantly. Or you might even have wondered how he came to be photographed outside Buckingham Palace with his girlfriend's family, and why a newspaper like the *Cardiff Times* had taken so much interest in an Australian infantry private.

Well, for those of you who don't already know, I'll tell you.

For actions performed in the heat of battle at Pozières on 23 July 1916, a month before he was severely wounded at the Battle of Mouquet Farm, Private John Leak became the first Queenslander, and the only member of the 9th Battalion, to be awarded the Victoria Cross for bravery. The full citation reads:

> He was one of a party which finally captured an enemy strong point. At one assault, when the enemy's bombs were outranging ours, Private Leak jumped out of the trench, ran forward under heavy machine-gun fire at close range, and threw three bombs into the enemy's bombing post. He then jumped into the post and bayoneted three unwounded enemy bombers. Later, when the enemy in overwhelming numbers was driving his party back, he was always the last to withdraw at each stage, and kept on throwing bombs. His courage and energy had such an effect on the enemy that, on the arrival of reinforcements, the whole trench was recaptured.

While many acts of selfless heroism in war have been performed by men who were model soldiers—obedient, disciplined, well-trained men who put duty and service before self-preservation—not *all* acts of bravery are performed by such men.

Some are, as Tom McVeigh has noted, 'the actions of a loner, a courageous individual who has no great regard for life'.

It is, perhaps, possible to reconcile some of the more unsavoury and less socially acceptable elements of John Leak's character with his amazing and admirable act of bravery that occurred that day on the Western Front, and in who knows how many other similar instances in other battles in which he fought.

As Tom McVeigh says:

When he'd see a challenge he'd just respond to it, not thinking about the implications of what that action might be or anything you'd done previously.

We are none of us perfect.

FIGHTING OUR FRIENDS– THE BATTLE OF BRISBANE

This is the story of one of the strangest, and least savoury, events in Australia's 20th century history. World War II forced Australia out of isolation and also forced us to confront the puzzling dilemma of dealing with people of other nationalities, whose cultures and philosophies of life were remarkably different from ours.

The differences between our way of life and those of our then-enemy, the Japanese, were stark and obvious, especially when it came to the attitudes of soldiers towards the opposition. Australians struggled to understand the Japanese mentality and the common response was hatred and loathing, along with a certain level of paranoia, as invasion seemed imminent.

When Japan entered the war in December 1941, it had a well-prepared invasion force, or series of such forces, and a well-planned campaign to capture most of Southeast Asia very quickly.

The Japanese plan proved to be a great success. Within weeks, the Americans were driven out of the Philippines and the British out of Malaya as the Japanese tide moved south. By March 1942 the Dutch had surrendered the East Indies (Indonesia) and Papua New Guinea and the Solomons were being invaded.

It was in March that General Douglas MacArthur arrived in Australia after escaping from the Philippines with his headquarters staff. He immediately assumed supreme command of Allied Forces in the Southwest Pacific Area (SWPA). All of Australia's military combat units in this area were part of SWPA forces and, consequently, they were placed under MacArthur's command. Douglas

MacArthur replaced the Australian chiefs-of-staff as the Australian government's main source of military advice and influence until the war ended in 1945.

The relationship with our allies the Americans was generally cordial and successful. On the surface, our lifestyles and social philosophies appeared similar, and we had an understanding of the American way of life due to the invasive nature of Hollywood movies, American literature and popular songs, as well as a long history of visits from American entertainers of all kinds. We also, of course, shared a certain amount of history and culture from our common British backgrounds.

Just below the surface, however, there were major differences in Australian and American attitudes to life, social structures, economic development and opinions on how the war should be fought.

The USA was more modern, more developed and had an economy and population much larger than ours. The clash of cultures and attitudes, although perhaps not as big an issue as it might have been, was still sufficient to cause some minor problems when certain single-minded American military leaders were imposed upon us, and almost one million testosterone-laden young American men of fighting age were forced to assimilate temporarily into our society.

Although General Blamey was appointed the Allied Land Force commander, he was not permitted by MacArthur to command American forces. MacArthur also rejected requests from his own superiors in the United States to appoint Australians to senior positions at his general headquarters. Later in the war he would be accused of relegating Australian troops to minor mopping up campaigns.

In spite of this, Prime Minister Curtin and General MacArthur developed a good relationship that proved very beneficial to Australia after 1942, and Curtin used MacArthur as a direct line of contact for Australian requests for assistance to the US government.

Close to one million US military personnel spent time in Australia during the war. US military bases for both the US Air

Force and troop deployment were constructed in Australia during 1942 and 1943—mostly in Queensland—and Australia was the major supply base for US forces in the Pacific until the end of the war.

What must be said at the outset is that Australians and Americans, thrown together in large numbers for the first time during WWII, by and large found they had a similar outlook on life. Both were generally open and friendly and managed to get on quite well together. There was a feeling of gratitude towards the United States in Australian society during the war, and overall the Australian and American attitudes to life had more in common than they had differences.

However, at times there were difficulties between Australian commanders and their US counterparts, like the incidents surrounding the sinking of HMAS *Canberra* at the Battle of Savo Island, when the USS *Chicago* retired from the battle area and left the *Canberra* to her fate. These were mostly localised incidents, which were dealt with diplomatically in the long term.

Many in our military resented MacArthur's marginalising of Australian troops for use in 'unimportant' areas of war towards the end. It was felt that he wanted US troops to have the glory, but at least it was a change from our troops being used as 'lambs to the slaughter' by the British. MacArthur had a job to do and he did it well.

The impact and consequences of the US–Australian alliance were felt more keenly at home than on the battlefield. During WWII the Australian public had to undergo quite dramatic social changes due to the war effort. On top of this came the cultural clashes when large numbers of American troops arrived in Australia on their way to and from to various theatres of war.

Even before the war, the Australian social tradition was for towns and cities to virtually shut down from noon on Saturday until Monday morning. The war had restricted entertainment and sporting activities even more. In Brisbane, for example, where the bulk of the Americans were stationed after MacArthur moved his headquarters there from Melbourne, only Doomben operated as a racetrack, while Albion Park and Eagle Farm had become army camps. With thousands of troops in capital cities, there was huge pressure on local authorities to change their policies, and to open hotels, theatres, nightclubs and restaurants for longer and for more varied hours. This led to a boost in the local economy, and new tastes and fashions in entertainment and dining.

When MacArthur moved his headquarters to Brisbane, many buildings and areas around the city were taken over by the US military. Brisbane's population of 320,000 increased by more than 50 per cent during 1942. Almost 90,000 US service-men were stationed in the city. Normal life was disrupted, some schools and other public services were closed, crime increased, the city's infrastructure was barely adequate and electricity often failed, causing 'blackouts' and 'brownouts'. In response to these changes, many families left Brisbane and moved inland or back to rural areas where they had relatives. These social upheavals, and the presence of large numbers of non-Australian young men, inevitably led to resentment and rivalry.

There was considerable resentment and jealousy due to the American troops being better paid and having access to consumer items in their military-based PX Stores. These were stores set up exclusively for American defence personnel serving overseas, giving them access to some of the items they were used to having at home. Australians, who had possibly never seen such consumer goods before and were also suffering the strict rationing of essen-tials, considered many of these items to be luxuries.

Another feeling of strong resentment came from the belief among Australian men that 'the Yanks' often 'bought' the favours of Aussie girls with luxury items such as nylon stockings. While there is some truth in this, it must also be said that many women in Australia found the Americans to have a better attitude towards women than Australian men. Americans often had a more respect-ful, sophisticated and friendly approach to the opposite sex than was common in Australian society at the time.

As with many social problems in Australia's history, alcohol was a factor. The American PX stores also sold cigarettes and alcohol at low prices. Australian servicemen were not allowed into American PX stores. Beer was scarce and hotels had quotas and were only allowed to serve alcohol for restricted periods each day. This led to binge drinking and groups of servicemen roaming the streets in search of pubs serving beer, rushing from one hotel to the next and drinking as quickly as possible before it closed.

It was against this background of social upheaval and resentment that a number of clashes between Australian and American troops occurred. They occurred in Melbourne, Sydney, Rockhampton and Perth, but were probably most common in Brisbane where they climaxed in the infamous 'Battle of Brisbane'.

Just before 7 p.m. on 26 November 1942, Private James Stein of the 404th Signal Company of the US Army apparently left the Australian canteen where he had been drinking (though some versions say he had been in a pub), to walk to the American PX canteen on the corner of Creek and Adelaide streets. Stein was either chatting to or arguing with three Aussie soldiers when US military policeman Private Anthony O'Sullivan asked to see his leave pass and became impatient when the inebriated soldier couldn't find it. American military policemen (MPs) were not popular with the Australian soldiers, who traditionally disliked authority figures, and the three Australians told the MP to leave Stein alone. This started an altercation that attracted more Australian soldiers, a few civilians and more MPs from the American PX canteen. A fight ensued in which MP O'Sullivan was assaulted and his fellow Americans were forced to retreat into the PX canteen, carrying their wounded colleague.

A crowd gathered outside the PX, throwing bottles and rocks, and a parking sign was thrown through a window. By 7.15 p.m. there were about a hundred Australian soldiers trying to break through a makeshift cordon of American MPs around the PX canteen door. As the crowd grew, fights broke out along the street and the American Red Cross building, diagonally opposite the PX building, was also attacked.

Police Inspector Charles Price arrived on the scene and Queensland policemen and American MPs began barricading the doors to the PX canteen. By 8 p.m. a crowd—later estimated by some to be up to 5000 people, but probably around half that size in reality—was involved in the disturbance and more fights broke out in other streets in the city area.

Women working in the area were told not to use the streets until they could be escorted to safety by soldiers with fixed bayonets, theatres were closed by the MPs and service personnel were ordered back to their barracks or ships.

Rumours abounded in the days after the riot, including that Australian MPs removed their armbands and joined in the attack on the PX canteen and that the Brisbane Fire Brigade arrived but refused to use their hoses on the Aussie soldiers. Legend has it that, inside the PX canteen, a still-inebriated Private Stein was searching the pockets of the unconscious MP O'Sullivan looking for his leave pass when he was handed a baton and told to help protect the building. There were also reports of an army truck being stopped by Aussie soldiers and Owen submachine guns, ammunition and hand grenades being 'requisitioned' and handed to rioters.

What is certain is that some of the American MPs in the PX canteen armed themselves with 12-gauge pump-action shotguns and elbowed their way to the front of the building in an attempt to stop the riot. The crowd reacted angrily to the sight of firearms and US Private Norbert Grant was jostled and grabbed by some of the men attacking the canteen in an attempt to take the gun from him. As Grant jabbed one Australian soldier in the chest with the shotgun, another soldier from the crowd grabbed the gun and yet another grabbed Grant around the neck.

The shotgun discharged three times. The first shot hit Private Edward Webster from the 2/2nd Australian Anti-Tank Regiment in the chest and killed him instantly. Two male civilians and five other Australian soldiers, all privates, received shotgun wounds.

As Private Grant fought his way back into the canteen, he clubbed another soldier and damaged the shotgun butt. One of the MPs guarding the PX canteen suffered a fractured skull.

The Americans fled to safety deeper in the building and by

10 p.m. the riot was over. The front area of the ground floor of the PX canteen was demolished by the mob.

Officially, the Military Censor's Office did a great job of killing the story: although the Brisbane *Courier-Mail* newspaper ran a heavily censored article about a disturbance in which a person was killed, there was no mention of the nature of the event or the nationalities involved. No mention of the riot ever appeared in the American press, so the censors obviously did their job on letters home as well.

While there was a successful cover-up by the censors, that didn't stop the rumours and the resentment growing. Word-of-mouth quickly spread and exaggerated reports of the events appeared, such as fifteen Aussies being killed by American MPs with machine guns. These rumours fuelled the fires of resentment and prejudice against the US troops to the extent that the following evening was a low point in Australian military history for behaviour by our soldiers. In a night of shameful thuggery and violence, mobs of Australian servicemen prowled the streets of Brisbane beating and kicking any Americans they found.

Where the mob anger on the first night had been directed at the authority figures of the unpopular military police, any American was a target on the second night. A crowd of Australian servicemen, estimated at between 500 to 600, formed three circles at the intersection of Queen and Adelaide streets and any passing American soldiers were pushed into the centre of the circles and then punched and kicked. Another crowd gathered outside General MacArthur's headquarters on the corner of Queen and Edward streets and shouted abuse at the building. MacArthur was in New Guinea at the time.

Brisbane identity 'Big Bill' Edwards was closing his pharmacy that night when an American officer and his Australian wife left a cinema nearby and were spotted by a group of a dozen Australian servicemen. Bill heard shouts of 'There's a bloody Yank—kill him' and 'Kick his brains out'. Bill saw the woman knocked to the ground twice. The couple scrambled into Bill's shop and he closed the wire security door to keep the mob out. When one of the soldiers said,

'Give us the bastard, Bill, he killed our mate,' Bill evidently replied, 'He didn't kill anyone, and if you find the one who did, I'll kill him for you.' The mob then moved on.

More than twenty Americans, mostly MPs and officers, were seriously injured on the second night of the Battle of Brisbane and more than half of those were hospitalised. The units involved in the disturbance were relocated out of Brisbane and the number of MPs patrolling Brisbane streets at night was increased. The American PX canteen was relocated, while the Australian canteen was closed permanently. The MP who held the shotgun, Private Norbert Grant, was subsequently court-martialled on a charge of manslaughter in February 1943. He was found not guilty on the grounds of self-defence. Five Australians were convicted of assault and one of them served a six-month jail term.

The Battle of Brisbane showed the duality of the Australian attitude towards the Americans who were stationed here in WWII. On one side, there was gratitude and relief that General MacArthur and the US troops and personnel were in Australia, support-ing the Australians' involvement in the war. The paranoia and fear of a Japanese invasion generally overrode any animosity felt towards the American troops. There is no doubt that the majority of Australians warmly welcomed the presence of the Americans. This is evidenced by the number of American names used as street names in the suburbs of Australian cities in the post-war expansion.

On the flipside, there were major cultural differences that made the presence of the Americans problematic at times. The differences were as simple as smarter uniforms, access to luxury items, different manners and grooming. But there were also major differences in social attitudes to such things as public affection between dating couples and the right to bear arms. Conservative Australia found public affection, kissing and 'smooching' offen-sive. Australian servicemen were also critical of the wearing of handguns and the use of firearms generally by Americans. Even today the attitude towards gun control is one of the defining differences between Australian and American societies.

It is easy to dismiss the Battle of Brisbane as an isolated

incident, but wartime authorities stated after the war that many similar incidents occurred. There are reports of an incident at Rockhampton where two troop trains stopped side by side. One was full of US troops heading south on leave and the other full of Aussies heading north to fight, and a full-scale conflict developed. Censorship kept the truth of these incidents from being revealed at the time to the Australian public.

As a sign that the times had changed and perceptions had shifted slightly, after the war ended young Australians sought to emulate the American lifestyle and adopted the very habits that annoyed the more conservative elements of our society during WWII.

While the Battle of Brisbane revealed some of the nastier elements of the Aussie character, it was mainly the result of large numbers of young men from two different cultures, full of alcohol and testosterone, being forced into an alliance in a time of stress and difficulty.

TURNING THE TIDE

Sometime around the year 1030, Canute, King of England, Denmark and Norway, apparently had his throne carried down to the seashore and ordered his courtiers to watch as he attempted to turn back the tide. The point that Canute was trying to make, evidently, was that mortal men cannot achieve the impossible, there are some things that even a king cannot do.

We don't know exactly when this happened, because the story was first told a hundred years after Canute's death, by the historian Henry of Huntingdon, who may well have made up the whole thing.

There have, however, been times in history when men have turned the tide of events against all odds and achieved the seemingly impossible. On at least several occasions in the 20th century, this was done by Australian soldiers.

In World War II the first 'defeat' suffered by the German army was at Tobruk and the first Japanese 'defeat' was at Milne Bay, and both of those were inflicted by Australian troops. When I say 'defeat' what I really mean is that, in each case, the relentless advance of the two enemy powers was halted for the first time in the war.

At Tobruk, in April 1941, General Erwin Rommel employed the 'blitzkrieg' tactic that had not failed since the war began in September 1939. He attacked with 50 tanks, which were repelled by infantrymen of the Australian 9th Division, ably assisted by the British Royal Horse Artillery Division. Rommel was forced to leave the fortified enclave to be an isolated pocket of resistance for more than eight months.

Holding Tobruk was only possible for two reasons. Firstly, it could be supplied by sea and, secondly, the Australian 9th Division happened to be there when it was cut off by Rommel's advance.

But it proved to be a costly exercise. Twenty-two Allied ships, all part of what became known as 'the Tobruk Ferry', were lost in the hazardous exercise of getting convoys through in the face of constant attacks by the Luftwaffe and German U-boats.

While holding Tobruk, 832 Australians died, another 941 were captured and 2177 were wounded. British artillery casualties exceeded 2000 and, in the end, Tobruk finally fell to Rommel's forces, but only after the Australian troops had been withdrawn.

At Milne Bay in August 1942 the Japanese suffered their first defeat of WWII when an invasion force of 2000 men was completely crushed by the Australian 25th and 61st Battalions, assisted by the 46th Engineers Regiment and the 43rd US Engineers, and by Australian artillery and the RAAF.

What makes that engagement even more commendable is that the majority of the Allied troops at Milne Bay were not crack infantry troops. They were there building an airfield.

I mention these two highly significant victories of World War II merely to point out that achieving unexpected victories that prove to be the turning points in world wars is something that Australian fighting forces seem to be rather good at.

All of that is, however, really only a patriotic preamble to the story of what many believe to be Australia's greatest military achievement, stopping the German army at Villers-Bretonneux on two occasions and turning the tide of World War I irrevocably in the Allies' favour. This occurred during what is commonly known as the Battle of Amiens, in April 1918.

On 24 April 1918 Australia's official war historian, Charles Bean, made an entry in his diary which referred to the planned pincer movement to be made that night by the Australian 13th and 15th Brigades, in an effort to recapture the town of Villers-Bretonneux. It reads:

I don't believe they have a chance. Went to bed thoroughly depressed . . . feeling certain that this hurried attack would fail hopelessly.

Next morning, however, when the sun rose on the third anniversary of Anzac Day, Villers-Bretonneux was safely in Allied hands, the massive German offensive known as the *Kaiserschlacht* had been stopped in its tracks, the strategic cathedral city of Amiens was safe and the tide of war had been turned. The German army was in retreat from that moment until the end of the war.

The *Kaiserschlacht,* or 'Kaiser's Battle', was a series of strategic attacks along the Western Front, part of the final German major offensive of the war, known as 'Operation Michael'. The aim of this offensive was to win the war before the massive manpower and military resources of the United States could be mobilised and brought to bear against the Central Powers. The US had declared war on Germany almost a year previously, in April 1917, and the German High Command realised that the full force of the US war effort would be felt on the Western Front sometime in 1918.

The signing of the Treaty of Brest-Litovsk by the new Soviet Russian government and the Central Powers, on 3 March 1918, ended Russia's involvement in the war and freed up more than 40 divisions, which could now be used against the Allied forces on the Western Front.

Operation Michael began with the Spring Offensive on 21 March 1918. The plan was for a massive German army, reinforced by the divisions from the Eastern Front, to push due west along the British Front north of the River Somme, thus separating the French and British armies, pushing the British into the sea and capturing the channel ports.

The most important strategic target of the offensive was the cathedral city of Amiens, which had actually been taken by German forces in the very early days of the war but had subsequently been reclaimed by the French.

Amiens was the central hub of rail and road networks in northern France. It was a communication centre, supply base and headquarters for the Allies. The main north–south railway line ran through Amiens. If Amiens fell, the British could no longer move troops and supplies by rail, ensuring victory on the Western Front would go to Germany.

Sixteen kilometres to the east of Amiens, the town of Villers-Bretonneux sits on a ridge overlooking the valley of the Somme. The ridge was strategically important to the German offensive for, in order to win the *Kaiserschlacht,* they needed to establish safe artillery positions from which the shelling of Amiens could begin. This would have allowed their infantry to then sweep across the Somme Valley, the aims of Operation Michael would be achieved and a German victory on the Western Front would be assured.

Both the *Kaiserschlacht* and Operation Michael, however, ended at Villers-Bretonneux.

On 29 March, the 9th Brigade of the 3rd Australian Division was sent to Villers-Bretonneux to prevent the Germans from driving a wedge between the remnants of the British 5th Army and the French 1st Army to the south.

The first encounters with the German forces occurred the following day. Four battalions of the Australian 9th Brigade were sent to defend Villers-Bretonneux. One battalion, the 35th, was protecting the eastern front of the village while three other battalions lay in support behind, on the western side.

On 4 April the full force of the German operation was brought to bear against the villages of Hamel and Villers-Bretonneux and other strategic locations in the district.

The British 18th Division, fighting around Villers-Bretonneux, held fast, but the British 14th Division was overwhelmed and the village of Hamel, 5 kilometres north of Villers-Bretonneux, fell to the Germans. This forced the Australian 35th Battalion to swing back to the left to prevent being surrounded.

Meanwhile, down in the valley, the 15th Brigade of the 5th Australian Division, commanded by Brigadier-General Harold 'Pompey' Elliott, was guarding the bridges across the River Somme.

Harold 'Pompey' Elliott was a Victorian farmer's son who served with the Victorian Contingent in South Africa in 1900–02, was awarded the Distinguished Conduct Medal and mentioned in dispatches before returning to university where he attained two law degrees and was a champion athlete and footballer.

At Gallipoli he led a battalion that won four Victoria Crosses at Lone Pine and he served in most of the great AIF battles on the Western Front. He was awarded the Distinguished Service Order, the Order of St Michael and St George, the Russian Order of St Anne, the Croix de Guerre, and was mentioned in dispatches seven times.

Elliott, who cried openly when he saw how few of his men had survived the Battle of Fromelles, was extremely proud of the bravery of the Australians he led and their stoic acceptance of seemingly hopeless situations.

There is a story that he was once leading his men towards the enemy as a group of French women, whose homes had been destroyed, fled past them. Some of the women, noticing the men were Australian, stopped and cried, '*Vive l'Australie!*'

A gruff Australian voice from the ranks yelled back, in mangled French, '*Fini retreat madame, beaucoup Australiens ici.*'

Relating the story later Elliott said, 'I was never so proud of being an Australian.'

When large numbers of retreating British troops began arriving at his position on 4 April 1918, it became apparent to Elliott that things were desperate up on the ridge and, later that afternoon, he sent his brigade's two reserve battalions across the Somme to hold the strategically important high ground to the west of Hamel.

Meanwhile, a new German thrust against the British 18th Division brought the enemy frontline to the outskirts of Villers-Bretonneux and the town seemed certain to fall.

Just as the Germans seemed sure to capture the town, they were surprised to see hundreds of Allied troops emerge from the woods to the southwest and run towards them with fixed bayonets. This courageous charge was led by the 9th Brigade's 36th Battalion, which had been lying in wait behind the village. They were joined by a company of the 35th Battalion and some men from the British 7th Battalion of the Queen's Regiment.

There was a space of some 400 metres between the opposing forces, and at first the Germans held their ground and inflicted heavy casualties on the advancing troops. Finally, however, the audacious action achieved its goal. The Germans hesitated and then broke ranks and retreated into the woods. Villers-Bretonneux was saved.

Soon afterwards British troops, along with the Australian 33rd and 34th Battalions, secured the Allied line to the north of the town and the crisis was over.

Australia's 9th Brigade of the 3rd Division suffered 665 casualties in the battle.

Elsewhere, Operation Michael was going quite well for the Germans. They had taken the town of Hamel and established secure positions around the strategically vital Hill 104. If the Germans could take Hill 104, the bombardment of Amiens by their heavy artillery could begin.

Further along the line, to the northwest, the Germans pressed on through Armentieres, and the Portuguese divisions holding the front at the Lys River were also forced to retreat.

Two weeks after the defence of Villers-Bretonneux, it was obvious that the only thing left for the Germans to do, in order to achieve victory, was to capture Amiens. To do this they needed to secure Hill 104 and in order to do that they needed to take Villers-Bretonneux from the Allies.

On 24 April a huge German force, led by fifteen tanks, launched a massive attack against the British forces that were now defending the town. The tanks pushed through the British ranks and, in a savage and hard-fought battle, the town fell to the Germans.

This battle is also famous for being the first in which tanks fought against tanks. In a field to the south of the town, three British tanks successfully attacked three German tanks, one of which was destroyed while the other two retreated.

The situation was now desperate. If the Germans could secure the district and safely install artillery on Hill 104, Amiens would be an easy target. Villers-Bretonneux had to be retaken.

Within hours two Australian brigades were rushed forward, and a daring and unconventional plan was put into action. The

15th Brigade of the 5th Australian Division, led by 'Pompey' Elliott, swept around the north of the town, and the 13th Brigade of the 4th Australian Division attacked from the south. Meanwhile, the 14th Brigade of the 5th Australian Division, already holding the line to the northeast, in a forested area known as Vaire Wood, moved forward to cover the left flank of the advance.

Official war correspondent Charles Bean had every reason to be pessimistic about the outcome of this operation. In a break with conventional military wisdom of the day, it was decided that there would be no preliminary artillery barrage prior to the Australians advancing. This preliminary tactic, which was standard procedure in World War I, was designed to knock out or disrupt enemy defences in order to make an attack more likely to be successful.

In the case of Villers-Bretonneux it was thought that the only chance of success lay in surprise. It was hoped that the Germans would not expect such a sudden retaliation and therefore no artillery cover was given to the Australian battalions as they advanced in the dark on the night of 24 April 1918.

The 13th Brigade of the 4th Australian Division, led by Brigadier-General William Glasgow, had just arrived after setting off at 10 p.m. and marching 13 kilometres to reach the battle zone. Glasgow had been assured by the British that they had knocked out enemy resistance in D'Arquenne Wood, through which his men had to advance. As the 13th Brigade advanced, however, machine guns in the woods opened fire and inflicted heavy casualties and progress became impossible.

Two Western Australians, Lieutenant Cliff Sadlier and Sergeant Charlie Stokes, led a small band of six volunteers into the woods and managed to locate and destroy six German machine-gun nests. Sadlier, who was wounded twice, was awarded the Victoria Cross and Stokes was awarded the Distinguished Conduct Medal.

Glasgow's brigade encountered barbed wire, came under shellfire and were targeted by other machine-gun posts before they finally reached their objective and joined the battle. Although they did not connect up with Elliott's brigade as intended, they ended up close enough to ensure success.

The departure of the 15th Brigade was delayed when one company became lost in the dark when told to make a detour around a gassed area and were late arriving at the assembly point. As a result, the brigade set off almost two hours late but actually reached the road north of the town before Glasgow's men.

The 15th Brigade stopped to regroup just outside the town and were detected by the enemy who sent up flares. A German machine gun opened fire but the Australians waited until 23-year-old Captain Eric Young, a bookkeeper from St Kilda, gave the order to charge.

The Australians, who knew that it was now officially the 25th of April and the third anniversary of Anzac Day, charged forward with an ear-splitting roar. The noise, Lieutenant-Colonel Jack Scanlan wrote later, was 'sufficient to make the enemy's blood run cold'.

The surprised Germans were swiftly overwhelmed and the northern part of the pincer movement was successful, although some Germans escaped east of the town through a narrow gap that the Australians had not managed close up.

By dawn on 25 April, the town was surrounded and the remaining Germans were trapped.

By mid-morning the German army was evacuating D'Arquenne Wood and relinquishing its positions around Villers-Bretonneux.

The German garrison trapped in Villers-Bretonneux had all been killed or captured by the morning of 26 April. The German threat to Amiens was over.

Australian casualties were more than 2400 while the British lost 9500 men, most of who were captured on 24 April in the German advance. Including prisoners taken, German losses were about 10,000.

Villers-Bretonneux today is an unremarkable place. There are no ancient monuments or lovely old medieval churches for tourists to look at. In fact, it looks like every building in the town was constructed after 1920, which they were. There was not a lot left of the town after April 1918.

There is a small museum, however, and, if you're looking for those quirky, amusing, touristy photos, you can take a selfie beside the street sign in the main street, which is named 'Rue de Melbourne'.

Oh, and there is the 'Kangaroo Restaurant' and the 'Victoria School', the town's only school, which was paid for with money donated by the schoolchildren of Victoria. There are quaint old plaques in every classroom which read, '*N'oublions jamais l'Australie*', and painted in huge letters in English across a building in the playground are the words 'DO NOT FORGET Australia'.

Just out of town at Hill 104 is the main Australian War Cemetery and Memorial for the Western Front. Most of the 1200 Australians who died saving the village in 1918 are buried there. The town has never forgotten them.

Legendary Australian General John Monash was not involved in the First or Second Battles of Villers-Bretonneux, but the man who is credited with being instrumental in the Allied victory on the Western Front later said: 'In my opinion, this counter-attack, at night, without artillery support, is the finest thing yet done in the war, by Australians or any other troops.'

If you ever doubt that there *can* be some honour in war, or that Australia has little to be proud of in world affairs, apart from sporting success, I suggest you visit a small, rather dull-looking French town, population 5000, in the Nord-Pas-de-Calais-Picardie region, Departement de la Somme, L'arrondisement d'Amiens, Le canton de Corbie—it's called Villers-Bretonneux (that's *Vee-yers Bre-tonn-oh*).

Note: 'Pompey' Elliott stood for the Senate in 1919 and topped the Victorian poll. He harboured many grievances about his lack of promotion in WWI and, after being hospitalised for blood pressure, he took his own life in March 1931 and was buried with full military honours in Burwood cemetery. He was 52 years old.

THE MOST CONFUSED BATTLE AREA IN WORLD HISTORY

The Battle of the Coral Sea

This is the amazing story of how Australia's fate—and the outcome of the war in the Pacific—hung in the balance while more than 60 warships and hundreds of aircraft played hide and seek in the ocean to the east of Queensland.

We remember the Battle of the Coral Sea on 7 May 1942 as a defining moment in World War II and celebrate it each year because of its importance in our nation's brief history, but it was, in fact, a farcical series of events. Military historian Chris Coulthard-Clark described the battle as 'a series of confused and indecisive attempts by both sides to inflict serious damage on the other.'

American military historian Admiral Duckworth went even further. He described the Coral Sea as 'the most confused battle area in world history.'

Maps attempting to show the movements of the various fleets from 4 to 8 May 1942 are so complex and indecipherable that they more resemble the crayon scrawlings of toddlers who have overdosed on red lollies than they do maps of any naval or military campaign.

In order to understand the importance of such an indecisive and shambolic series of encounters, which some military experts have said hardly deserves the name of a 'battle' of any kind, it is necessary to remind ourselves of the situation that Australia and the United States found themselves in as Japan speedily and successfully took control of East Asia and the islands to Australia's north.

Once the Japanese had established Rabaul as a secure military and naval base, in February 1942, they were free to attack and invade the north coast of New Guinea as well as the Solomon Islands.

February 1942 saw the fall of Singapore, the destruction of the port at Darwin, successful Japanese invasions on Timor and Ambon, and the destruction of the Allied fleet in the Battle of the Java Sea.

These victories gave the Japanese virtual control of the entire region north of Australia, from Burma to Bougainville in New Guinea. The Japanese fleet, air force and various invasion forces were free to move and attack as they wished in this area.

On 8 March, Japanese invasion forces established garrisons at Lae and Salamaua on Australian territory on the north coast of New Guinea. The only territory north of Australia left unoccupied by the Japanese was the eastern end of New Guinea, where Port Moresby, on the southern coast, was the last strategically important bastion of Allied resistance.

To the east the Japanese needed to gain control of the Solomon Island chain and then they intended to occupy Fiji and Samoa.

As part of their war strategy, some of Japan's General Staff had suggested an invasion of Australia to prevent Australia becoming a base against their operations in the South Pacific. The idea was rejected on the grounds that Japan's forces and naval strength would be too thinly spread and could be better used elsewhere. The idea that *was* adopted was a four-part strategy that had been around since 1938 and called for the establishment of an air base at Tulagi Island, near Guadalcanal, the occupation of Port Moresby, an assault on Fiji, New Caledonia and Samoa, and the presence of a large naval carrier force in the Coral Sea to attack Townsville and Cairns at will.

The Coral Sea lies between the east coast of northern Australia and the Solomon Island chain. Control of this area would give Japan a free hand to operate to Australia's north and east and would place the eastern seaboard of Australia at the mercy of the Japanese, whether they chose to invade or not.

This strategy was called 'Operation MO' and, early in 1942, Vice Admiral Inoue, commander of the Imperial Japanese 4th

Fleet, also known as the South Seas Force, suggested it be implemented in May that year. The plan called for the invasion by sea and occupation of two key strategic bases, Port Moresby and Tulagi (in the southeastern Solomon Islands). Tulagi was to be invaded on 3 May and Port Moresby on 10 May. These two bases would then be used to strengthen the ring of defence around the main Japanese base at Rabaul and expand Japanese air and naval control further into the Pacific.

Australian bases for Allied bombers, such as Townsville and Cooktown, were beyond the range of Japanese bombers stationed at Rabaul and Lae. If Operation MO succeeded, Australia's northern ports and airfields would be within easy bomber range, then New Caledonia, Fiji and Samoa could be invaded and the Allied supply lines across the Pacific effectively cut.

A secondary operation was also planned as part of Inoue's strategy; codenamed 'RY' this operation was to see the invasion of Nauru and Ocean Island and the capture of their valuable phosphate deposits.

In order to make Operation MO effective and successful, Inoue needed aircraft carrier support until the captured bases were established as airfields. He requested carriers from the Japanese Combined Fleet to provide the air power he needed.

Meanwhile, Naval Marshal General Yamamoto, commander-in-chief of the Japanese Combined Fleet, was working on a plan of his own. He needed to destroy, or render ineffective, the US carrier fleet, which had not been damaged in the attack on Pearl Harbor.

Yamamoto's plan was to draw the US carriers into a major sea and air engagement near Midway Atoll and use his superior strength and better-trained aircrews to put the US carriers out of action. Midway, as the name suggests, was a strategically vital base halfway between Hawaii and Japan in the Pacific.

General Yamamoto had built up his fleet with this objective in mind but, in response to the need for Operation MO to be successful under the command of Vice Admiral Inoue, Yamamoto sent two fleet carriers, a light carrier, a cruiser division and two destroyer divisions to support the operation.

The Japanese planned to take Port Moresby in the same way that they had taken so many other places in Southeast Asia. An invasion force embarked on twelve transport vessels at Rabaul in the first few days of May 1942. It departed early on 6 May, bound for Port Moresby. Vice Admiral Inoue, based at Rabaul, was in charge of protecting this invasion force and the other, which had sailed on 2 May to occupy the Australian advanced operational base on the island of Tulagi in the Solomons. Inoue had at his disposal no less than 51 warships, which were divided into six operational groups.

Allied vessels available to counter the Japanese fleet numbered about twenty, most of which were located south of Guadalcanal when the Japanese invasion convoy sailed from Rabaul. What the Japanese did not know was that the US Navy had cracked their communication ciphers and codes and picked up references to Operation MO in March 1942.

On 13 April, the British deciphered a message to Inoue that the ships he needed were on their way. This made it clear to the Allied Forces that Port Moresby was the likely target for the Japanese operation.

Newly appointed commander of Allied Forces in the Pacific, Admiral Chester Nimitz, took charge of the situation and ordered all four US fleet carriers based in the Pacific to head to the Coral Sea. These would be organised into three task forces (TF), named as TF11, TF16 and TF17, in an effort to form a three-pronged attack to pre-empt the invasion by the Japanese fleet.

TF17, commanded by Vice Admiral Fletcher and centred around USS *Yorktown*, was already heading towards the Coral Sea; while TF11, under Rear Admiral Fitch and centred around USS *Lexington*, was between Fiji and New Caledonia. These two forces, which joined north of New Caledonia, comprised 27 ships (two carriers, nine cruisers, thirteen destroyers and three support vessels) and 128 aircraft. TF16, based around the carriers USS *Enterprise* and USS *Hornet*, was not ready, having just returned to base at Pearl Harbor. Although the Coral Sea was under the control of General MacArthur, the naval commanders of the three task forces were answerable to Nimitz, who was also based at Pearl Harbor.

A series of airborne naval engagements was fought between Inoue's fleet and the Allied ships, commanded by Rear Admiral Jack Fletcher, between 4 May and 8 May 1942. This became known as the Battle of the Coral Sea. In hindsight, this battle was a confused series of engagements and near-misses and the consequences of these events affected the course of the war dramatically.

TF17 refuelled and headed north on 2 May. TF11 completed refuelling on 4 May and headed into the Coral Sea to rendezvous with TF44, a joint US–Australian force of three cruisers (HMAS *Hobart*, HMAS *Australia* and USS *Chicago*) and three destroyers under the command of Australian Rear Admiral John Crace. TF44 was part of the forces under General MacArthur's control. TF11 and TF44 joined up due east of Cape York, southeast of the tip of New Guinea, on 5 May.

The Japanese fleet supporting the invasion was in several groups. Some warships, under the command of Admiral Goto, accompanied the troop ships from Rabaul while most left from the base at the island of Truk, northeast of Bougainville. Some Japanese warships entered the Coral Sea from south of Bougainville to support the invasion fleet sailing from Rabaul. The main Japanese strike force, commanded by Admiral Takagi, with Admiral Hara in charge of air strikes, proceeded down the eastern side of the Solomon Islands. Some ships then supported the invasion of Tulagi, which was easily accomplished under the command of Admiral Shima on 3 May after the Australian reconnaissance force evacuated before the Japanese arrival. The main carrier fleet entered the Coral Sea from south of San Cristobal Island (now Makira), at the bottom of the Solomon Islands.

The Japanese had mistakenly assumed that only one US carrier was in the area. They also assumed that the Allied ships were to the east, when they were actually inside the Japanese area of operations, to the west.

Rear Admiral Fletcher was notified of a sighting of the Tulagi invasion force on 3 May. He changed course and launched air strikes against the Japanese ships and the forces attempting to build an airstrip and seaplane base on Tulagi on 4 May. These air strikes sank a destroyer and four minesweepers and destroyed four seaplanes; despite this, the Japanese were operating seaplanes from Tulagi by 6 May. The Japanese force situated north of Tulagi sent planes to find the US carrier, but they searched to the east of the Solomon chain of islands and found nothing as the Allied ships were all to the west.

On 5 May the Allied task forces all joined up and refuelled 600 kilometres (373 miles) south of Guadalcanal. Rear Admiral Fletcher was informed by Pearl Harbor that deciphered messages suggested the Port Moresby invasion fleet was due to arrive on 10 May. In response, Fletcher merged all the Allied ships into task force 17, which he then split into two groups called TF17 and TF17.3.

TF17.3 was the old TF44, Rear Admiral Crace's six warships. This group was sent northwest, without air support, to the south-east of Port Moresby in order to block the passage of the Japanese invasion fleet. TF17 then headed northwest where Fletcher believed he would find the Japanese warships.

Unbeknownst to either side, after the Japanese force had rounded the southern tip of San Cristobal, entered the Coral Sea and moved south, the two main fleets were within 130 kilometres (81 miles) of each other. It was the closest they ever came to meeting. The Japanese assumed the Allied fleet was to the south-east and the Allies assumed the main Japanese force was in the vicinity of the transports heading to Port Moresby from the north.

On 6 May, a Japanese seaplane from Tulagi sighted TF17 about 550 kilometres (342 miles) south of Takagi's force that had moved north again. The Japanese were refuelling and this distance range was at the extreme limit for their aircraft. They finished refuelling and then headed south to close the gap. As they were doing this, TF17 moved in a northwesterly direction.

Carrier Battles—7 May

At 7.22 a.m. on 7 May, a Japanese reconnaissance plane from the main Japanese carrier fleet south of Fletcher's TF17 spotted the two support vessels, which had refuelled TF17 and headed south. He wrongly reported that he had found an American fleet and, in a major error of judgement due to his faulty reporting and the assumption that the Allied fleet was to the southeast, the Japanese Admirals Hara and Takagi sent the full weight of their air power, 78 fighters and bombers, to the south.

The aircraft were launched between 8 a.m. and 8.15 a.m. At exactly 8.20 a.m., a Japanese aircraft flying out of Rabaul spotted the Allied TF17 to the northwest of the Japanese strike force and reported back to base. The message was passed on to Hara and Takagi who were confused and assumed that there were two Allied fleets operating in the Coral Sea. They decided not to recall the 78 aircraft they had despatched five minutes earlier, sending their entire air strike force to attack a fuel oiler, USS *Neosho*, and a destroyer, USS *Sims*.

Just as the last aircraft departed from the Japanese carriers, a US aircraft from TF17 spotted the Japanese warships escorting the invasion task force to Port Moresby to the north of the Allied fleet. The pilot reported back in code that he had seen 'two carriers and four heavy cruisers' when he actually meant to say 'two cruisers and four destroyers'. Fletcher assumed that the main Japanese carrier force had been found and prepared his aircraft to attack.

All was ready two hours later when a flight of American B-17s sighted and reported the same invasion convoy, 'ten transports and sixteen warships', just south of the first sighting. Although no large carriers were sighted, Fletcher took this sighting as confirmation that this was the main strike force.

All 93 available aircraft were ordered to attack and by 10.15 a.m. they were gone to the north. At 10.19 a.m., the pilot who had made the first sighting landed back on the USS *Yorktown* and realised he had made a coding error. There were, in fact, no confirmed sightings of Japanese fleet carriers to the north.

The Japanese had mistakenly sent their full airborne firepower in the wrong direction, against the wrong target, and the Allies had done the same. The Japanese planes found the two support vessels and searched in vain for the main Allied fleet.

Finally realising there had been a mistake, they reported back to Admiral Takagi who immediately understood that he had acted on the wrong report and the American fleet was now in between his ships and the invasion convoy.

All aircraft were ordered back to the carriers except for 36 dive-bombers who were to attack the two American ships.

USS *Sims* was sunk and USS *Neosho* was crippled and drifted until found by the destroyer USS *Henley* on 11 May. The survivors of the USS *Neosho* and USS *Sims* were taken on board and the supply ship USS *Neosho* was sunk by torpedoes. USS *Neosho* sent a garbled message to Admiral Fletcher saying they were sinking, but gave out the incorrect coordinates. Only fourteen men from USS *Sims* survived. One hundred and twenty of the USS *Neosho*'s crew were rescued. The death toll from the two ships was 180 men.

The American strike aircraft sighted the Japanese support force for the invasion fleet at 10.40 a.m. The light carrier *Shōhō* was the only aircraft carrier they could find, as it was the only one in the convoy. The *Shōhō* had only eight planes ready to launch in her own defence. *Shōhō* was a small aircraft carrier with a crew of 834 and, ironically, her other ten aircraft were below decks being prepared for an attack on TF17, whose general whereabouts was now known to the Japanese.

Although surrounded by the Japanese cruisers giving anti-aircraft support, *Shōhō* was hit by thirteen 1000-pound (454-kilogram) bombs and seven torpedoes and sank at 11.30 a.m. The Japanese support fleet withdrew to the north, hoping to get out of range of further attacks. Later that afternoon a Japanese destroyer was sent back to look for survivors from the *Shōhō*. Only 203 of her crew of 834 were found.

The Americans lost only three aircraft in the attack while all of *Shōhō*'s eighteen aircraft were lost.

The American aircraft had returned to USS *Yorktown* and USS *Lexington* by 2 p.m. and were re-armed by 2.30. Although Fletcher was tempted to attack the invasion convoy and the support fleet again, he was worried that there were other Japanese fleet carriers somewhere in the Coral Sea that he hadn't found yet.

As the weather was overcast and his fleet screened by cloud, he decided to wait until scout aircraft found the main Japanese strike force before launching another attack. TF17 turned southwest.

After the loss of *Shōhō*, Inoue ordered the invasion convoy and its supporting warships to withdraw to the north and prepare for a sea battle with the Allied fleet, which he assumed was still headed northwest.

The Japanese invasion convoy was attacked by US Army land-based B-17s but not damaged.

Admiral Takagi was told to find and destroy the Allied carrier fleet. However, a Japanese aircraft from Rabaul had sighted Admiral Grace's TF17.3 fleet of six warships, heading north to blockade Port Moresby, and made a mistaken report that it contained two carriers. Based on this report, Takagi, whose aircraft had not returned from attacking USS *Neosho*, turned his fleet to the west at 1.30 p.m. and reported to Inoue that the Allied fleet was too distant for him to attack them that day.

Two attacks were mounted against Admiral Crace's TF17.3 by aircraft based at Rabaul, but Crace's ships were undamaged and managed to shoot down four Japanese aircraft.

A short time later, three US Army B-17s mistakenly bombed TF17.3, luckily causing no damage. Understandably fed up with being isolated from air support and running low on fuel, Admiral Crace radioed Fletcher that he was unable to reach the planned position. He then retired to a position 400 kilometres (248 miles) southeast of Port Moresby. This was a compromise designed to increase the distance between TF17.3 and Japanese carrier-based or land-based aircraft and yet still be close enough to intercept any Japanese convoy using the Jomard Passage or China Strait to reach Port Moresby. To add to the general confusion, Admiral Crace did not know that Admiral Fletcher was maintaining radio silence and consequently had no idea what was going on elsewhere in the Coral Sea.

At around 3 p.m., a Japanese reconnaissance aircraft reported that Admiral Crace's TF17.3 had altered course, but the new bearing was wrongly reported as being southeasterly. Admiral Takagi made another major error. Based on the pilot's error about

TF17.3's direction, and assuming that the aircraft had spotted the main Allied fleet, Takagi calculated that, on the course wrongly reported, the Allied ships would be within striking range of an air attack before dark.

Eight torpedo bombers were sent as scouts to search the sea to the west. Naturally, they did not find TF17 although they certainly flew past Fletcher's ships as they headed west.

At 4.15 p.m. twelve Japanese dive-bombers and fifteen torpedo bombers were launched to join the search for the Allied carrier fleet. This was a risky decision, as the planes would have to return to the carriers in darkness. As these planes flew toward a non-existent target, they were actually on a course that took them directly over the real target.

TF17 was now 370 kilometres (230 miles) to the west of the Japanese fleet under thick cloud and the American radar picked up the oncoming Japanese formation. At around 6 p.m. Fletcher launched eleven Wildcat fighters, making a surprise attack against the Japanese planes and shooting down eight of the torpedo bombers and a dive-bomber for the loss of three Wildcats.

The Japanese planes scattered and aborted their mission. They jettisoned their bombs and attempted to return to their fleet carriers. In a twist of fate that is almost comical, several Japanese planes found TF17 after dark and, mistaking the Allied fleet for their own, attempted to land on the American carriers until driven off by anti-aircraft fire from escorting destroyers.

The day ended with both sides preparing for extensive scouting flights at dawn next morning. Admiral Fletcher took TF17 to the west and Admiral Takagi decided to take the Japanese fleet north to be closer to the invasion convoy, which he assumed was about to engage in a sea battle with the Allied fleet.

Carrier battles—8 May

Admiral Hara, in command of aircraft on Admiral Takagi's fleet, said he could never believe his bad luck on 7 May 1942 and felt like quitting the navy. On 8 May, however, luck was to turn against the Allies. To begin with, the cloud cover that had protected TF17 moved north and covered the Japanese fleet, leaving TF17 easily detectable under clear skies with visibility at 30 kilometres (19 miles).

An American plane from USS *Lexington* spotted the Japanese fleet through a break in the clouds at 8.20 a.m. and a Japanese plane found TF17 two minutes later. The two fleets turned towards each other and launched their dive-bombers, torpedo planes and fighters almost simultaneously at 9.15 a.m. Sixty-nine Japanese planes headed southwest as 75 American planes headed northeast.

The planes from USS *Yorktown* found and attacked the Japanese carrier *Shōkaku* just before 11 a.m. Two 1000-pound (454-kilogram) bombs hit *Shōkaku* and caused massive damage to her forecastle and flight and hangar decks. The other Japanese carrier, *Zuikaku*, was hidden under a bank of low clouds in a tropical rainstorm.

USS *Lexington*'s planes arrived at 11.30 a.m. Two of USS *Lexington*'s bombers found the *Shōkaku* and she was hit with another 1000-pound bomb. Two other bombers found *Zuikaku* and attacked her without doing any damage, but the rest of USS *Lexington*'s dive-bombers could not find the Japanese ships in the low cloud.

In the air-to-air battle, two of the thirteen Japanese Zeros protecting the fleet were shot down and five American planes were lost.

Shōkaku was severely damaged and unable to land aircraft. With 223 of her crew dead, she withdrew from the battle and headed northeast, escorted by two destroyers, bound for Japan.

USS *Lexington* detected the Japanese aircraft approaching by radar at a distance of 126 kilometres (75 miles) and Wildcat fighter planes were launched to defend the US carriers. The savage air battle helped deflect the Japanese attack to a large extent, but two torpedoes hit USS *Lexington* and an armour-piercing bomb hit USS *Yorktown* and exploded four decks beneath her flight deck.

As aircraft from the two enemies returned to their fleets, they met in mid-air and another battle ensued in which two Japanese planes were shot down, including that of their flight commander, Kakuichi Takahashi.

Forty-six of the 69 Japanese planes returned to land on *Zuikaku*, of which only 36 were able to fly again without repairs.

Admiral Takagi made another error when he reported to Inoue that two American carriers had been sunk. He also reported that, as his aircraft losses were heavy and he was low on fuel, he could not provide air cover for the invasion fleet. Admiral Inoue, aware of the presence of Admiral Crace's TF17.3, recalled the invasion convoy to Rabaul and ordered his warships to head northeast of the Solomons to prepare for the RY Operation.

Meanwhile, Admiral Fletcher was assessing the damage to his strike force. Although both USS *Yorktown* and USS *Lexington* were badly damaged, they were still able to land the returning aircraft. The Allies lost 23 aircraft in the action and another eight during recovery. However, the worst was yet to come for Admiral Fletcher.

USS *Lexington* had suffered damage to aviation fuel tanks in the bombing, and petrol fumes had leaked through much of the ship. The first of a series of explosions, caused by sparks from unattended electric motors, rocked the vessel just before 1 p.m., as planes were returning and landing. Further explosions between 2.45 and 3.45 p.m. resulted in a massive fire, and the crew began to abandon ship around 5 p.m.

With the fire out of control and the ship listing heavily, the destroyer USS *Phelps* was ordered to sink the carrier with torpedoes just after 7 p.m. Thirty-six aircraft went down with the USS *Lexington*. Despite the sudden loss of the USS *Lexington*, only 216 out of a crew of 2951 died in the loss of the carrier. Sadly, some of them died by jumping from the decks before it was really necessary to leave the ship.

Fletcher had already decided to take TF17 out of the Coral Sea before losing the USS *Lexington*. With the oiler USS *Neosho* sunk, he had no fuel supply, so he radioed General MacArthur suggesting an attack on the Japanese fleet by land-based army bombers. MacArthur radioed back that B-17s had attacked the invasion convoy and it was retreating northwards. TF17 headed south then east to refuel at Tonga before the damaged USS *Yorktown* headed to Pearl Harbor for hasty repairs.

Meanwhile, Admiral Crace and his TF17.3 were unaware of any of the battles of 7 and 8 May. TF17.3 patrolled until 10 May and then returned to harbour in the Whitsundays on 11 May. At the time, Crace had no way of knowing how important a role sightings of his fleet had played in creating errors of judgement and poor strategy by Japanese commanders.

Both sides claimed victory in the Battle of the Coral Sea. The sinking of USS *Lexington*, and the amount of luck involved in keeping the battle from being a major Japanese victory, gave the Japanese Imperial Navy a false sense of superiority and confirmed their poor opinion of Allied naval capability. They believed that future sea-to-air battles against the Allies would be easily won.

In simplistic terms, looking at the battle losses over the five days of conflict, the Japanese scored a major hit against the Allied fleet by sinking USS *Lexington*, one of only four American fleet carriers in the Pacific. They also sank a destroyer and a fuel oiler, while the Allied tally was a light aircraft carrier, a destroyer and four minesweepers. The Allies lost 70 aircraft, half of which went down on the USS *Lexington*, while the Japanese lost 92 aircraft. In terms of numbers killed, Japanese losses were 970 dead and the Allies lost 660 men.

The real results of the battle had nothing to do with numbers of ships or aircraft or lives lost. Most importantly, the sea-borne invasion of Port Moresby failed. For the first time a Japanese invasion force was made to turn back without achieving its objective. Subsequently, the Japanese made plans to invade the eastern end of New Guinea from the north and then attack overland and around the coast to capture Port Moresby.

In order to mount an overland attack on Port Moresby, the Japanese needed to use the only available overland route, the narrow 100-kilometre (62-mile) pathway over the Owen Stanley Ranges known as the Kokoda Track.

The fact that Japan did not win a decisive victory in the Coral Sea meant that the threat to the supply lines between the United

States and Australia was removed. This lifted morale among Allied forces, which had suffered a continuous series of defeats by the Japanese since Pearl Harbor.

The most important result of the Battle of the Coral Sea, however, was not apparent until after the Battle of Midway.

The Battle of Midway

Shōkaku, *Zuikaku* and *Shōhō* were all scheduled to be part of General Yamamoto's planned showdown with the American carriers at Midway. Now all three were lost from his battle line-up. One was gone, one was being repaired and the other was waiting on new aircraft to replace those lost in the Coral Sea. *Shōkaku* required almost three months of repair in Japan. *Zuikaku* needed new crew and aircraft and was not considered for use at Midway by Yamamoto, although it has been suggested that surviving *Shōkaku* aircrews combined with *Zuikaku's* aircrews could have seen her with sufficient air power to take some part in the battle.

Also, Yamamoto wrongly believed that two US carriers were lost in the Coral Sea.

USS *Yorktown* was, in fact, still operational. She was sufficiently repaired at Pearl Harbor in late May to be able to take part in the Battle of Midway in the first week of June 1942, one month after the Coral Sea battle. USS *Yorktown*'s aircraft helped sink two Japanese fleet carriers at Midway and the patched-up carrier was a third target for Japanese aerial attacks, which meant the Japanese strike force was thinned out considerably rather than being concentrated on the other two American carriers.

Historians and critics say that Yamamoto, having decided that the decisive naval battle was to take place at Midway, should never have diverted any of his fleet carriers to a secondary operation such as Operation MO.

Inoue and Yamamoto missed significant factors in the Coral Sea battle. The unexpected appearance of American carriers and planes in the right place was partly due to luck, but it was also due to the improving use of radar by the Allies.

Although not as well trained and experienced as their Japanese counterparts, US aircrews demonstrated skill and bravery in the Coral Sea encounters. The United States was training men faster than Japan and had superior industrial strength to build ships and planes, which meant that, once the Japanese lost their numerical naval superiority, as they did at Midway, they could never regain it. Every Japanese aircraft, airman and ship lost was irreplaceable.

The Allies learned more from the Battle of the Coral Sea than the Japanese and these lessons would count at Midway where Japan lost four fleet carriers, the mainstay of her Pacific naval force. It was at Midway that Japan lost the initiative in the Pacific War. The Battle of the Coral Sea made victory at Midway achievable for the Allies.

Close Ties

The Battle of the Coral Sea is celebrated annually around Australia as one of the most important events of WWII. One thing that came out of the event was a renewed optimism about the alliance with the United States and a strengthening of the bonds between the two nations. There was a feeling that Australia had managed to cooperate successfully and US naval involvement is still a feature of annual Battle of the Coral Sea celebrations in Australia.

It is certain that most Australians who join these celebrations accept that this battle was a major victory and believe that Australia was saved from the Japanese and the tide was turned in the Pacific War. However, few understand that the importance of this battle can only be viewed in hindsight.

It is not technically true that Japan intended to invade Australia if victorious in the Coral Sea and successful in the planned invasion of Port Moresby. Japan's plan was to establish a safe theatre of operations in the Pacific and then invade Fiji, Samoa and other Pacific Islands.

The fear of occupation was a major element of Australia's feeling of relief after the Coral Sea and Midway battles. There was a fear of the Japanese, who were seen, by a nation steeped in the White Australia Policy and feelings of British cultural superiority, as an inferior race, as well as the knowledge of the suffering and cruel treatment of Australian prisoners of war at the hands of the Japanese troops.

While the Japanese had no detailed plans to invade Australia, their plans to conquer the Pacific and separate us from our American allies were real and obvious, and the long-term results for Australia, had this occurred, would have been similar to an actual invasion on home soil.

The Coral Sea is off the coast of Australia. This battle was seen to be at home. The war was no longer being fought in strange foreign places with exotic names.

The incident that reinforced the importance of the Coral Sea battle in the Australian psyche was the invasion of Sydney Harbour by midget submarines three weeks later. This was an indication to Australians, even more so than the constant bombing of distant Darwin, of just how close we were to being on the frontline of war with Japan. The northern bombings and the furious debate about the rumoured 'Brisbane Line' plan to defend the southeast of Australia and abandon the north, added to the fear and hysteria Australians felt at the time about a Japanese presence very close by.

The Battle of the Coral Sea gave some hope for security and safety to a terrified nation. Australia's memory of the battle and its importance in the big picture of the war is coloured, even today, by this perspective. Similarly, the bond between Australia and the US, which was forged in the Pacific, was seen to be operating effectively in the Battle of the Coral Sea.

Our memory and celebration of the battle serves as a reminder that Australian foreign policy was moving from a reliance on Britain to closer ties with the Americans, a trend that was to continue after the war and that still affects the Australian life-style today.

THE ENEMY WE SIMPLY DIDN'T UNDERSTAND

During World War II, Australia's conflict with Japan was more than just a war between two armies, it was a war between two vastly different cultures and attitudes to life. Where the Australian soldiers were generally tough, laconic and easy-going, their Japanese opponents were obedient, fanatical and raised in the *bushido* tradition of 'death before dishonour'.

Nowhere is this better illustrated than in the amazing true life story of Matsuo Fuchida, the man who not only led and planned the bombing of Darwin, but also was the architect and leader of the infamous raid on Pearl Harbor.

The Darwin raids on 19 February were larger than the Pearl Harbor raid and more bombs were dropped than at Pearl Harbor. It was the first time since European settlement that mainland Australia had been attacked by a foreign enemy. The operation has often been described by military historians in retrospect as 'using a sledgehammer to crack an egg'.

Fuchida led the first group of 188 attack aircraft, which were launched from *Akagi*, *Kaga*, *Hiryū* and *Sōryū*, the four Japanese carriers of the First Carrier Fleet, commanded by Admiral Nagumo and stationed 350 kilometres (217 miles) from Darwin in the Arafura Sea near Timor.

Fuchida later said in his report that the operation 'seemed hardly worthy' of his highly trained strike force and that: 'A single pier and a few waterfront buildings appeared to be the only port installations. The airfield on the outskirts of the town . . . had no more than two or three small hangars, and twenty-odd planes of various types scattered about the field . . . were destroyed where they stood. Anti-aircraft fire was intense but largely ineffectual, and we quickly accomplished our objectives.'

Four months later Fuchida was about to be involved in the Battle of Midway when he had to undergo an emergency appendix operation on board the carrier *Akagi*.

Akagi was hit and exploded and sank during the battle, and Fuchida broke both ankles when the explosions threw him from a rope ladder he was using to leave the ship onto a deck metres below. He survived and spent the rest of the war as a staff officer.

Fuchida was again apparently singled out by fate to survive against the odds when he was part of a group sent to Hiroshima the day after the atomic explosion to assess the damage. While all other members of Fuchida's party died of radiation poisoning, Fuchida suffered no symptoms.

In 1947, Fuchida met a group of returning Japanese prisoners of war and among them was his former flight engineer, Kazuo Kanegasaki, who was believed to have died at Midway.

Kanegasaki told Fuchida that, as prisoners of war, Japanese soldiers captured by the Allies were well treated and not tortured or abused. He related how a woman whose missionary parents had been murdered by Japanese troops in the Philippines had cared for the Japanese POWs. Hearing this, Fuchida, raised in the *bushido* belief of revenge for honour, was stunned and became obsessed with trying to understand Christianity, although at first he couldn't find a bible translated into Japanese.

His obsession eventually led to a meeting with the Christian evangelist Jacob De Shazer and conversion to Christianity. Fuchida became a member of the Worldwide Christian Missionary Army of Sky Pilots and spent the rest of his life evangelising in the United States, becoming a US citizen in 1960. He died of a diabetes-related illness in 1976, aged 74.

Fuchida's total bewilderment at having to confront a completely different cultural philosophy, one he had been despising and attempting to destroy for a large part of his life, was a state of mind not uncommon among individuals on both sides during the Pacific War.

When 1000 Japanese prisoners staged a mass riot and breakout at the prisoner of war camp at Cowra, in central New South Wales, Australians were terrified and paranoid. What we didn't understand was that they wanted to destroy themselves . . . not us.

In fact, they had been ordered to do no harm to Australian civilians.

There were POW camps all around Australia during WWII. In New South Wales there were camps at Liverpool and Long Bay Gaol and others at Bathurst, Orange, Hay and Yanco, as well as Cowra.

Although the Japanese rarely surrendered alive, there were, by August 1944, 2220 Japanese prisoners of war in Australia, including 550 merchant seamen. In the *bushido* code, which was part of the Japanese military ethos, surrender was a sign of shame and disgrace; death was more honourable than surrender.

There were also 14,720 Italian POWs in Australia, most captured in North Africa, and 1600 Germans, mostly naval or merchant seamen.

Just outside Cowra, in the central west of New South Wales, about 300 kilometres (186 miles) by road from Sydney, was No. 12 Prisoner of War Compound (Camp 12), which housed 4000 military personnel and detained 'alien' civilians. At that time the town's population was just over 3000, so the prisoners outnumbered the locals.

Camp 12 was a large compound, covering 30 hectares, and was divided into four sections with well-lit, barbed-wire-fenced spaces in between for security. Two sections, A and C, held Italian prisoners. Camp D held the Korean and civilian detainees and the Japanese officers, and the 1100 Japanese non-commissioned officers (NCOs) and other ranks were held in Camp B.

Almost half of the Japanese prisoners of war in Australia were at Camp 12, along with 2000 Italians, some Koreans who had served in the Japanese military, and civilians from the Dutch East Indies (Indonesia) detained at the request of the Dutch.

POWs in Australia were treated in accordance with the Geneva Convention but cultural differences made relations between the Japanese prisoners of war and camp staff very unfriendly.

A riot by the Japanese at a New Zealand POW camp in February 1943 led to security being tightened at Cowra, and machine guns were installed to add to the rifles carried by the 22nd Garrison Battalion Militia who guarded the camp. They were mostly old or disabled veterans or young men considered physically unfit for frontline service.

In early August, partly in response to the New Zealand riot, plans were made to separate the Japanese NCOs from the other ranks in Camp B and relocate all but the officers and NCOs to the POW camp at Hay.

The Japanese inmates had discussed escape plans for some time and, after the prisoners were informed of the relocation plans on 4 August, Sergeant Major Kanazawa, commander of Camp B, told hut leaders to explain the situation to their men and conduct a vote to see if there was support for a mass breakout. Evidently the final decision to break out was far from unanimous and some of the twenty hut leaders distorted the results, but the decision was made for a mass escape.

Strict ground rules were laid down. Any injured or disabled prisoners who could not join in were asked to restore their honour by committing suicide when the rest escaped. The huts were to be burned so there was nowhere for recaptured prisoners of war to return to, and it was agreed that civilians would not be harmed.

Weapons were to be made from cutlery, baseball bats, timber, nails and wire; blankets would be carried to cover the barbed wire.

The men were divided into four groups. Two groups would climb the outer perimeter, which consisted of three fences and 10 metres (33 feet) of barbed wire entanglement. The other two groups would break into the space between the four camps, known as 'no man's land' or 'Broadway' due to the powerful bright lights. One of these groups was designated to link up with the Japanese officers in Camp D and the other was to attack the outer gates and the 22nd Garrison Battalion Militia barracks. A bugle would sound at 2 a.m. to start the operation.

The Japanese obviously saw the whole operation as a military exercise to restore their honour in death, rather than an escape to reach their homeland or annoy their enemies.

At 2 a.m. a lone Japanese prisoner of war ran to the gates of Camp B and shouted a warning to the sentries. A bugle sounded and 1000 prisoners, in three separate mobs and all shouting 'Banzai', began attacking the wire fences to the north, west and south.

The sentries started firing as soon as the Japanese warning was shouted, firstly a warning shot was fired and then, as the mob appeared, the sentries started shooting to kill. The militia garrison was awake within minutes and two privates, Benjamin Hardy and Ralph Jones, soon manned the truck-mounted No. 2 Vickers machine gun and started firing into the mob.

By sheer weight of numbers the two guards were soon over-whelmed and killed by a frenzied mob described later by Prime Minister John Curtin as having a 'suicidal disregard of life'. Hardy was clubbed to death and Jones stabbed. However, Private Jones had removed and hidden the machine gun's bolt while the Japanese were attacking and the gun could not be used by the prisoners against the guards. Both men were posthumously awarded the George Cross for bravery.

Another guard, Charles Shepherd, was also stabbed to death near the top end of 'Broadway' during the riot.

The two groups who broke into 'Broadway' failed to breach the main gates or link up with the Japanese officers in Camp D. They attempted to storm the guard posts at either end but were in direct firing line and remained pinned down for several hours.

Of the 378 Japanese who broke through the outer perimeter wire fences of Camp B, all those who remained alive, some 334, managed to escape.

It took ten days to round up the survivors of the breakout. The RAAF, police, Australian Women's Battalion stationed at Cowra and army trainees conducted the round-up operations. Some escapees made it across country as far as Eugowra, more than 50 kilometres (31 miles) away.

Many of the Japanese chose death rather than be recaptured. Two threw themselves under a train and some hanged themselves.

Two prisoners were shot by local civilians and several others by military personnel. Some pleaded to be shot when they were recaptured and some surrendered peacefully. Some died in suicide pacts, killed by their comrades.

Lieutenant Harry Doncaster of the 19th Australian Infantry Training Battalion was the only Australian killed in the pursuit, when he was attacked by a group of Japanese 11 kilometres (7 miles) north of Cowra.

In total, 231 Japanese soldiers were killed and 108 were wounded. Four Australians died, and another four were injured. No civilians were harmed.

Cowra is the largest prisoner of war breakout ever recorded.

Inquiries were held into the breakout and the reactions of the media and the general public were twofold. There was an increase in the level of general distrust and paranoia about the enemy; the same sort of reaction that had been experienced over the Darwin bombings and the midget submarine attack. There was also puzzlement and a failure to understand the Japanese psyche. These men seemed so different, with their focused and conditioned obedience to authority and narrow-minded cultural thinking, that most Australians simply thought they were weak-minded or insane. To many Australians, the Japanese appeared to be childlike, cruel and uneducated aliens.

When the camp was dismantled after the war, the puzzlement lingered on in the district and enough people were curious about the Japanese and their beliefs to begin to take steps to understand. Cowra was developed into a Centre of World Friendship.

Those Japanese who died on Australian territory now lie in the Cowra War Cemetery, which was opened in 1963 and, in 1979, Cowra's famous Japanese Gardens were established. Tourists can also visit the ruins of POW Camp 12 and an avenue of cherry blossom trees links the Cowra War Cemetery and Japanese Gardens to the site.

Part Four
THOSE MAGNIFICENT WOMEN AND MEN

In the entire history of *Homo sapiens* there has never been a notion as fanciful and unbelievable as the idea that mankind could fly in the air.

I can still recall the sense of wonderment that filled my young mind as I read of the exploits of the early explorers and navigators, from Vasco da Gama to James Cook and Matthew Flinders, who risked their lives, and the lives of all who sailed with them, venturing in fragile, wooden, manmade vessels across the trackless oceans to the ends of the earth and beyond.

But the idea of exploring the planet by travelling through the sky in heavier-than-air flying machines was even more wonderful and mind-boggling. It filled me with a sense of wonderment that eclipsed even the exploits of the great navigators and sailors.

Powered flight was still really in its infancy when I was child—the idea was less than 50 years old and I can still remember the first jet-powered aeroplanes coming to Australia.

A friend of mine, the legendary entertainer Frank Ifield, travelled on the first-ever commercial jet flight out of Sydney—and that was as recently as 1959. In fact, it was Frank's Australian father, Richard Ifield, who invented and perfected the fuel pumps that made jet engines possible.

Richard Ifield did this while he was working as an engineer for the Lucas aeronautical company in Coventry in the UK, just before World War II, which explains why Frank, a proud Aussie, was born in the UK and not here in Australia.

Most people of my grandparents' generation were born before 12 November 1894, when an Australian, Lawrence Hargrave, flew 16 feet in a sling seat attached to four of the box kites he had invented, proving that heavier-than-air flight was possible and providing a cornerstone for other inventors and pioneers.

My grandfather was a WWI veteran, born in 1891. He took my mother to see Charles Kingsford-Smith land in Sydney and he was part of the last generation to know what it was like to live in a world without planes, airports or an aviation industry. There were people still living as recently as the last decade who were born *before* powered flight existed!

The first man to be transported into the air and held there by a manmade device was Jacques-Etienne Montgolfier who, along with his brother Joseph, is credited with being the inventor of the hot air balloon, although archives unearthed in the Vatican in 1917 show that a Portuguese-Brazilian priest, Bartolomeu de Gusmão, demonstrated a working hot air balloon as early as 1708, although it never lifted a human being into the air.

That momentous event occurred on 15 October 1783, when Jacques-Etienne ascended 24 metres into the air in the basket of a balloon, which was tethered to the ground. Later that same day two French noblemen, Jean-François Pilâtre de Rozier and the Marquis D'Arlandes, made the first-ever free flight in a hot air balloon.

Lifting off from the grounds of a château near the Bois de Boulogne, the two gentlemen flew for 25 minutes, reaching a height of 3000 feet and travelling a distance of 9 kilometres. They had enough fuel to keep the fire going and travel even further, but were forced to land near some windmills outside the city walls when the fabric of the balloon caught fire. Monsieur de Rozier took off his coat and used it to put out the fire.

The events of 15 October 1783 were preceded by an ascent on 19 September of that same year when a sheep, a duck and a rooster were passengers in a hot air balloon that lifted off in the presence of King Louis XVI of France and Marie Antoinette.

Ballooning became the wonder of the age and the Montgolfier

brothers were the toast of Paris. The king elevated their father to the nobility as a reward for their achievements.

Jean-François Pilâtre de Rozier did not fare so well. He experimented with hydrogen as fuel for balloons and became the first victim of a fatal mid-air explosion when his hydrogen balloon blew up near Calais in 1785.

We even know the identity of the first woman to fly in a hot air balloon. Her name was Élisabeth Thible and, on 4 June 1784, eight months after the first manned balloon flight, she flew in a balloon financed by a group of merchants in Lyon and called *La Gustave*, in honour of King Gustav III of Sweden's visit to the city. The young opera singer managed to persuade one of the balloon's designers, the Comte de Laurencin, to let her take his place in the basket.

Madame Thible (described by some sources as 'the abandoned spouse of a Lyon merchant') was dressed as the Roman goddess Minerva and during the 45-minute flight, during which time they travelled 4 kilometres and reached heights estimated at up to 1500 metres, she and the balloon's other creator, a painter and designer named Fleurant, sang two arias from the opera *La Belle Arsene* by the composer Pierre-Alexandre Monsigny.

Sadly, the landing was rather bumpy and Madame Thible twisted her ankle as the basket hit the ground. Monsieur Fleurant said that the success of the flight was due to Madame Thible, who not only displayed courage and sang, but also fed fuel into the balloon's firebox to keep them airborne.

Parachuting arrived on the scene just fourteen years after the first balloon flight. Although Leonardo da Vinci had designed a parachute in the 15th century, André Jacques Garnerin was the first man to jump from a balloon using a parachute in October 1797 in Paris. He was 27 years old at the time and had first flown in a balloon he'd made himself when he was twenty.

In 1794 Garnerin, a public servant with the Department of Supply, had been seconded into the army of the French Republic, sent to negotiate with the Allied Forces then invading France, and promptly imprisoned in a castle.

He set about collecting materials and designing a parachute in order to escape, but was released and sent back to France before he could finish it.

The French government gave him funds to keep working on the idea and considered using balloons and parachutes to attack England, but eventually realised the idea lacked substance as the prevailing winds were from the west.

Garnerin's parachute, held open by whalebone, did not have a hole in the centre of the canopy so the parachutist had to rock from side to side to release the air, which tended to make him air sick. The French astronomer Joseph-Jérôme Lefrançois de Lalande suggested the idea of a central hole and Garnerin soon realised the whalebone was unnecessary.

He went on to make four more descents, including one from 8000 feet in London in 1802 with a 23-foot canvas parachute.

Garnerin's wife, Jeanne Geneviève Labrosse, was the first woman to make a parachute jump, on 10 November 1798, and his niece Elisa Garnerin became a professional parachutist, and made more than 40 parachute jumps around the world between 1815 and 1836.

In the mid nineteenth century, aviation pioneers like French-born American Octave Chanute and George Cayley in Britain, developed heavier-than-air machines which 'hopped' and glided short distances and 'almost flew'. Between 1880 and 1914, there was progress in the development of both heavier-than-air flying machines (which became known as aircraft, airplanes or aero-planes) and rigid bodied lighter-than-air machines (known as zeppelins or dirigibles).

As technology, building materials and engines developed, inventors and aircraft designers like Lawrence Hargrave in Australia, Horatio Phillips and Percy Pilcher in Britain, the Wright brothers in the USA, Brazilian Alberto Santos-Dumont and the Voisin brothers in France and Count Von Zeppelin in Germany paved the way for these flying machines to become more viable and reliable.

World War I saw a rapid advance in the development of planes and zeppelins as fighting machines. Britain developed fighters and bombers so quickly that the aircraft were named 'BEa1', etc—which stood for 'British Experimentals' a, b, c, . . . etc, number 1, 2, 3 and so on. The men who flew them called them 'Bloody Emergencies'.

By the end of the war both planes and zeppelins were developed enough to be used as reliable forms of transport and by the late 1920s international commercial flights by zeppelins and reliable air services by planes were a feature of modern life.

We take aviation for granted today, but the entire wonderful adventure of powered flight and air travel, with all its amazing and unbelievable stories of human endeavour, is really just over a century old.

SOME AUSSIE UPS AND DOWNS

It was 75 years after the Montgolfier brothers' flights that Australia's first successful hot air balloon ascent took place on 1 February 1858 at Richmond, which was then a semi-rural area outside Melbourne. An Englishman named Joseph Dean became the first person in Australia to fly when a 60-foot-high balloon, made in England by balloonist Charles Brown and inflated with gas supplied by the City of Melbourne's gasworks plant at Black Swamp, lifted him into the air.

Originally both Brown and Dean were to make the flight but it was a windy day and it became apparent that the balloon would support only one. After what was reported to be a 'vigorous argument', Brown allowed Joseph Dean to make the flight alone.

The flight lasted a little less than half an hour and the balloon descended near Heidelberg, having travelled about 8 kilometres.

Two weeks later, Charles Brown made a short flight and was then reportedly assaulted by an angry mob of Melburnians, who believed that it was wrong for humans to fly.

Balloon ascents and angry mobs were nothing new in the Australian colonies. At least one demonstration of balloon flight as a moneymaking 'entertainment' had been attempted in Australia before Joseph Dean's success. In fact, our first 'aviation death' had occurred in 1856, as the result of a failed balloon demonstration in the Domain in Sydney.

Monsieur Pierre Maigre, a French balloonist and entrepreneur, sold hundreds of tickets and erected a grandstand so that spectators could watch the first flight in Australia. The wind was rather too strong, however, and the balloon took ages to inflate; Monsieur Maigre attempted to postpone the event, but the crowd was having none of it.

Realising he had no choice but to attempt the ascent, Maigre tried to inflate the balloon sufficiently but it all went disastrously wrong when the balloon was swept along the ground and then caught fire and didn't rise.

The crowd began to riot and, in the crush, the grandstand was wrecked and a pole anchoring the hot air balloon was knocked down. It struck Thomas Downes, aged eleven, on the head. He was taken to the Sydney Infirmary and Dispensary, in Macquarie Street, where he died from his head injuries. Monsieur Maigre took refuge in Government House.

At the inquest, the jury unanimously decided that 'if any person is to blame, it is Monsieur Maigre, the perpetrator of the sham balloon ascent'. But, by then, Monsieur Maigre was nowhere to be found.

Thus, Thomas Downes became the first victim of an aviation accident in our history. He is buried at Camperdown Cemetery and, in what seems a particularly puzzling and unfeeling footnote to his tragic death, there's a hot air balloon carved on his headstone.

The first parachute descent in Australia was actually an accident.

On 14 April 1879 the Australian aviation pioneer and daredevil, Henri L'Estrange, had ascended in his balloon *Aurora* to well over a mile above the Agricultural Society's grounds in Melbourne. Suddenly the fabric of the balloon burst and the balloon plummeted earthwards. The silk parachute tied to the centre of the balloon quickly inflated, slowing the descent of the basket, which was further checked when it struck the side of a fir tree at the rear of Government House. L'Estrange survived intact.

On Saturday 8 December 1888 one Mr J.T. Williams, a 33-year-old watchmaker, who had migrated from Birmingham as a teenager and was a 'better than average gymnast', made the first intentional parachute jump in Australia from the Ashfield Recreation Ground in Sydney.

A crowd of more than 4000 watched him ascend in a balloon for seven minutes to 4000 or 5000 feet and then jump, using a parachute that 'resembled a Chinese pagoda'.

Loud cheers rang out as he attempted to guide his descent back to the waiting crowd, but he was carried away by the wind and came to earth near Homebush. The huge balloon he had used ended up at Greenwich, on the upper reaches of the harbour and was recovered in good order and the event was deemed 'a pronounced success'.

Mr Williams challenged a visiting daredevil calling himself Professor Baldwin to a contest during the American parachutist's visit to Australia in 1889, but it never eventuated.

The first woman parachutist in Australia was an American named Valerie De Freitas, alias Valerie Van Tassel, and her amazing story appears in this section.

Aussie inventor Lawrence Hargrave can be called the father of the aeroplane. He is credited with being the most important contributor to the development of the powered heavier-than-air (non inflated) flying machines and he quite possibly made the world's first powered flight in 1894. Perhaps inspired by the boomerang, he had discovered that curved surfaces lift more than flat ones and subsequently built the world's first box-kite, hitched four together, added an engine and flew five metres.

Hargrave was born in 1850 at Greenwich in England into a wealthy family. His uncle was a landowner in northern New South Wales and member of the colony's parliament. When Lawrence was six, his father left to join his brother and subsequently became a judge and attorney general of New South Wales. Young Lawrence went to a private school in Kent, where he lived with his mother until he was 15, and then joined his father in Sydney.

The lad was destined for a career in law but went on a sailing voyage around Australia and New Guinea, with his father's permission, and failed his matriculation examination. So, in 1867, he was apprenticed in the engineering workshops of the Australasian Steam Navigation Company and worked there for five years before heading off on several scientific expeditions to the islands and surviving the wreck of the brig *Maria* in the Coral Sea, in which 36 lives were lost. After several rather more successful expeditions, including exploration of the Fly River jungle, he was elected a member of the Royal Society of New South Wales in 1877.

Hargrave then went to work for five years as an astronomical observer at Sydney Observatory until his father died, leaving him property at Point Piper and Coalcliff. Lawrence was independently wealthy before he was 30 and, with income from land and coal of about £1000 a year, he gave up work and became an inventor.

Late in 1894 he lifted himself from the beach at Stanwell Park in a four-kite construction, attached to the ground by piano wire and, after he developed the design further and published his designs, almost all early experimental aircraft used Hargrave-type box kite structures.

Hargrave opposed the idea of patents and believed in sharing discoveries and ideas. He did not patent or copyright his inventions and designs, but allowed others, like the Wright brothers in the USA and Alberto Santos-Dumont, Gabriel and Charles Voisin and Louis Bleriot in France, to use them freely.

What is so commendable, and perhaps almost unbelievable in the modern commercial age, is that Hargrave actually encouraged others to use his ideas and develop them. Octave Chanute, the man who wrote the definitive history of early heavier-than-air flight, said of Hargrave:

> If there be one man, more than another, who deserves to succeed in flying through the air, that man is Mr. Lawrence Hargrave, of Sydney, New South Wales. He has now constructed with his own hands no less than 18 flying machines of increasing size, all of which fly, and as a result of his many experiments he now says, in a private letter to the writer, that: 'I know that success is dead sure to come.'

Hargrave is remembered as flying his box kites and aircraft at Stanwell Park but he also flew them many times over Sydney Harbour from where he lived at Point Piper.

Hargrave died of peritonitis aged 65, in July 1915, just two months after his only son, Geoffrey, was killed at Gallipoli. After his death his wife and four daughters went to live in England.

In later life Hargrave had offered his archive of papers and models to the state of New South Wales but, after there was little interest, he gave them to some German academics who donated them to the Deutsches Museum in Munich. Most were destroyed by Allied bombing in World War II and those remaining are now in the Powerhouse Museum collection in Sydney.

William Hudson Shaw, a Qantas Airlines executive and aviation historian, wrote numerous articles about Hargrave, whose daughters and grand-daughter gave Shaw many letters, papers and photographs which were donated to the Powerhouse Museum, which now has a display honouring the man regarded by many, including Santos-Dumont, Voisin, Bleriot and other European aviation pioneers, as the father of powered flight.

The Wright brothers used Hargrave's ideas, and even patented some of them, and never acknowledged him. He was featured on the Australian $20 note from 1966 to 1994.

The first controlled heavier-than-air flights in Australia recognised as 'officially first' occurred in Narrabeen in Sydney, on 5 December 1909.

On that day George Augustine Taylor successfully flew in a glider he designed and built. His wife Florence and their friend Emma Schultz also flew in the glider, which makes them the first Australian women to fly an aircraft. Florence had to tuck up her skirts in order to make the flight and later commented, 'My dress-maker never realised I was a budding aviatrix.'

As far as our pioneers of powered flight are concerned, there are three conflicting 'claims to fame' as the first man to fly a powered aircraft in Australia.

George Augustine Taylor, the man who made that historic glider flight at Narrabeen and later wrote the official history of Australian aviation for the first edition of *The Australian Encyclopedia*, gave the credit to Ehrich Weiss, who flew his French Voisin biplane at Diggers Rest, near Melbourne, on

18 March 1910. Weiss, who was better known to the world by his stage name, Harry Houdini, made a number of flights around Australia at that time.

There is well-documented evidence, however, that on 9 December 1909, just four days after George Taylor made his heavier-than-air flight in the glider at Narrabeen, a young Englishman, Colin Defries, left the ground in a Wright Model A aircraft at Victoria Park racecourse, near Kensington in Sydney. Defries flew the aircraft, named *The Stella* after his wife, 'straight and level' at a height of about 20 feet (6 metres) for a distance of 115 yards (105 metres) in front of a crowd of 150 people.

A reporter from the *Sydney Morning Herald* reported that Defries had actually flown 300 yards (274 metres) when his hat blew off and, in his effort to retrieve it, he crash-landed the aircraft, which was badly damaged.

Defries was not mentioned by George Taylor in his 'official' history and it was not until the 1960s that Defries was officially recognised as the first man to make a powered controlled flight in Australia. There are three possible reasons why George Taylor did not consider him worthy of the honour.

One reason could have been simple professional jealousy, but it may also be true that Taylor did not consider the flight made by Defries to have been 'controlled'. The third reason may be the fact that the flight was made in an aircraft designed by the Wright brothers. Taylor, and many other Australians, resented the fact that the Wright brothers used Lawrence Hargrave's ideas and never acknowledged the fact.

In 1960, aviation journalist Stanley Brogden suggested that the first powered flight in Australia actually occurred in South Australia, at a town called Bolivar, near Salisbury just north of Adelaide, when Fred Custance flew a Bleriot monoplane on 17 March 1910, just one day before Houdini's flight at Diggers Rest.

In 1967, Brogden retracted the claim as there were no independent authorities that witnessed the flight and there was no clear evidence that Custance, who had never flown before, had 'proper control of his machine'.

The owner of the property on which it took place, Mr F. Jones, who had imported the Bleriot, and several of his neighbours witnessed the flight. Custance made a second attempt but crashed, damaging the plane.

Custance was a skilled mechanic and motoring pioneer who migrated to South Australia with his family from England as a child. With his partner, Gilmore White, he drove from Melbourne to Adelaide in 20 hours and 6 minutes in March 1909 and from Melbourne to Sydney in 21 hours and 19 minutes in December 1909.

During WWI Fred Custance joined the Royal Flying Corps and flew BE2s in Palestine. He set a record by flying from Cairo to Romani in 40 hours and after the war became a successful 'Caterpillar' tractor dealer. He continued his motoring exploits until he perished in the South Australian outback after a car breakdown. He was just 33 years old.

In 1909 the new Australian government, carried away by all the excitement about flying, offered a prize of £5000 to anyone who could invent 'a flying machine suitable for use in war'. There were more than 40 entries, but none were practical and so the prize was never collected.

The men who developed the Australian aviation industry in the 1920s were almost all survivors of WWI. These were men who learned to fly during the war and survived to develop aviation in Australia.

Many of the young men who enlisted in the army in WWI saw the chance to join the flying corps as a wonderful piece of luck. They would never have had the chance to learn to fly back home on the farm or in their city jobs.

The majority of them died, in training, in battle, or just in the normal course of flying. The few who survived mostly wanted the chance to keep flying as civilians.

This small group became the foundation of the emerging aviation industry. They begged and borrowed money to purchase or lease surplus army planes after the war. They badgered governments for sponsorship, set up aviation companies that delivered mail, freight and passengers. They tested new machines and new technology and helped design and develop bigger and better aircraft, and many died doing it.

The list of the men who were members of the Royal Flying Corps in WWI and went on to pioneer our aviation industry includes Charles Kingsford-Smith, Keith Smith, Ross Smith, Charles Ulm, Bert Hinkler, Hudson Fysh, Frank McNamara VC, Wally Shiers, Hubert Wilkins, Fred Custance, Raymond Parer, Jim Bennet, Francis Briggs and John McIntosh.

When you consider that the life expectancy of a new pilot on the Western Front in 1917 was five weeks, it makes you realise how lucky these men were to survive the war and help build Australia's aviation industry.

'Smithy' always said that being shot through the foot and repatriated to England to be a pilot instructor was the thing that saved his life in World War I. He often commented on the irony of the fact that he was given a medal, as well as having his life saved.

It is a chilling afterthought to consider that six of the men listed above were killed in aviation accidents within twenty years of the end of WWI.

As usual, it was different for women.

In Australia women were not granted pilots' licences until 1927, which was about seventeen years after most other English-speaking countries.

Hilda McMaugh, an Australian nursing sister who worked in Britain during World War I, passed her flying test in Britain in 1919. She was the only female among 400 who received their wings that year, yet when she returned to Australia, she was not allowed to fly.

Millicent Bryant was the first woman to hold a pilot's licence in Australia when she was granted licence number 71 in March 1927. Sadly, Millicent, who was 49 years old when she was given her licence to fly, died just eight months later, along with 39 others, when the ferry *Greycliffe* was cut in half by the steamer *Tahiti* on Sydney Harbour.

By 1930, eighteen women had gained pilot's licences in Australia and the arrival of Amy Johnson in May 1930 inspired another ten to do so within months.

Freda Thompson became the first Australian female flying instructor in 1934. She was also the first woman in the British Empire to become a flying instructor.

Maude Bonney, who was married to a cousin of Bert Hinkler, is reputed to have taken flying lessons when her husband refused to let her drive a car. Legend has it that the local milkman drove her in secret to Eagle Farm airport to take lessons.

Her husband, Henry, a wealthy Brisbane businessman who owned a leather manufacturing business, became far more supportive once he realised what his wife had achieved. He bought her a DH 60 Gipsy Moth, which she named *My Little Ship*.

Maude Bonney went on to be the first woman to fly from Australia to Britain, and made the first flight from Australia to South Africa in 1937. She also circumnavigated Australia and set a record for the longest one-day flight by a woman when she flew 1600 kilometres from Brisbane to Wangaratta in 1931. Her Gipsy Moth was requisitioned by the defence forces during World War II and scrapped after the war.

It is true that the majority of early women flyers in Australia came from relatively privileged backgrounds and had the time and money to pursue their interest in aviation. This was certainly not true, however, in the case of Nancy Bird, who operated charter services in outback New South Wales and Queensland, flew doctors to remote areas and saved many lives.

Nancy once commented that 'other women who flew were women of independent means, but I had to do something with it'. She was the first woman to work in commercial aviation in Australia, pioneered air ambulance services and formed the Australian Women's Pilots' Association. She was a wonderful, feisty woman.

I telephoned her once to check some details for a story about her. She was in her 90s at the time but chatted to me and shared stories and laughed about how shocked people were when she was driven to Mascot Airport each day by Charles Kingsford-Smith, who taught her to fly and was divorced at the time. She graciously agreed to be my guest on a radio program and concluded the conversation by saying, 'Just send the article over to me and I'll proofread it for you.'

In 1970 Mary O'Brien became the first Australian woman to work as a pilot for a major international airline, Singapore Airlines. In 1974 Christine Davey became the first female passenger-airline pilot in Australia, flying with Connair out of Alice Springs.

Deborah Wardley, who eventually piloted passenger aircraft for KLM, had to battle through the equal opportunity board in Victoria before Ansett Australia included her in their pilot training program.

In 1992 Sharelle Quinn became Australia's first international female flight captain with Qantas.

Madame Thible would have been pleased!

THE SCANDALOUS FLYING TASSELS

The headline in the *South Australian Register* read A DROP FROM THE CLOUDS—DARING FEAT BY A FAIR AERONAUT. It referred to an event that took place at the Adelaide exhibition grounds on the afternoon of Saturday, 3 May 1890, when the American entertainers, the daring Van Tassel sisters, performed acrobatics on a trapeze suspended below a 78-foot pear-shaped calico balloon. The 'fair aeronaut' was Gladys Van Tassel, who hung by her feet from a trapeze suspended beneath the balloon and did acrobatic tricks, which 'displayed great daring and skill'.

When the balloon reached 4000 feet and was 'just a speck in the sky', Gladys jumped and, opening a muslin parachute, descended to the ground in the square outside the Wellington Hotel where a local band was in place to play 'See The Conquering Hero Come' as Gladys, clad in a skimpy sequined costume, landed safely in the square.

This was all too much to bear for the more conservative elements of Adelaide society. After all, this was the City of Churches in the colony that had never been sullied by convict transportation, and the Flying Van Tassels were evidently more than enough to outrage the more prudish, dare we say 'wowserish', citizens of Adelaide.

The performance and the costume were denounced as immoral and there were calls to cancel any further such demonstrations.

Gladys Van Tassel defended her costume stoutly, telling the gentlemen of the Adelaide press that it was simply 'what professional athletes wore' and 'could not be more wanting in decency than a costume which society demanded in the way of dress'.

The Van Tassel troupe, as we shall discover, were quite used to scandal and sensationalism, to them it was water off a duck's back—especially when you realise that the whole exercise in Adelaide provided them with a net profit of more than £400, an enormous amount for a day's work in 1890.

It was not, however, the first parachute descent to thrill the good citizens of Adelaide.

The Christmas celebrations at Adelaide Oval in 1888 included a 'death defying parachute leap from a balloon' by the 'American champion aeronaut, Professor Bartholomew' who looked 'very Mephistophelian in his sombre garb', which was 'a close fitting black costume with blue trunks'. The Professor's reputation for narrow escapes preceded him, according to the Adelaide press, and he had, evidently, previously landed in reservoirs, on the tops of churches and even in the Atlantic Ocean.

With such a reputation, it is no wonder that crowds waited all day to see him ascend, in his 60-foot balloon, to a reported height of 3000 feet, and then parachute to the ground, at which point the crowd 'rushed to greet their hero'.

Gladys's younger sister Valerie had made the first descent by a woman from a balloon in Australia, at Newcastle Racecourse on Saturday 8 February 1890, not long after the troupe arrived from the USA via Hawaii.

Gladys made the second parachute jump and descent by a female in Australia at the Newcastle Cricket Ground two weeks later. There was also another performance at Maitland before the Flying Van Tassels moved on to Sydney, where they were booked to perform at the Bondi Aquarium.

The *Sydney Morning Herald* gave a graphic and colourful account of the event:

Miss Val Van Tassel made a very successful balloon ascent from the grounds of the Bondi Aquarium, and descended by the aid of a parachute on Saturday afternoon. Some thousands of persons were attracted to the grounds to witness the daring performance; for this was the first time a woman had undertaken such a feat in Sydney.

The entertainment venue commonly known as Bondi Aquarium was a major amusement park, zoo, skating rink and dance hall situated in Fletcher's Glen at Tamarama Beach. It went by the official name of 'The Royal Aquarium and Pleasure Grounds' and was later developed to become Sydney's 'Wonderland City' after it was bought and expanded by the entrepreneur William Anderson in 1906.

Once public bathing was permitted by law, in 1903, and surf life-saving clubs were formed around 1906, conflict arose about public access to the beach and the venue finally closed in 1911. In its heyday it was a precursor to Luna Park with a roller coaster, skating rink, ghost train and zoo featuring Alice the elephant and a seal pool.

A group of swimmers eventually took a deputation to the Minister for Lands, James Ashton, who issued an order in 1907 for the resumption of a 12-foot strip of land fronting the beach to 'give free access for all time to the beach at Tamarama Bay'.

The swimmers then formed the Tamarama Surf Life Saving Club and in February 1908 the first surf carnival (called at the time a 'surf gymkhana') was held at Wonderland on Tamarama Beach. These events were held annually until Wonderland City closed.

Back in 1890 the Van Tassels were a big drawcard at the Bondi Aquarium, although the *Sydney Morning Herald* noted that a seaside location was not the safest place for pioneering aeronautics:

> Bondi Aquarium Grounds are on the sea beach and it cannot be said that they are by any means the safest place for such a thing as a parachute descent; still no accidents have ever happened at this favourite pleasure resort. The feat was advertised to come off at 4 o'clock, and there was a large crowd present at that hour to see the promised exhibition.

The balloon 'Australia' was lying on the grass, and no attempt at inflation had up to that time been made. There was a strong breeze blowing out to sea, and some distance up in the air it was known that the wind was blowing very strong.

For a while it looked as if the event may not happen, and the *Herald* reported that 'the spectators became weary'. Those who waited patiently were, however, finally rewarded when 'the wind veered round a bit, and at half-past 6 o'clock a start was made to inflate the balloon'.

Half an hour later Miss Valerie Van Tassel appeared 'looking as happy as if she had been going on a pleasure trip ... ready to make her journey into the clouds':

> The young lady stood holding a trapeze, which was fastened to the balloon. When the word was given to let the balloon go, away the parachutist was borne skywards amidst the cheers of the spectators.

The balloon ascended rapidly, but the prevailing breeze carried it away towards Coogee. Before she disappeared partially from view, Valerie 'performed on the trapeze, and hanging on to the bar by her toes she looked downwards, kissing her hands to the spectators'.

When the balloon became stationary, only the top of the parachute was visible, but then it was 'seen to open, and it was then known that the young lady had commenced her descent'.

At this point the balloon 'shot into the air, and continued its course' and that's the last any of the spectators at the Bondi Aquarium knew of the deed until 35 minutes later when 'Miss Van Tassel was within the grounds at Bondi again'.

On her return to the starting point of her adventure, Valerie was able to tell the crowd what had eventuated after they saw her drop from the balloon. The *Herald* related the story to its readers this way:

> The balloon was at a height of about 4000ft., when the parachutist dropped. From a conversation with Miss Van Tassel, it seems that

the balloon went up steadily until crossing the cliffs at Bondi, when a heavy gust took it slightly to the south-east. It was just after this that Miss Van Tassel performed on the bar, but she found that the wind was too strong, and the young lady had to give it up.

She travelled along by the sea shore, and then passed over a cemetery about half a mile in shore. The parachutist knew that she was safe after this, there being previously a danger of drifting out to sea, but she was 'not nervous'.

When over Little Coogee, the balloon remained stationary, and the parachute becoming open, the young lady cut away.

The parachutist had to guide her parachute when descending to prevent her alighting on the top of a house.

She came down in a field where some cricketers were at play. Miss Van Tassel then secured her parachute and returned in a cab to Bondi.

What I find truly amazing about the whole thing is that, in the year 1890, it was possible to ascend in a hot air balloon from Bondi, jump out over Coogee, pack up your parachute, find a cab, and return to Bondi in 35 minutes. I'm sure you could not possibly manage that today.

When she was interviewed about the jump at Bondi some two months later in Adelaide, Valerie gave her personal recollection about her fears and her embarrassment at having to face the crowd back at Bondi, after her cab ride, in a rather bedraggled condition:

When I made the ascent at Bondi near Sydney, the wind was blowing very strongly, and I drifted right across the bay, which perhaps you know. It was a queer sensation when I looked down and saw the angry waves immediately beneath me. I wondered if I should be blown out to sea, because you can never depend upon the upper currents; but, thank, goodness, I wasn't.

I was wafted right over to little Coogee, when I descended into a large mud hole. I cut a pretty figure, I can assure you, and when, in response to the cheers of the people back at the Aquarium,

I had come forward and bow my acknowledgements, I looked as though I had just been fished out of a ditch.

This particular interview, which appeared in the *Adelaide Advertiser* on 24 April 1890, is the most detailed and personal of all the interviews conducted while the Van Tassels were in Australia. We're not certain who the 'special reporter' was, but he appears to have been rather taken in by Valerie's charming personality and humility:

Miss Valerie Van Tassel is a young lady whom you would be likely to pass by in the street without supposing for the moment that she was the daring aeronaut who has been thrilling the public of the sister colonies by her aerial flights.

She is of medium height, good figure and face, a wealth of auburn hair, and a genial style about her that is very taking.

When I called upon her at her hotel on Wednesday afternoon she was engaged superintending the manufacture of a parachute by means of which she or her sister, Miss Gladys van Tassel, will descend from the clouds on Saturday afternoon next.

'You know,' she said, 'you can't be too careful about an apparatus on which your life depends, and you feel ever so much easier in your mind when you have had it constructed under your own supervision. There is a great deal more work about a parachute than you would imagine, and whilst being light at the same time it has to be constructed of the very best and strongest material. But I'm sure you won't care to stay here listening to the incessant whirr of the sewing machines, so if you've no objection we'll adjourn to my sitting room, where we can have a quiet chat.'

Once safely ensconced in the privacy of Valerie's sitting room, the special reporter was able to ask such hard-hitting questions as, 'Have you been following the aeronaut business long, Miss Van Tassel?' to which Valerie gave an interesting answer which indicated that, although she and her sister were trapeze artists or acrobats professionally, the business of jumping out of balloons equipped with handmade parachutes was a new enterprise in their lives, one which had only begun when they arrived on our shores:

No, Gladys and myself only adopted it since we came to Australia. I first went up a few months ago at Newcastle, and since then I have made several successful ascents in the other colonies.

I am the first lady who has ever done any of this balloon work in Australia. When I first went up I somehow didn't feel at all nervous, but I must say I was very excited. My sister and myself have for some years past been engaged in aerial work, notably in connection with the flying trapeze business, and we always perform on the trapeze in making ascents and before cutting away the parachute. In reference to aerial work I do not mean balloon business.

In response to the question, 'What is the sensation like when you cast yourself adrift from the balloon?', Valerie answered:

Well, in the first place you dive through the air at such speed that you can hardly think. It is like falling from a steeple and as the balloon soars away you experience a feeling of loneliness—like having an old friend taken away from you. You fall, as a rule, from 50 to 100 feet before the parachute expands, and then as you gradually descend the feeling is a very pleasant one. You have the whole surrounding country stretching around you for miles, and the extensive panorama grows clearer and more distinct as you near the earth.

The sensation experienced in ascending is very queer when performing on the bar on account of the rush through the atmosphere. About 6,000 feet is the highest elevation to which I have ascended. My brother always fires a gun when he considers I have gone sufficiently high and I then cut away the parachute and descend.

At this point in the interview Mr Park Van Tassel entered the room and was interviewed by the reporter about his achievements as a balloonist in the USA. The article concluded with the prediction by the reporter that, 'When Miss Van Tassel makes her ascension on Saturday afternoon next there is sure to be a big crowd to witness her daring feat.'

What he did not predict was the public outcry over the shockingly immoral nature of Miss Van Tassel's skimpy costume and the calls from certain sections of the outraged Adelaide citizenry for such demonstrations to be banned.

Another thing that the completely besotted young reporter apparently failed to ascertain during his interview was the fact that Mr Park Van Tassel, the mastermind behind the whole venture, was not Valerie's brother at all. In fact, Valerie and Gladys were in no way related to Park Van Tassel, although it is true that they were sisters.

Their real name was De Freitas and it appears that they were from a family of acrobats, perhaps circus people, and had been hired by Van Tassel sometime during his travels while performing in mainland USA, or perhaps in Hawaii, and joined the troupe as his 'sisters'.

Park Van Tassel was born in Indiana and was a typical 19th century American flamboyant opportunist, what was known in the US as 'a huckster'. Tall, blond and good-looking Park was the owner of the Elite Saloon in Albuquerque, New Mexico, and was around 30 years of age when he began his ballooning exploits, which were calculated to make a quick buck.

He bought a balloon made from cattle intestines for $850 in California, called himself 'Professor' (which he later upgraded to 'Captain') and planned to make the first manned balloon flight in New Mexico's history at Albuquerque's Fourth of July festivities in 1882.

The balloon, christened *The City of Albuquerque*, required 30,000 cubic feet of coal gas to inflate and he managed to talk the residents of Albuquerque into giving up access to their home supplies of gas so the feat could take place on 4 July.

The launch was planned for 10 a.m. but the balloon was still only partially filled at 6.15 p.m. when Professor Van Tassel and a local reporter prepared to lift off. Nothing happened so the reporter stepped out.

Still nothing happened so Van Tassel tossed a heavy sandbag over the side, which managed to land on the head of a spectator who later sued him.

At last the balloon slowly rose to 11,000 feet, according to the Professor's 'on-board instruments', at which point he threw out more ballast and climbed to 14,207 feet. With the air becoming thinner and colder, Van Tassel panicked, opened a valve too quickly and made a bumpy landing in a corn field near the fairgrounds.

Within a week he attempted another ascent during which he crashed, wrecked the balloon and immediately started looking for another.

Park Van Tassel was hooked on the 'balloon business' and made many ascents, the longest being some 300 miles in a 6 hour 45 minute flight that carried him from Salt Lake City right over the Wasatch mountain range. At the time parachuting was becoming the latest daredevil craze in Europe, so Van Tassel made his own parachute, using a diagram he found in a book in a library, and made his first jump in Kansas City sometime around 1885.

Around this time he married Jeanette 'Jenny' Rumary, who soon became a prime attraction in the Van Tassel touring troupe and was scheduled to attempt the first parachute jump by a woman, in Los Angeles, on 4 July 1888.

During a practice run she landed on the roof of the home of a former mayor and knocked down his chimney, which led to the police trying to stop her upcoming jump.

A police detective was assigned to follow her and prevent the attempt, but she eluded him and made her historic leap from 6000 feet. After the event, the 75-kilogram Jenny was quoted as saying, 'I ain't exactly a bird nor an angel, but it's just about what I imagine the sensation of flying is. It was beautiful!'

There were several encounters with death. In 1889, Park Van Tassel's parachute lines became tangled over the ocean just west of San Francisco and he barely escaped drowning. More scandal followed in Hawaii where it was reported that Van Tassel had died when his parachute failed to open over shark-infested waters.

When the Professor was seen quite alive and well after the incident, it was revealed that the man who died was a certain Joe Lawrence from Albuquerque, who travelled with the Van Tassel troupe and had done all the jumps credited to Park Van Tassel, who apparently hadn't jumped since his near-fatal experience off San Francisco.

Van Tassel had a good philosophy when scandal or disaster struck—'move on'. So he took his troupe on a 'world tour' to Australia and Asia, and they managed to generate controversy at just about every stop, which was usually good for business.

In Australia the 'Van Tassel' sisters wore skimpy, skin-tight, sequinned outfits and caused a sensation with their acrobatics while dangling from trapezes below the gondola before dropping to earth using their homemade muslin parachutes.

The biggest scandal of the entire trip to Australia occurred when they performed in Townsville and were accused of 'assisting to desecrate the Sabbath'.

For the performance which took place on Sunday 22 June at Acacia Vale Gardens, Townsville, Gladys wore her usual 'circus-style' costume—a blue bodice and tights—which had caused trouble in Adelaide previously. She was described by the press in Townsville as being 'scantily-clad'.

The factors which led to the scandal in the press, apart from North Queensland prudishness, were the costume; the fact that it was a Sunday and people were charged a fee to be entertained on the sabbath; and that 500 of the 2000 spectators were soldiers, members of the Queensland Defence Force, who were in Townsville for their annual training encampment.

A trench was dug from the balloon to a wood fire and covered over with earth to make a tunnel and the balloon was tied to the ground by ropes. As it gradually expanded it had to be held down until it was ready to be released by some of the defence force troops, assisting with the permission of the commandant, Colonel French. Major des Vœux of the defence force also presented Gladys with a bouquet of flowers.

As the balloon began to rise, Gladys performed her usual stunts on the trapeze bar and then released herself and descended to earth using the parachute.

A scandal erupted after the performance because not only had Miss Van Tassel performed this feat on a Sunday, it was also witnessed by almost the entire Queensland Defence Force and there were unofficial reports that one military critic claimed the soldiers were so mesmerised by the scantily clad skydiver that there would be 'an outbreak of masturbation that would ruin their collective manhood'.

A visiting evangelist, the Reverend James Stewart of Brisbane, arrived on the scene and attempted to prevent the ascent from going ahead by waving a copy of a religious act concerning the observance of the sabbath, which he claimed to be 'the creed of the people of Townsville'.

Stewart was a vocal member of the 'Sabbatarian' movement which was closely allied to the Temperance Movement and attempted to preserve the religious and pious nature of Sundays by preventing any commercial or entertaining activities from taking place on what was, for working people, their only day of rest and recreation.

The defence force officers and police refused to stop the exhibition and several people in the crowd loudly reminded Mr Stewart of certain scandals regarding money raised for hospitals in Brisbane, in which he was accused of being implicated.

The *Townsville Daily Bulletin* reported that the Reverend Stewart addressed the crowd with these words:

> In the name of the right-thinking citizens of this colony I protest against the members of the Defence Force—which costs this colony £60,000 a year, and to the support of which we largely contribute—being allowed to assist in desecrating the Sabbath.

The scandal snowballed out of all proportion and was eventually debated in the Queensland parliament, where the National Party Premier, Boyd Morehead, was condemned for not having stopped the event and earlier ascents in Brisbane.

Colonel French defended himself by stoutly claiming that he was defamed in the *Townsville Daily Bulletin*:

> The whole of the leading article referred to is more or less a tissue of falsehoods and scarcely requires denial in detail. I may state, however, that I drove to the ground with a private party and saw most of what went on there.

The poor colonel, caught in a web of what we might today call 'overly politically correct nonsense', attempted to defend himself by explaining that he was merely attempting to provide his red-blooded soldiers with the kind of recreation they heartily enjoyed and had earned after days of military exercises and drill:

> It was represented to me by some of the senior officers of the local forces that their men generally wished to be present to see the balloon ascent and having also been informed that the Government had made no objection to the performance, I gave the necessary permission. A long military experience has convinced me that the religious principles of the men, or the absence thereof, are matters with which superior officers had better not interfere.

The colonel went on to state that his own views regarding the sabbath were irrelevant, as he was acting as the commanding officer of his troops. He therefore gave permission for a 6-mile route march to proceed from the defence force camp to Acacia Downs, where the ascent was to take place. He then gave orders that:

> . . . the men could rest in that vicinity, those who desired to see the balloon ascent being allowed to enter the gardens . . . those who did not wish to enter the gardens were to remain outside. I myself gave the senior officer positive orders on this point, as I thought it likely that some of the men might not care to go in. I may add that as I looked on the whole matter as one to be settled for the convenience of the local forces, any further details were

left to the local officers. No staff officer accompanied the force, or took any part in their proceedings.

Colonel French then went on to specifically deny newspaper claims that his men were ordered to attend the event, that hundreds of school cadets were forced to attend, and some to assist with the balloon or that 'a gentleman honoured by the Queen's commission, and wearing her uniform, went on his knees to a female acrobat with apparently the approval of the Commandant and of his brother officers'.

In defending himself from accusations that 'he went down on his knees and presented a female acrobat with a bunch of flowers', Major des Vœux, wrote:

> I have the honour to report, for the information of the Chief Secretary, that they are totally untrue. Attached is a paragraph from the copy of the Northern Age, published on the same date, 23rd June, which correctly relates the incident: 'We are informed that the true story regarding the handing of the bouquet to Miss Van Tassel by Major des Vœux was as follows:—The Major was standing by while preparations were being completed for the ascent. An assistant was holding a bouquet of flowers and having to do something else asked Major des Vœux if he would mind holding the flowers. This he did, and when all was ready, Miss Van Tassel looked round for her bouquet which was then handed to her by Major des Vœux.'

Colonel French then attempted to take the moral high ground and, in answer to the accusations of the 'editor of the *Townsville Daily Bulletin*, in the issue referred to, and certain clergymen who from the pulpit have thought fit to vilify me from their idea of a highly moral and religious standpoint', he made a statement which I am sure would find sympathy with those thousands of innocent people who have found themselves to be victims of either overzealous clergyman or newspapermen seeking to sensationalise an otherwise perfectly ordinary incident:

To these I can only with the utmost humility reply in the words of Moses the lawgiver, 'Thou shalt not bear false witness against thy neighbour.'

Sadly, as is often the case, common sense did not prevail and the result of the beat-up was a pyrrhic victory for the wowsers.

The Chief Secretary's Department, responsible for legal and parliamentary matters in the colony of Queensland, refuted the colonel's claims and the poor fellow was hung out to dry by official statements from the chief secretary which included:

I cannot regard the Commandant's explanation of the circumstances which occurred on the Sunday in question as in any degree satisfactory.

. . . that Colonel French was further informed that the Government had no objection to the performance being given is equally inadmissible in justification of the arrangements to which he gave his authority as it does not appear that he made any inquiry from the proper source as to whether or not the information was correct. Had Colonel French done so he would have learned that the Government had a most decided objection to any such course being pursued as that which he though fit to adopt.

The chief secretary then went on to question Colonel French's claim that staff officers were not officially involved and stated that, while he accepted Major Des Vœux's explanation of the incident with flowers, he disapproved of the 'tone and language adopted by that officer in giving his explanation'.

He then took the side of the 'Sabbatarian' and the wowsers and roundly attacked 'Colonel French's remarks concerning (it is assumed) the Rev. Mr Stewart':

I consider them most injudicious and uncalled for. In protesting as he did against what he regarded as a public desecration of the Sabbath, the reverend gentleman was only doing his duty, and his efforts, in my opinion deserved the assistance and not the censure of any right-minded man.

I desire again to express my opinion as to the unsatisfactory nature of the explanation which I cannot regard as adequate to release Colonel French from the charge of neglect of duty in not preventing what I hold to have been nothing less than a public scandal.

Premier Morehead was a pioneering cattleman who owned thirteen cattle properties in the Mitchell district, and who represented that district in parliament. He was, no doubt, well aware of the hard-line prudish feelings of rural Queenslanders.

He eventually caved in to the Chief Secretary's Department and the wowsers, whose complaints were constantly voiced by the *Brisbane Courier Mail*, which pompously printed 'I-told-you-so' editorials with statements like:

Had the Government dealt wisely with our appeal of a few weeks ago, touching female parachuting in Brisbane, the colony would have been spared the scandal of the Sunday exhibition just made at Townsville.

And:

Innocent exhibitions might easily be tolerated on Sunday; yet these are the very exhibitions which would shrink from presenting themselves. Exhibitions on the contrary which are inherently demoralising, and objectionable therefore on any day of the week, are precisely those which come boldly forward to outrage the sacred convictions of the people.

In order to prevent himself from becoming even more of a target for the forces of outraged righteousness, inside and outside parliament, the premier made it clear to Colonel French that he would be removed from his position unless he apologised.

Sir George Arthur French was 49 at the time of the scandal. Educated at the Royal Military College, Sandhurst, and the

Royal Military Academy, Woolwich, he had served with distinction in Canada and became the first permanent commissioner of the North West Mounted Police (later Royal Canadian Mounted Police).

Under his command the mounted police established their worldwide reputation for honesty, justice and fair play. He was knighted in 1877 and appointed Commandant of the Queensland Defence Forces in 1883. He helped to develop the defence forces in Queensland and New South Wales, and drafted the Defence Act for the new federal parliament in 1901.

To the eternal shame of Queensland, this fine military man was forced to apologise in 1890 for allowing soldiers to see a balloon and parachute demonstration. He sent the following letter to the chief secretary:

> Having now obtained legal opinions on the matter, I understand that, although I imagined I was acting quite within my powers in giving those under my command permission to attend the Acacia Vale Gardens on Sunday, the 22nd June, and affording facilities for their so doing, I was clearly in error in giving such permission through ignorance of the civil law on the subject. In view however of the fact that the law in question is as I believe a very old one, dating I understand from the time of Charles I, and that no answer was received to the application to the Government to have the proposed proceedings stopped, and that the local authorities took no steps, and I believe refused to take any steps in that direction, I trust that I may be acquitted of any wilful intention to disregard the law.
>
> I have now to express my very great regret for placing myself in the wrong even technically in the matter, and for permitting orders to do so, and in the event of your thinking proper to modify the severe remarks in your minute of the 7th instant, I beg to request that any censure may be confined to myself as I now take the whole responsibility for the presence of members of the Defence force on the occasion referred to, and the consequences thereof.

Park Van Tassel and his troupe moved on, as usual, but a repeat Sunday performance a week later in Charters Towers was stopped when the colonial secretary, prompted by the objections of local Sabbatarians, banned the proposed event.

The stupidity of the whole situation was highlighted by the fact that, in order that the public could witness the parachuting and trapeze acts, a half-holiday was granted to Charters Towers during the following week.

Having spent six months in Australia, during which time they performed their acrobatic and parachute feats dozens of times and managed to scandalise the city of Adelaide and the colony of Queensland, the Van Tassel sisters faded away into the mists of colonial history.

Premier Morehead battled on until August 1890 when, perhaps tired of Queensland politics, wowsers and political and military affairs generally, he resigned as premier in order to spend more time with his cattle. He had, after all, borne the burden of leading the colony of Queensland for almost two years.

Colonel French survived the scandal and went on to be a most competent and useful servant to the Australian people, leading the committee that designed the national defence forces for the new federal government.

Park Van Tassel and his wife Jeanette moved on, as usual, and performed their ballooning and parachuting feats in Siam, India and Burma.

In 1892, Park and Jeanette were invited to participate in a grand celebration by the Nawab of Dhaka, which involved the first balloon ascent in East Bengal. The plan was to launch the balloon from the riverbank of the Buriganga River, float north and land on the roof of the main building of the nawab's compound at Ahsan Manzi. Instead of landing on the palace roof, however, the balloon came to rest in a tree at Ramna Garden, nearly 3 miles away.

As police were attempting to a rescue Jeanette by means of a bamboo pole extended to the gondola of the balloon, the pole snapped and she crashed to the ground. She was severely injured and died a few days later.

It seems that Park Van Tassel lost the barnstorming spirit once his wife died. He returned to the USA and lived in Oakland, California, where he operated the Captain P.A. Van Tassel Toy Balloon Manufacturing Company until he died in October 1930, at the age of 78.

Note: Female parachutists didn't all come from the USA back in our wild colonial days. I want to make mention of the Aussie pioneer, Millie Viola, who pioneered parachuting in Perth and was certainly the first woman to parachute in Western Australia, which she did many times in 1891. She often made up to three descents a week and survived landing on the edges of roofs several times and having her parachute collapse in a whirlwind once, when she was subsequently saved by landing in a tree. She later went on to make many descents in eastern Australia.

There are a lot more women like Gladys, Valerie and Millie these days, but there were not many gals like them in 1890 and 1891.

THE BOY WHO WATCHED
THE IBIS

Herbert John Louis Hinkler was a short, modest man who spent hours as a boy in his hometown of Bundaberg in Queensland watching ibises fly.

Herbert, who was enrolled as 'Bertie Hinkler' at the North Bundaberg State School in 1898, finished his formal education at age fourteen. Young Bertie worked in sugar mills and a foundry and became a competent photographer, taking many photographs of ibises in flight.

From early childhood Bertie had just one ambition: to spend his life flying. As a teenager he built gliders, modelled on the ibis.

There is a story that, when he was a teenager, he left home and headed to Richmond, near Sydney, where he washed down the plane making joy-ride flights over Sydney every night in return for just one flight. Unfortunately his mother followed him from Bundaberg and prevented him from having his first flight.

But nothing could stop Hinkler. He talked his way into a job as a mechanic for the American aviator Arthur Burr Stone, who brought his Bleriot monoplane to Bundaberg in 1912. He then accompanied the American flyer on his tour of southern Australia and New Zealand.

There were no flying schools in Australia so Bert worked his passage on a freighter to Germany, when still only twenty, and made his way to London, where he eventually landed a job as a mechanic with the Sopwith aircraft company.

When war came, he joined the Royal Naval Air Service. Hinkler was an excellent rifle shot and became the commanding officer's observer and a petty officer by the end of 1915. He flew on many daytime and night raids in Handley-Page bombers and DH4s and is credited, as a gunner, with destroying six enemy aircraft. He also invented a dual-control system, which enabled the gunner to take control of the plane when the pilot was wounded.

By the end of the war Bert had been awarded the Distinguished Service Medal, gained a commission, and joined the Royal Flying Corps.

In December 1917 the banns for his marriage to Hannah 'Nance' Jervis were read in St Giles Church, Camberwell, but, although they lived together for many years, the marriage was never proceeded with, perhaps because Hannah was previously married with a daughter.

After the war Hinkler bought a 35-horsepower Avro Baby and flew from London to Turin over the Alps, a feat for which he was awarded the Britannia Trophy.

Mechanical problems prevented him from attempting to fly on to Australia, but he and his plane travelled home by ship and he made a series of pioneering flights around Australia, including the first direct flight from Sydney to Bundaberg.

Returning to England in 1922, he spent four years as chief test pilot for the Avro company. One of the aircraft he tested was the Avro Aldershot, the first plane in the world to have an engine capacity greater than 1000 horsepower. During this time he also won the light aircraft trials in 1923 and the Grosvenor Challenge Cup in 1924, flew his Avro Avian from London to Latvia, was decorated by the Latvian government, and made an unsuccessful attempt on the London to India air record.

Bert Hinkler flew into history in February 1928, when he piloted an Avro Avian from London to Darwin in fifteen and a half days, smashing the record of 28 days for the journey. At the time it was the longest solo flight ever made.

He flew the 1100 miles nonstop from London to Rome, a first leg that demonstrated his determination. He continued flying long stages every day, with a regularity that made it seem inevitable that he would achieve his goal.

Hinkler's rapid progress and endurance seemed incredible at the time. He was small of stature and quiet and modest by nature, but he was physically strong and was a gifted and expert pilot with thousands of hours experience testing aircraft.

From Rome he flew direct to Malta, then crossed the sea to Benghazi the following day and on to the North African coast to Tobruk that afternoon. Three days from England to the continent of Africa was a record at that time.

On 11 February, Hinkler flew from Tobruk to Palestine and the next day he set off for Baghdad, but actually made such good time that he kept going on to Basra, covering 950 miles in a nonstop flight of nine and half hours.

On 14 February, after a flight in beautiful weather down the Persian Gulf, the Avro Avian landed in Karachi, seven days after leaving England. This established a new record—5000 miles had been flown in seven days at an average of more than 650 miles per day.

The fastest normal travel time from London to the edge of the British Empire at Karachi was then about three weeks, by train and ocean liner. The idea that this could be reduced to less than a week was a source of wonderment to the ex-patriots, colonial officers and civil servants who suddenly began to think of the possibility of being able to read English newspapers only a week old.

The only problem experienced up to this time was a slight leak in an oil tank, which Hinkler discovered as he flew down the Persian Gulf. This was quickly repaired by RAF mechanics and caused no real delay to the flight schedule.

As Hinkler crossed India in two stages, from Karachi to Cawnpore and from Cawnpore to Calcutta, he passed the halfway point of his journey. It took him just two days to cross the sub-continent.

On the next stage to Rangoon, Hinkler encountered the first really bad flying conditions of the trip when he was forced to fly through two tropical storms and heavy rain. The next stage to Burma was relatively uneventful but, on the next day, on the stretch to Singapore, he again struck several heavy rainstorms and, just before reaching Singapore, he found it necessary to make a wide detour to miss a thick storm belt.

From Singapore, Hinkler flew on to Bandung, in Java, on 20 February, and the next day he brought the Avian to Bima, his last stop before facing the final stage, across the lonely Timor Sea to Darwin.

That night Hinkler tried to get as much sleep as he could in a native hut, but mosquitoes kept him awake and tropical rain pelted down.

At dawn he took off, with just a drink of water for breakfast and no food or water on board. Darwin was still 1000 miles away as he climbed with great difficulty through the turbulent tropical air and over the mountains to the south of the landing place at Bima.

For most of the stage across the vast ocean, clouds gave him some anxiety, but he maintained an altitude of 2000 feet, and a speed of 92 miles per hour. Despite no visibility for most of the flight, Hinkler's compass reckoning proved very accurate, and he sighted the coast of Australia at 4 p.m. on 22 February.

Following the coast to Darwin, the pioneer airman came in over the jungle to Darwin and circled the Ross Smith Memorial twice. He landed at Fanny Bay, 3 miles from the town, just after 6 p.m. local time.

A rather sunburnt and very tired Bert Hinkler gave a speech that evening at a civic dinner in his honour. In the speech, a typically modest and unpretentious Hinkler said that the most critical day of the whole trip was the first, when he flew for three hours in darkness before reaching Rome, and his only real moment of anxiety was when fading daylight caused a forced landing in the North African desert and some rather menacing natives approached him, but a gift of cigarettes solved the problem.

The king sent the following message:

Please inform Mr. Hinkler that I have received the news of his safe arrival in Australia with great pleasure. I have personally watched the progress of the great flight with great interest and am delighted that it has been successful.

Australia went Hinkler-crazy. The government sent a cruiser to stand by as Hinkler flew his final leg, across the Arafura Sea. Composers wrote songs about him, and the nation's hit tune was briefly 'Hustling Hinkler'. People wore Hinkler buttons, girls wore Hinkler flying-helmet-type hats, federal parliament stopped to welcome him, the Queensland government gave him £500 and the Australian government £2000, plus the Air Force Cross and the honorary rank of squadron leader in the Royal Australian Air Force.

Bert Hinkler never used the rank or wore the uniform.

Hinkler later returned to England and invested his money in a company making an amphibious aircraft named after the bird he used to study, the ibis. The prototype of this new aircraft proved very successful, but the Wall Street crash and depression derailed the project commercially.

Undeterred, Hinkler headed off to Canada in 1930 where he acquired a Puss Moth aircraft, which he flew to New York and later to the West Indies and South America. He then flew over the Atlantic from east to west, which was considered to be the greatest piece of solo navigation in aviation history.

Times were tough in Britain, and Bert returned to America. In May 1932, in Connecticut, he married Katherine Rome, about whom little is known except that she was probably originally British and lived in the USA. She was living in Glasgow when he was killed. Their marriage was to be sadly brief and childless. She returned to America after his death and died at Long Island in 1976.

On 7 January 1933, Bert Hinkler took off from London in an attempt to break his own record to Australia. It was the last flight of his career. Hinkler's body and plane were finally found in a remote part of the Apennine Mountains in Tuscany at the end of April. It is believed that he attempted an emergency landing after losing a propeller blade in flight.

The Aero Club of Florence and the Italian fascist government gave Hinkler a hero's funeral. He is buried in the English Cemetery in Florence. There is a monument to him near the fatal crash site on Mt Pratomagno in Italy.

A federal electorate in Queensland is named after him, as are quite a few streets and parks in that state, along with others in Darwin and in various places in New South Wales. Songs were written about Hinkler, including 'Hustling Hinkler', recorded by Len Maurice and Fred Monument, and 'Hello! Hinkler' sung by Frederick George.

In December 2008, the $7.5 million Hinkler Hall of Aviation was opened to the public in Hinkler's hometown of Bundaberg.

Bert's Home Comes 'Home'

Hinkler planned most of his epic solo flights from his home, a cottage named Mon Repos on the Thornhill Estate, in Southampton in the UK, near where he worked as a test pilot and where he lived for many years with his de facto wife Hannah 'Nance' Jervis.

Mon Repos is a detached residence of cavity-brick construction. The flooring, frame and roof rafters are of Baltic pine and the interior fittings are European redwood. The ceilings are plaster and lathe and it has a Welsh slate roof.

In spite of it seeming an impossible task, a group of dedicated Queenslanders, inspired by the knowledge that Captain Cook's childhood family home had been moved holus-bolus from Yorkshire to Melbourne in 1934, decided that Mon Repos, the English cottage that had been home to Bert and Nance, should be demolished, shipped to Australia, and rebuilt in Bundaberg.

A prohibitive $60,000 was needed but Bundaberg's Bicentennial Committee liked the idea and three local councils and the Bundaberg District Tourism and Development Board decided to make it happen.

The Southampton City Council planned to demolish the Hinkler house late in 1982 and desperate approaches were made to the council to defer the demolition, which they did, but the deadline was set: the house had to be removed by 30 June 1983.

A team of three, including the initiator of the project, local Hinkler historian Lex Rowland, went to Southampton to dismantle Bert and Nance's old home, and they managed to do it in four weeks.

The project was aided by British Aerospace, the Royal Australian Navy, the Royal Navy, the Royal Dutch Navy, Qantas and many other sponsors, and the house was shipped to Australia and reconstructed in the Bundaberg Botanic Gardens by members of the Rotary Club of East Bundaberg and members of the dismantling team.

During the demolition of the house, Bert and Nance's kitchen sink was retrieved from a well in the backyard next to an old shed. Amazingly, Hinkler's logbook of his 1928 flight to Australia had been found in a wing stub of Bert's Ibis, still stored in the shed in 1953, after Nance had sold the house in 1952 and moved to South Africa.

On 16 June 1984, Mon Repos was officially opened by the Premier of Queensland Sir Johannes Bjelke-Petersen and the former mayor of Southampton, Councillor Dorothy Brown.

A popular children's rhyme in 1928, by that popular author 'Anonymous' was:

Hinkler, Hinkler, little star
15 days and here you are

The two poems by C.J. Dennis that follow were written during the last days of Hinkler's historic solo flight to Australia and on his landing, they appeared in the *Melbourne Herald Sun* in February and March 1928.

The Singing Ace

by C.J. Dennis

Utterly fearless, small, active, and with a schoolboy grin, Hinkler (now crossing the Timor Sea on his final hop) is an ideal long-distance flier. He has unique endurance, enabling him to make a solitary flight for hours, singing as the mood moves him. —*The London Daily Mail*

There's an Aussie in an Avian high o'er the Timor Sea,
Flying on and singing as he flies
For the honor of his country, for the sake of you and me,
And the spirit, true and bold, that never dies.
He is speeding, he is singing, as the boys in old days sang
When the High Adventure beckoned them along,
Where the frowning cliffs of Anzac to their lilting voices
    rang,
And the crags of Sari Bair gave back their song.

There's an Aussie in the zenith where the Timor spills its
    flood.
Alone with sea and sky, he rides the air.
He is homing to his own land with her spirit in his blood,
And only sea-birds mark his passing there.
But he's singing, gaily singing with a heart aflame with hope,
And his eyes fixed on the far horizon's rim
Where tropic skies to tropic seas in azure glory slope
And the nearing shores of Homeland beckon him.

Where the Timor basks in sunlight there's an Aussie all
    alone—
Alone with sea and sky—a speeding mite,
Who flies o'er Asian seaways as no other man has flown
And finds but true adventure in the flight.

And he's singing—still he's singing, while the nations
    breathless wait
And count the hours of waiting all too long,
Till he ends his long adventuring beside his mother's gate
And his kinsmen catch the burden of his song.

There's an Aussie in an Avian—a speck within the blue—
Who puts to shame old tales of fabled ships.
For honor of his land he sails, for proof for me and you
Who wait with greeting trembling on the lips.
And he's singing—ever singing as he drops the leagues
    behind—
The man who ventured half a world to roam,
And thankfulness shall mingle with the welcome he will find
When at last the Singing Ace comes winging home.

Out of the Blue

by C.J. Dennis

Speaking in welcome of the famous airman, Bert Hinkler, yesterday, the Premier, Mr Hogan, said 'Today Mr Hinkler has come to us out of the blue'.—*Melbourne Herald Sun*

Out of the blue. A glimmering speck
Draws on while the thousands cheer,
With straining vision, with craning neck,
Each one fearing he yet may wreck,
They gaze as his ship looms near,
Bringing, from half a world away,
Something to each man here today.

More than honor and more than fame,
More than a triumphing song
More than the tale of a well-won name
More than the title of high acclaim,
Brings he to the clustering throng.
'Tis Vision, and Pride, and a Hope that's new
He brings with him shimmering out of the blue.

Strange, vague promptings of waxing Pride,
Vision for me and you.
Men who yet never may learn to ride
Into the void o'er a whole world wide,
Venturing into the blue—
Yet in the bosom of every one
Comes hope, because of a deed well done.

Is it that we of the age and race
Into which he was born
Seers for the moment, only trace

Something there of a hidden grace
Salve for a world forlorn?
As a sign and a portent of places new
Comes he thus winging it out of the blue?

Doubly an 'Ace' in that he, alone,
Played for the stake and won.
By such high deeds have the seeds been sown
Out of which Empire and glory have grown:
Thus are new worlds begun.
Was it something of this that we sensed today
When out of the blue he came winging his way?

Comes a new era for men of the earth
That the 'Lone Ace' flies this way?
Cook, Columbus were men of worth,
Drake knew much of the wide world's girth—
But night has followed their day:
A night of blackness that gave men fear,
When the gods of war strode all too near.

'Tis but the Dawn. Yet skies grow clear,
And the new Day breaks full fair.
But, as year follows on glorious year,
And the 'Tale of the Air' is an old tale here,
The name of Hinkler, Pioneer,
Shall shine while the skies are there—
Writ indelibly into the Blue—
'This Boy who had made his dreams come true'.

THE GIRL FROM HULL

JILLIAN DELLIT AND JIM HAYNES

Had I been a man I might have explored the Poles or climbed
Mount Everest, but as it was my spirit found outlet in the air.

Amy Johnson, 1938

The name Amy Johnson is etched deeply into Australia's aviation
history. At a time when Australia was known in world affairs only
as a distant outpost of the British Empire, she, more than anyone
else, made the world aware of our nation.

To this day, she is remembered in more than a dozen streets
and parks named after her in Britain. KLM named a plane after
her, popular songs were written about her and movies made.
A fictional account of her life even featured in an episode of
Doctor Who. A highway in Darwin is named after her, as is a street
in Brisbane. The names 'Amy Johnson' and 'Australia' are forever
inextricably linked—and she wasn't even an Australian.

The girl from Hull visited Australia only once. Yet every year
in her hometown, the Mayor of Hull presents a gold trophy to
recognise the bravery of a local child. Amy Johnson purchased
the trophy with funds raised for her by the children of Sydney in
honour of her arrival 'down under' in 1930.

As a girl Amy, whose family were fish merchants in Hull, loved
active sports, especially those regarded as 'boys' games'. She loved
to compete and, while playing cricket one day in the street, a ball
struck her in the mouth. She lost her front teeth and spent the rest of
her brief but amazing life being self-conscious about her false front

teeth. As a young English woman in the 1920s, Amy was certainly atypical. She was fit, a good swimmer, and able to box and wrestle.

One day she spread out a map of the world, pointed to the uncharted spaces of the large open country in the southern ocean that was Australia and said, 'I'm going there!'

No doubt many others of her generation had dreamed of such things, but Amy Johnson fixed her mind on this goal and worked until she reached it. In the process she altered forever the way Australians thought about that map.

Amy left Hull's Boulevard Secondary School in 1922. With first-class honours in Latin in the Oxford Senior Local Examination, she went to Sheffield University to become a teacher.

At Sheffield, Amy changed her mind, graduated with a Bachelor of Arts degree in economics, and went to London to work as a private secretary with a law practice but spent her spare time working in the field that had become her obsession: aviation.

Each day, when her law firm work was finished, she did voluntary work at Astor House in Aldwych, the office of the Air League of the British Empire. In 1928 she joined the London Aeroplane Club and learned to fly.

Her Class A pilot's licence covered basic engine mechanics, which was all most amateur pilots, like most car drivers, wanted. Amy, however, cribbed time to strip, clean and mount engines with other members of the mechanics section of the Aero Club at their Stag Lane workshops in order to get her ground engineer's licence.

After finishing for the day at the law firm, she worked on planes for as long as the workshop would stay open, then was back again at six the next morning to put in another hour and a half before she had to get to the office. She knew and understood every part of the plane and its engine, and tested her work with her life, by test-flying the planes she worked on.

Amy became the only woman to hold a British ground engineer's licence.

Sometimes Amy was able to manage to fit in a full day working as an apprentice engineer. Here is her own account of an average day in the workshops, written for the Magazine *Air*:

Seven forty-five a.m.!

'Good morning'—me, brightly.

'You're late,'—Boss boomingly: 'We start work at 7.30 sharp.'

On with the overalls-slightly soiled, I'm afraid—and up the steps I go, armed with grease gun, oil squirt, spanner, and the like, for an engine waits my personal attention. First I wash it down— with every minute the engine grows cleaner and I dirtier!

Tug-tug-tug—petrol filters do so object to being unscrewed! There! I've knocked flat the last of my once-pointed finger.

My, but I'm hungry. Landladies don't cater for breakfast at 7 a.m. Hurrah, it's time for our cup of tea. In we all troop to the kitchen and take up our stand round the table. A huge cup of tea and thick cheese roll refresh and strengthen us for the rest of the morning's work.

Back roll the hangar doors and a procession of six yellow machines, each tail, hoisted high on the shoulder of a mechanic, marches out on the tarmac. 'Props' are swung, and engines are left to warm up. Meanwhile I don scarf and cap, ready for running up my engine, for it's some cold job. Then over to the petrol pump, the machine must be taxied, and back again to the sheds, where I line it up with the rest—all awaiting for the arrival of the two instructors for test at 10 a.m.

One part of the day's work over. I return to the hangar for instructions, 'sweep out the hangar and tidy up the office.'

Ugh, I thought I'd fled from housework to learn engines. But Engineer No. 1's word is law; so, armed with a broom bigger than myself, I set to work. The hangar has never before seemed so immense. Howsoever, patience is at last rewarded, and I reach the far corner (not to leave the rubbish there—I tried that once . . !).

My next job is to scrape carbon off a cylinder head. (Two of these should be finished in an afternoon, I'm told.) Mine looks like taking a week. Anyhow, it is dinner time before I have made any noticeable impression on its blackness. (The blackness, incidentally, has made a most notable impression on me!)

We have an hour for lunch, and it flies all too quickly in eating, joking and talking shop. The afternoon passes uneventfully, except for a newspaper man who arrives and asks to see the 'lady engineer'!

Everyone looks blank. No lady here. I emerge, rubbing dirty hands on the seat of my overalls, and join in the search. But when I wash my face and hands for tea, my secret is discovered.

'You want to know what I have done? No . . . ? Oh, . . . what I wear!? Oh, I see. Well, I wear overalls over my clothes, and over my overalls oil, grease, dirt.'

But he's gone! He didn't seem to like the things I tell him! So away he trots to make it all up for himself.

Now comes a photographer. Oh hurry, where's my heart-shaped helmet, my manicure set and my powder puff. Where can my powder puff be? There's a spanner in my stern pocket, a few loose nuts, screws and bolts in every other pocket, but where, oh where, is my powder puff pocket? You see, I must look nice for the photographer, for I've been told that every pilot has several proposals weekly. So I must spread abroad my beauty!

I've had no proposals yet, so I suppose I'm no pilot. But while there's life there's hope. Maybe the stronger sex don't like my brawny fist . . . or brawny arm, is it? I don my smart flying suit and appear for once as others would have me be, but the minute the camera has clicked, off it comes . . . for in roll the machines to be put to bed for the night.

Hangar doors are closed, 'Good Nights' are all said, and off we go to our various pursuits.

Do I go to the pictures with my sweetheart? Oh no, indeed. At 6 p.m. I have a lecture, and after that I hope to do some reading for my next examination. A hard life, but, by Jove—it's a good one!

If I didn't do it all voluntarily and for nothing I should, of course, consider I was grossly overworked, ill-treated, underfed and underpaid . . . but don't let the Boss hear this, or I'll have to change this story to a 'Day as a Sacked Engineer'!

When Amy persisted with her idea of flying alone to Australia, most experts were sceptical. It was not unusual for amateurs to get their first licence on only eight hours of flight and crash the first time they tried to fly any distance.

And this amateur was a woman, attempting to fly to Australia. She had only been flying for two years and had clocked up less than 100 hours as a pilot.

Her attempts to interest newspapers, experts and officials in sponsorship were unsuccessful. Tom Clarke, managing editor of the *Daily News* and *Westminster Gazette,* later told it this way:

Her scheme of flying to Australia alone stirred nobody to enthusiasm. It was first heard of towards the end of last year (1929), but no one could be got to aid with the financing of the project.

To fly to Australia was not exactly original. And who was this obscure girl anyhow? Quite an ordinary person by all accounts. She could not be serious.

Lord Wakefield was approached early in January. He felt it was a hopeless job for the girl to tackle. Miss Johnson next saw Mr. Fenton, the Australian Minister for Trade and Customs, who was visiting London. He patted her on the back as a kindly uncle would, and said: 'Go to Australia by steamer, my girl. You would be foolish to try to fly there.'

Then she got in touch with Fleet Street through my Australian journalist friend. He rang me up one day in March and asked if we were sufficiently interested to assist with the financing of a flight to Australia by a young woman

So I said, 'Who is she? Anyhow, flying to Australia is not very original, and the last woman who went took months.'

'Her name is Johnson. She means to do it—and alone. She's her own mechanic. Will you see her?'

I was not impressed, but I wrote asking her to come to see me at any time to discuss the matter. I wanted to dissuade her. To have any responsibility for a young girl's going alone on such a perilous journey was not to my liking.

She came one day when I was out. My secretary saw her, and has since given me the following note of their interview:

The most noticeable thing about Miss Amy Johnson was her complete independence. She said she did not want any newspaper publicity—she was making the trip for her own amusement, and if anyone cared to write about her in the papers—well, that was their affair. She had been told her venture was worth a lot of money to any paper who would buy it, but was not particularly interested; and she tossed her head with its long, swinging ear-rings.

She is small and slight, blue-eyed, fair-haired, but with an air of strength and will-power—something almost masculine, given the lie by the earrings which continually thrust themselves on the notice. They seemed to be there for the purpose of accentuating each toss of the small, haughty head, and showing the determination of their owner. They said, in their nodding way, what Miss Johnson did not put in words:

'You may not think much of me, but I'll show you I can do it.'

We had one more letter from Miss Johnson, a rather delightfully petulant protest against the announcement of her project.

What Amy wrote was in answer to an article in the *Daily News*, which Tom Clarke edited. Her letter to him stated:

I am not 23, and my age is of no importance. The longest flight I have done is not 200 miles; anyhow London to Hull is only 147 miles by air. I am not making a high-speed flight, and, although I have a large fuel capacity, I do not intend making 1,000-miles non-stop hops. My ambition is not to surpass the record time set up by Mr. Hinkler—in fact, I am positively certain that his time cannot be surpassed in a light aeroplane. My route is not across France and Italy and I do not touch Egypt.

Clarke said later, 'I heard no more from her. We probably felt she would do a nice flight or two and then come down with some sort of trouble, and hurry back home.'

Only one expert, Major Travers, the chief pilot of the London Aero Club, watched her training and thought she'd do it, because, he said, 'She knows her job'.

Amy attempted to find better-paying jobs in the aviation industry to finance the flight, even a job testing the new 'ejector seat', but finally relied on savings from her secretary's pay of £3 a week.

The man known as 'Patron Saint of Civil Aviation', Lord Wakefield, who was head of the Wakefield-Castrol oil company, sponsored her by paying for petrol. Her father bought the plane, and Amy paid the rest.

At that time the most dangerous stage of flying from Britain to Australia was seen as the last stretch across the Timor Sea. Several aviators had died on the 900-mile journey from Sumbawa to Darwin, out of sight of shipping and effective communications. Hinkler went missing there for several hours. Crossing the Timor Sea was the very loneliest kind of flying.

To address such risks, Amy had followed her ground engineer's licence in 1929 with a full navigation licence in 1930. The slight girl with the earrings was a woman to be reckoned with.

She learned quickly, and adapted to new ideas. Three days before she started from Croydon on 5 May, she reduced another risk by making use of a new technology: the parachute.

Tropical storms might well be unavoidable once out of Europe. In a tropical storm, with her Gipsy Moth overloaded with fuel at every take-off, she ran a high risk of an uncontrollable spin ending inevitably in death. In the last few years RAF pilots had saved their lives in similar conditions by the use of parachutes. Amy had never worn one, but she went to the manufacturer to ask advice. They trained her in half an hour.

The seat-pack parachute she settled on was light—a mere 18 pounds—specially fitted to her size. The harness fitted over her shoulders, round her waist and legs so it would brace her whole body against the opening shock. She wore it, using its body as a seat, all the time she flew.

Along with all the other things she was doing to prepare, she read books on navigation, building up a good knowledge and confidence enough to choose the most direct 11,500-mile route across Europe, via Vienna and Constantinople, over the Balkans.

This route was complicated by the need for visas and immigration clearances for landings in several European countries, which was why most pilots avoided it.

The only thing she failed to do in preparation was to make full load tests before her flight. This is probably the reason it took her two attempts to get off the ground when she left Croydon aerodrome on 5 May 1930.

Three people saw her off. There were no speeches or publicity, just a farewell kiss for her father. The Gipsy Moth started immediately but she had not allowed herself enough distance for the weight of petrol she was carrying for the ten hours to Vienna. Cautiously, she slowed and turned round.

The second time, Amy lifted off easily. Five machines from the London Aeroplane Club escorted her out over Surrey.

On that day few planes took off, due to reports of fog all the way to Cologne. Amy met rain at one stage but otherwise covered the 800 miles in fine weather, landing on Vienna's Aspern Aerodrome in just under ten hours of continuous flying.

The next day, Tuesday 6 May, she left Vienna for Constantinople via Belgrade and Sofia, another 800 miles, with more good weather apart from some rainstorms over the Balkans. There was a crowd to welcome her, when, after another twelve hours of solo flying, she landed in what is now Istanbul.

Now the world was interested. Amy had never crossed the Channel before, or flown more than 200 miles in a straight line. When she repeated the performance the next day, people began to understand the extent of her determination and flying ability. Fleet Street had underestimated her.

Speed was her focus on the 550 miles to Aleppo, down the Bosphorus on the third day. By the time she arrived she had spent 27 hours in the air and covered more than 2000 miles in three days.

Then, in the 500-mile stretch across the desert to Baghdad, a sandstorm forced her down into the desert, where, for two hours she fought to hold the Gipsy Moth to the ground, piling her luggage against the machine's wheels to prevent the wind taking it. She did this with a revolver in her hand, in case of trouble. The revolver wasn't for show; Amy had learned to shoot and was an excellent shot.

Fortunately, without having to use the revolver, she got underway when the storm subsided and made Baghdad by nightfall on her fourth day. Bert Hinkler's England to Australia light plane record that she had thought unbeatable looked like it was about to be smashed.

On the fifth day, in Basra and Bushire, the towns where most pilots put down as daylight failed, locals waited for Amy, but she passed them by, making it to Bandar Abbas, 830 miles along the Persian Gulf. On her sixth day, 10 May, she got to Karachi, breaking Hinkler's England to Karachi record of eight days.

To cut two days off his time for the 5000 miles between London and Karachi had been unthinkable and was not explained away by her shorter route. She had beaten the record mile for mile.

In an age of records, it was big news. Hull, in particular, recognised a hometown hero.

Hull was an aviation town. With a flying club organised by the National Flying Services, it was one of the first English municipalities to have an aerodrome. The navy's torpedo planes and flying boats were built at an aircraft factory along the Humber and a few miles out of town—near Kingston-upon-Hull—the Airship Guarantee Company (with Vickers as its major shareholder) built the new R100 airship to the design and under the supervision of Barnes Wallis—famed for his Dam Busting Bouncing Bomb in World War II. Before the R100, the R38, although built at Bedford, had been, in 1921, the first airship disaster after WWI, when during a trial flight it broke apart and fell in flames over Hull, killing 44 of the 48 British and United States passengers.

So the people of Hull depended on aviation, understood its risks and recognised a pioneering achievement when they saw one.

Like it or not, Amy was now in a popular competition with Hinkler's record as she left Karachi for the 1000-mile leg to Allahabad, en route to Calcutta. Her personal, single-minded focus on flying solo to the isolated country at the bottom of her atlas was now public property.

Then, after 700 miles, as she neared Jhansi, she ran out of petrol, and had to put down there for the night. On the eighth day, 450 miles beyond Allahabad, she was in Calcutta, the halfway mark, 7000 miles from England and still two days ahead of Hinkler's time.

Beyond Calcutta, on the ninth day, in heavy rains and against strong headwinds, she faced the Arakan Yomas ranges, the lowest of Burma's western mountains. For a while she flew high—up to 12,000 feet—but as the day drew on and visibility deteriorated further, she was flying at no more than 150 feet, first above the coastline and then the railway line, in order to find Rangoon where the racecourse served as the airfield.

Anxious to find the racecourse, and unwittingly 12 miles short, she initially mistook the playing field of Insein for the racecourse, but as it appeared too small she continued south. Today Insein is a suburb of Rangoon, home to Myanmar's only railway workshop and notorious for its prison, but in 1930 it was a country town. So when Amy was unable to sight Rangoon, and with no visible alternative, she turned back to the playing fields.

Once back over the Insein playing field, she brought the plane down square between the goal posts, only to run into a ditch and damage the Gipsy Moth's undercarriage in the unmarked field. Fortune, in the form of the Government Technical Institute workshop right next to the field, gave her a lucky break.

The repair time, however, eroded her good lead over Hinkler, and the media interest became more intense. It was now 13 May, her ninth day.

All the following day, the local technicians helped repair the damage to the undercarriage and wing. Amy tore up army surplus shirts and used two products from the local chemist to repair the wing—pink sticking plaster and a product that later turned up across the world as nail varnish.

To test the repairs in the air, she organised for the plane to be moved by road to the racecourse at Rangoon where she had the room she needed for take-off. She was losing time in this middle section of the journey.

On the morning of 16 May, as the good weather suddenly changed to heavy rain, she set off for Bangkok, 356 miles away.

From the coast, her course to Bangkok took her over treacherous mountains of rainforest where there was little chance of survival if forced to land. There was a passage through the ranges but many aviators had failed to find it. In the heavy rain she climbed to 10,000 feet, trying to fly blind over the peaks, and seeking clear patches. When she did find a clear patch, she was still on the western side of the range.

Keith and Ross Smith got through these ranges by going to 13,000 feet. In a Gipsy Moth this was not an option.

It took Amy seven hours to cover the 356 miles from Rangoon to Bangkok—a long time on your own with basic instruments in the mist and rain over mountains, but on the twelfth day, exhausted by her long struggle, and approximately level with Hinkler's record, Amy reached the Don Muang air force base in Bangkok.

She prepared her machine immediately for an early morning continuation towards Singapore. The keen, highly skilled Thai airmen helped. Their respect for her was based on their local knowledge of the terrain that she had just conquered.

Down the Malay Peninsula on her thirteenth day she held the plane on course against headwinds and tropical rainstorms. Local networks followed her ragged progress until, after six hours of flying, Amy was finally forced to land at Singora, modern Sonkhla, in southern Thailand.

On the following day she was in Singapore, looking happy at her reception. Two of Singapore's Gipsy Moth seaplanes escorted her in. The Singapore Royal Airforce Squadron operated Gipsy Moth seaplanes, so this stopover could provide experienced aero-mechanics and the comfort of an aviation community.

It was her fourteenth day and she had now lost the contest for Hinkler's record. On her own terms, however, she had already performed miracles and at her present rate of progress she knew she would still arrive at Darwin in excellent time.

By now Amy was famous. People around the world followed her with intense interest, waiting for news of her arrival at the end of each long day of flying, anticipating the dangers of the final stage across the Timor Sea.

When pilots planned flights to Darwin, they knew that the last hop of 1500 miles was the most risky for land planes. Fitting seaplane floats to the Gipsy Moth would have added another third to the cost of the plane—not in Amy's price range.

Before Amy set off, the local Singapore aviation club fitted a new bottom wing on her plane. Then she departed for Surabaya, hugging the edge of the Java Sea. The bad weather and fuel shortage forced her, after nine hours flying, to use an emergency landing-place. She was holding out to reach Samarang but eventually made a forced landing at a sugar plantation 60 miles short.

Local factory workers were quickly recruited to help patch the holes made in the Gipsy Moth's wings by the sugar canes. The next morning, she found a better place for take-off, and with all unnecessary items removed from the plane, she flew out of the sugar and on to the better space where the plane was reloaded for take-off to Samarang.

It was now her sixteenth day and, in the company of the Dutch mail plane, she barely touched down at Samarang before heading for Surabaya, another 200 miles, where crowds came to watch her land. They wanted to see and touch this woman who defied their weather and terrain as the monsoons turned to the east. She seemed relaxed, showing no signs of the fatigue expected of a woman who had been flying alone for more than two weeks.

Still, Amy's priority was preparing her plane for the final, most feared stage of the journey. She was attuned to the sound of her engine and found the magneto trouble that an irregular noise had alerted her to on the way in. After Surabaya, she could expect no help if her engine failed. She had two long, dangerous sea stretches to go.

Bert Hinkler had crossed the Timor Sea at its widest part— 1000 miles from Bima on the island of Sumbawa—and locals assumed Amy, too, would land at Bima. They watched for her but, when she was sighted in the middle of the day, they had to be satisfied with a glimpse of her plane. She did not land.

It looked as if she had chosen Atamboea, on Timor, as her last stop, with its promise of a shorter sea flight to Darwin.

Then nothing. The watchers on the tiny islands, some with landing strips built in 1919 to help aviators in the first England to Australia air race, caught no glimpse of her.

Night fell around 5.30 p.m.

The Dutch administrators kept their communication system open.

No news.

Local authorities prepared for a sea and land search. The government steamer *Gemma* was instructed to search the Timor Sea. Two flying boats were ready to start out from Surabaya.

First thing in the morning a telegram arrived from Amy.

She had landed in Haliloelik, in Timor, 12 miles from Atamboea and the nearest telephone. She got herself into Atamboea late at night and found accommodation. In the morning she had to return to the village to fly her machine to Atamboea aerodrome.

The whole world had been waiting for that news.

The 'lone girl flyer' had come to stand for independence, hope, defying the odds, and a quiet refusal to accept imposed limits of distance, engineering, navigation or gender. Plenty thought she had proved a point and should stop before the Timor Sea, but Amy Johnson was not flying for the approval of others. She had come 10,000 miles to fly this last 500, and fly it she would.

Radio listeners stayed tuned.

She left at dawn. Her only contact was about halfway over, when she sighted the Shell oil tanker, *Phorus*, which radioed her progress to Darwin. Several aircraft then set out to meet her.

The biggest crowd Darwin had ever recorded was waiting to welcome her. It was 3 p.m. on the nineteenth day of her journey. She was behind Hinkler's 1928 record time, but a week ahead of Keith and Ross Smith's 1919 time.

Amy had defied her critics. They could dismiss her pilot's licence, even discount her ground engineer's licence, but none of them had even considered the possibility that her navigation skills and persistence would enable her to reach Darwin.

Amy carried no wireless. She navigated the Timor Sea using a compass and ruler. She had simply tuned the engine, strapped on her parachute and flown.

Over nineteen days the Gipsy Moth's four-cylinder, air-cooled engine had proven reliable in rapid changes of temperature and with almost constant servicing by Amy.

Australia has a warm heart for heroes. Bundaberg had declared a holiday for local boy, Bert Hinkler, when he passed through. Darwin adopted Amy and did the same. The whole town, multi-cultural even then, turned out for the parade and speeches in order to catch sight of the young woman most experts thought would never make it.

Like her engine, Amy had operated for nineteen days with little rest. Newspapers fully expected she would want to rest in Darwin for several weeks, but within a few days she headed across the Northern Territory to Brisbane. On her arrival in Brisbane, on 29 May, in a misunderstanding with an escort, she overshot the runway and the Gipsy Moth turned over, sustaining damage. Amy escaped without injury.

Amy and Jim Mollison, the Scottish aviator she was to later marry, flew over Sydney into Mascot airport in one of Charles Kingsford-Smith's planes, accompanied by 'Smithy' himself in another. There is a famous photo of the two planes over the incomplete Sydney Harbour Bridge.

A group of Australian women pilots flew to meet Amy and accompany her in. Undaunted by discovering they had accompanied the wrong plane, they took off again and repeated the gesture!

The 'lone girl flyer' had made it, despite the indifference and patronising assumptions of the male-dominated establishment. And for that Australians loved her.

King George sent the following telegram:

The Queen and I are thankful and delighted to know of Miss Johnson's safe arrival in Australia, and heartily congratulate her upon her wonderful and courageous achievement.

The Australian Prime Minister, James Scullin, said, 'Heartiest congratulations on your achievement which has won the admiration of the world,' and invited Amy to attend a session of parliament.

Tom Clarke, the managing editor of the *Daily News* and *Westminster Gazette*, who had been so dismissive before her flight, had the grace to apologise, noting wryly:

> Mr. Fenton [the Australian Minister of Trade and Customs] . . . will meet her in his own country, to which he has gone by the steamer he advised for her.

Perhaps the most fitting tributes were the London newspaper placards announcing her arrival in Darwin to the British public. Reflecting how personal the flight had become, the placards simply stated . . . 'SHE'S THERE.'

Note: In 1932, Amy married Scottish aviator Jim Mollison and, that same year, broke the record for a flight from London to Cape Town which had been held by her new husband. In 1933 they set out to fly together from South Wales to New York, but crashlanded at Bridgeport Connecticut and both sustained minor injuries. When they recovered they received a ticker-tape parade down Wall Street. The couple divorced in 1938.

Amy lost her life while delivering planes to RAF bases to support the British war effort. On 5 January 1941, while flying from Prestwick to Kidlington Airbase near Oxford, she went off course in bad weather, ran out of fuel, and bailed out as her aircraft crashed into the Thames estuary.

The crew of HMS *Haslemere*, a balloon barrage vessel, saw her parachute come down and saw her alive in the water, calling for help. There was a heavy sea and a strong tide and it was snowing. The *Haslemere* attempted to turn but ran aground and had to put its engines into 'slow astern' to get free.

Ropes were thrown to Amy by the crew but she failed to grasp them and disappeared under the stern of the ship.

Captain Walter Fletcher, the commander of *Haslemere*, dived into the water and attempted to rescue Amy. The ship's lifeboat was launched but, as that was happening, the Luftwaffe attacked the barrage ships.

Fletcher was rescued from the water by Lieutenant George Wright, who swam to him and got him back on board. Captain Fletcher died in hospital later that night from hypothermia and was posthumously awarded the Albert Medal for bravery.

Amy's body was never recovered.

ACKNOWLEDGEMENTS

I would like to thank Jillian Dellit for permission to use our co-written story on Amy Johnson and for her suggestions and proofreading. Thanks also to all at Allen & Unwin, especially Rebecca Kaiser for her support and encouragement of this project, Genevieve Buzo for her enthusiastic and professional proofing, and Romina Panetta for her excellent cover design. Thanks to Susin Chow for her perceptive editing and attention to detail, and to George and Paul at 2UE for their encouragement and friendship over 15 years.